PROJECT-BASED LEARNING IN THE FIRST YEAR

PROJECT-BASED LEARNING IN THE FIRST YEAR

Beyond All Expectations

Edited by

Kristin Wobbe and Elisabeth A. Stoddard

Foreword by Randall Bass

Copublished with

Association
of American
Colleges and
Universities

Sty/us

STERLING, VIRGINIA

Published by Stylus Publishing, LLC.
22883 Quicksilver Drive
Sterling, Virginia 20166-2019

Library of Congress Cataloging-in-Publication Data
Names: Wobbe, Kristin, editor.
Title: Project-based learning in the first year : beyond all
    expectations / edited by Kristin Wobbe and Elisabeth Stoddard ;
    foreword by Randall Bass.
Description: Sterling, Virginia : Stylus Publishing, LLC, [2018] |
    Includes bibliographical references and index.
Identifiers: LCCN 2018017635 (print) | LCCN 2018019664
    (ebook) | ISBN 9781620366905 (uPDF) | ISBN
    9781620366912 (ePub, mobi) | ISBN 9781620366882 (cloth
    : alk. paper) | ISBN 9781620366899 (pbk. : alk. paper) |
    ISBN 9781620366905 (library networkable e-edition) | ISBN
    9781620366912 (consumer e-edition)
Subjects: LCSH: Project method in teaching. | College teaching--
    Methodology.
Classification: LCC LB1027.43 (ebook) | LCC LB1027.43 .P75
    2018 (print) | DDC 371.3/6—dc23
LC record available at https://lccn.loc.gov/2018017635

13-digit ISBN: 978-1-62036-688-2 (cloth)
13-digit ISBN: 978-1-62036-689-9 (paperback)
13-digit ISBN: 978-1-62036-690-5 (library networkable e-edition)
13-digit ISBN: 978-1-62036-691-2 (consumer e-edition)

Printed in the United States of America

All first editions printed on acid-free paper
that meets the American National Standards Institute
Z39-48 Standard.

Bulk Purchases
Quantity discounts are available for use in workshops and for
staff development.
Call 1-800-232-0223

First Edition, 2019

CONTENTS

Foreword

Do Project-Based Learning—Save The World

That rallying cry, "Do Project-Based Learning—Save the World," is one that I conclude with every year when I speak at Worcester Polytechnic Institute's annual summer institute. I'm only half joking and offer it as only partial hyperbole. Project-based learning (PBL) that is thoughtfully designed and equitably executed is, I believe, as central to the paradigm of higher education in the twenty-first century as inquiry and research has been for the past 200 years. This is not to say that "inquiry" is not still the central activity of the university. Rather, at this point in the evolution of higher education, we have now expanded the paradigm of critical inquiry to include what we might think of as critical action. More than just thinking *and* doing, PBL is *doing* that arises from and leads to better thinking.

By arguing that PBL is part of a paradigm expansion in higher education, I am asserting that this is not merely another pedagogical strategy, trend, fad, or one of many approaches that faculty might use to enhance their teaching. True enough that this volume is filled with concrete strategies, approaches, and thoughtful ideas that can be adopted by faculty in varying levels of course redesign; but there is something much more game-changing going on in this volume and, indeed, the larger sphere of work around PBL. This work is about a fundamental change in the kind of graduate we want to shape and produce. Chad Wellmon (2016) argued the university strove to produce a new kind of learned individual, what he termed the *disciplined self*, characterized by specialization in a branch of organized knowledge, shaped by ways of knowing the kinds of problems addressed and shared methods and processes. At the heart of PBL is an analogous cultural project, one that seeks to produce a similarly disciplined *actor*, an agent of positive change in the world that brings to that agency certain highly cultivated characteristics of critical thinking, creative problem-solving, empathetic engagement, and ethical judgment.

To put this another way, if we were designing the university for this moment in history—given everything we know about learning and understanding, the shifting demographics of our students, the global challenges that face them, and the positive long-term impact of sustained mentored work on a lifetime of engagement—I believe we would build a university education on a foundation of PBL. We would ask, what does it take to make a graduate who can be effective in the world in the ways that advance the common good, can conceptualize and engage the other in noninstrumental ways, and has the capacity to take on complex problems with creative resilience. We are, at best, at the barest beginnings of understanding this cultural project.

This volume, *Project-Based Learning in the First Year: Beyond All Expectations*, goes especially to the heart of this expanded paradigm because it takes up the need to seed project-based learning in the very foundation of a college education. This volume loudly asserts that these capacities, so critical to the future of our society, should be the place where this kind of education should begin, not end. To think otherwise would be tantamount to wanting students to engage in critical thinking, writing, and inquiry *only* at the end of their college careers. No, if you want students to culminate at a place of proficiency in skills and abilities, you have to take those end-point outcomes and "backwardly design" all through the curriculum to the very foundations to achieve them. And indeed we do this for those traditional outcomes. We want students to write from the first year forward. We consider numeracy and scientific literacy and many other skills and abilities to be foundational, and we put them in general education for that reason. The time has come to understand *critical action* as a fundamental skill that has to be developed from the beginning of a higher education.

Project-Based Learning in the First Year contributes significantly to making the goal of developing critical action and actors real and attainable for faculty at all kinds of institutions. Such signature work is often saved for the later years if not the very end of an undergraduate education. Yet, as Boudreau and Wobbe argue in the first chapter, their objective is "to convince you that projects, in particular interdisciplinary projects, can be just as valuable in the first year and provide a wealth of advantages to students who participate in them" (p. 11, this volume). To focus on PBL at all is to say that this is now central to a college education; to focus on project-based learning *in the first year* is to say it is not only central but also foundational and transformative.

Cumulatively, the perspectives in this volume highlight the dissolution of the traditional binary between liberal and professional education, content and skills, and theory and practice. The contours of this more integrative or fluid paradigm take shape in discussions of what it means to engage students in authentic problems and projects, be responsive to clients and diverse partners, and receive feedback and assessment that are situated and tied closely to student judgment and actions. These chapters speak to the holistic nature of PBL—cognitive, affective, interpersonal—and its transdisciplinary and integrative nature.

Through PBL, the "character traits" that we know are keys to long-term success are pulled into the foundations of a college education. In the first chapter, Boudreau and Wobbe name many of them, such as "persistence through failure (grit), optimism, curiosity, gratitude, conscientiousness, and self-control" (p. 12, this volume). To these we might add creativity, compassion, humility, and resilience. These traits cannot be taught. You cannot *instruct* someone directly in these traits. They arise from personal context. As Howard Gray, S.J., the eminent Jesuit educator once said to me when we were discussing this very topic, "Humility, for example, is *always* experiential." Yet, even if these traits cannot be directly taught, one can design and provide the support for environments in which they are more likely to be cultivated. PBL contexts are the epitome of such designs.

No one is arguing that all of higher education should be project based. But, in this holistic context, PBL, taken seriously and executed well, has the potential to help students connect relevance and purpose in profoundly formational ways, shaping all of the parts, as well as the whole, of an education.

One could argue on many grounds that we are at an inflection point for higher education. The personal lifetime impact of a college degree has never been clearer; the role that higher education can and must play in our society has never been more necessary. Yet, it is also arguable that the credibility of higher education has never been lower. Given all of that, the focus of higher education must turn to those paradigmatic practices that fundamentally, thoughtfully, and inclusively engage students with the world in empowering ways. It is in this urgent context that *Project-Based Learning in the First Year* takes a stand, makes its claims, and provides a most valuable contribution.

Randall Bass
Georgetown University
Washington DC
February 15, 2018

ACKNOWLEDGMENTS

The creation and sustaining of a program that is so different from what came before is the result of contributions, large and small, from a great many individuals (and even some committees!). We owe many thanks to Art Heinricher and John Orr for designing the structure of the Great Problems Seminar, our first-year project-based-learning (PBL) course, and also for their work in shepherding its approval through faculty governance. Thank you to Dennis Berkey, Worcester Polytechnic Institute's (WPI's) former president, whose early support and enthusiasm helped solidify our program. Thank you to Laurie Leshin, WPI's current president, whose continued vocal support has helped the program grow and develop even further. The Eric Hahn Family Foundation provided substantial contributions that allowed us to fund the initial course offerings. Thank you, Fred Molinari, '63, for your substantial contributions that allowed us to bring in speakers to enhance the program. Thank you to the Davis Educational Foundation for funding work that allowed the development of assessment materials for the program.

Our program has been successful in large part because of the efforts of a great many offices and individuals across campus. We owe a great deal to Jes Caron and Christine Drew, formerly of WPI's Academic Technology Center (ATC) and Gordon Library, respectively; they were instrumental in the development of the program. The current ATC and library staff, including Jess Baer, Jim Monaco, Lindsey Van Gieson, Laura Robinson, Jess O'Toole, Lori Steckervetz, and Paige Newman, continue to provide essential support to the program. Thank you to Ryan Smith Madan and others from the WPI Writing Center for your support of the program and our students as well. Thank you to Paula Quinn for the thorough assessments of the program that led to many improvements. Thank you so much to Peggy Isaacson, our rigorous, dedicated, and humorous copy editor. Thank you to WPI's Morgan Center for Teaching and Learning for funding multiple faculty learning grants that made much of this work possible. Thank you to the #SWEETSquad: Tiffiny

Butler, Matthew Foster, Adrienne Hall-Phillips, Anne Ogilvie, and Charlana Simmons, who helped develop key ideas around equitable team formation and management tools.

To all the GPS faculty, Brian Savilonis, Helen Vassallo, Kent Rissmiller, Sharon Wulf, Beth Eddy, Paul Kirby, Rob Krueger, Joe Beck, Courtney Kurlanska, Mohamad (Soroush) Farzinmoghadam, David DiBiasio, Curtis Abel, Leslie Dodson, John Bergendahl, John Sullivan, Glenn Gaudette, Sarah Wodin-Schwartz, and our authors, we are indebted for all their contributions to our understanding of how best to deliver PBL in the first year.

Finally, a heartfelt thank you to the over 2,400 enthusiastic students who taught us so much about how to teach them.

INTRODUCTION: A LITTLE BIT OF HISTORY

The Worcester Polytechnic Institute Plan and the Great Problems Seminars

Arthur Heinricher

Picture three first-year students working in the lounge area of their residence hall about three weeks before the end of their first semester at college. They have a draft version of a 3' × 4' poster on the table and are discussing the layout. Their resident adviser, a junior, walks in and says, "Hold on. You're not supposed to be able to do that yet!" The first-year students were doing something that, until 2007 and the creation of the Great Problems Seminars, had been reserved for juniors and seniors at Worcester Polytechnic Institute (WPI). We had assumed that first-year students were not ready. We were wrong.

When the faculty working on the first-year pilot for the Great Problems Seminars heard this story, we knew we were onto something important. The faculty had held long and detailed discussions of the goals and learning outcomes for project work in the first year. They had developed activities that would help students achieve the outcomes, along with ways to assess student achievement of those outcomes. And yet, I don't think that we had fully understood the power of that moment, the critical importance of the first semester of the first year. Students expect college to be different, and faculty need to use that expectation.

This book contains the collected wisdom and experiences of the faculty who helped build the Great Problems Seminars. The Great Problems Seminars, which have become known as "the GPS," have now been part of the first-year experience for more than 10 years. More than 20 different faculty have teamed up to engage students in problems ranging from food to energy to health to learning. Almost 2,500 students have completed more than 500 different projects in the seminars.

1

Projects at WPI

The story of project-based learning (PBL) at WPI really begins, in some sense, more than 150 years ago when the institute was founded. WPI was founded in 1865 with the motto "*Lehr und Kunst*," which translates roughly as "Theory and Practice." From the very beginning, the academic programs intentionally mixed, on a daily basis, theoretical course work in science and mathematics and engineering with practical work in the machine shops. The curriculum was not three years of theoretical work followed by a year of practical work. Theoretical studies in the Boynton Hall classrooms were made real in the Washburn Shops. Practical work in the Washburn Shops provided concrete motivation for the next stage of theoretical work in Boynton Hall. The term *PBL* was never used, but the mind-set was in the foundation of the institute.

The institution grew, and the programs evolved and eventually added more structure; improvement always seems to add structure and constraint. By the late 1960s, WPI's president, Harry Storke, saw an institution that had become rigid and stagnant. Many faculty, especially a group of young faculty, were dissatisfied with the traditional engineering curriculum and were ready to make a change. In 1968, President Storke created "the faculty planning committee" and challenged this small group of faculty to envision an entirely new WPI.

Of the many paths considered by the planning committee, the path chosen had some of the flexibility of the "tutorial" approach long used in Oxford and Cambridge. The goals for the new program, which became known as "the WPI Plan," were framed in the following statement:

> The WPI graduate of the future must have an understanding of a sector of science and technology and a mature understanding of himself and the needs of the people around him. While an undergraduate, he must demonstrate that he can learn and translate his learning into worthwhile action.

A completely new undergraduate program for our then all-male school was designed with this end in mind.

The faculty did something else unusual: Instead of building from the ground up and constructing a scaffolded sequence of courses that would define the path to a degree, they really did start at the top of the pyramid and focus on what graduates should be able to do at the end of their four years at WPI. They did not discuss content to cover or courses to require. They focused on project work and what students should be able to do with their learning.

The WPI Plan made two significant projects the core graduation requirements:

- *Project 1: The Major Project:* This project, usually completed in the senior year, is a design or research project in the student's major area of study. It is a nine-credit project, roughly one quarter of the senior year. The major project, actually called the Major Qualifying Project or MQP, is the place where each student would integrate and demonstrate that he or she can apply disciplinary knowledge.
- *Project 2: The Interdisciplinary Project:* This project, usually completed in the junior year, carries nine credits and asks the student to address a problem at the intersection of science and technology with societal need. This interdisciplinary project, actually called the Interactive Qualifying Project or IQP, makes a clear statement that technical knowledge alone does not define an educated person—or a WPI graduate.

Each required project has a faculty adviser working closely with an individual student or a small team (usually three to five students). For the major project, the adviser is a faculty member in the major discipline. For the interdisciplinary project, even though many of the projects have some aspects of social science research, faculty from all departments serve as advisers. This point is important to emphasize: Disciplinary boundaries were low and kept low by faculty engagement and continuous collaboration in the junior-year projects.

One other note of historical interest. Support for the WPI Plan was not universal among the faculty. When the faculty met in May 1970 to discuss the new curriculum and vote, the WPI Plan was approved in a vote of 92 in favor, 46 against, with 3 abstentions. It was close: The motion had passed with *exactly* the 2-to-1 minimum required. If one "yes" were changed to a "no," the plan would not have been adopted.

The WPI Plan and the First-Year Experience

Project work remained the core of the undergraduate program for the next 40 years. When faculty talked about the undergraduate program, they focused on project work. The projects defined faculty expectations for student achievement.

Student expectations were also framed by projects. If we asked a WPI student why he or she chose to come to WPI, the answer was almost always "for the project work." Prospective students read about the major projects and saw pictures of students working on interdisciplinary projects in London or Venice or Bangkok or Ecuador or Washington DC. Here was the rub: When students arrived at WPI, they found a first year filled with fairly traditional course work. The schedule was unusual (all classes last seven weeks), but the subjects were familiar. One common complaint about the WPI first year was that courses were "just like high school." The first year did not meet student expectations for college and WPI.

The WPI faculty sensed that the first year was not living up to the goals of the WPI Plan, and data from the National Survey of Student Engagement (NSSE) confirmed that feeling. NSSE data showed that WPI seniors were well above benchmark peers at institutions focused on science and engineering in all measures of engaged learning. The same measures for first-year students were well below those of our benchmark peer institutions. The first year did not live up to, or even really support, the excitement and engagement of the project work in the junior and senior years.

The WPI Plan started when President Storke charged the faculty planning committee. When Dennis Berkey became WPI's 15th president in 2004, he charged a new faculty committee to reimagine the first year. The report from *President's Commission on the First-Year Experience* crystalized five goals for the new first year at WPI, but perhaps the most important was a challenge to *engage first-year students with current events, societal problems, and human needs.*

That commission recommended, and President Berkey supported, the creation of a new administrative office to support the development of new first-year programs. In the spring of 2007, I, as the new associate dean for the first-year experience, sent an e-mail to all faculty asking for volunteers to pilot some new project work in the first year. Eighteen faculty responded; 11 were tenured professors, and 5 of these were department heads or associate departments heads. There was strong interest from some of WPI's most senior and most respected faculty.

Faculty working to design the first seminars identified three design goals for the pilot. First, each seminar should start with an interesting and important (GREAT) problem; academic engagement is the main goal. Second, the course should emphasize discussion and written argument. Third, even though the enrollment was set at 60 to 80 students in each course, the students should spend most of the "contact time" in small groups (15–20 students).

Professor Kristin Wobbe, the department head in chemistry and biochemistry, partnered with Robert Traver, the head of the Massachusetts Academy of Mathematics and Science (a public high school associated with WPI), to develop a seminar focused on food:

Feed the World: This seminar was built around a sequence of projects (team and individual) tied to food, ranging from the biology of genetically engineered corn to the ethics of price supports and fair trade. Sample questions include the following:

- Where does the food you see in the grocery store come from? Where does the money you spend for that food actually go?
- What does the food we waste tell us about people today? What will waste look like in 100 years?
- What are the promises and dangers of genetically modified foods?

Brian Savilonis from the mechanical engineering department partnered with historian David Spanagel to develop a GPS focused on energy:

Power the World: This seminar focused on various forms of energy resources and the history of their technologies. Sample projects include the following:

- The thermodynamics of energy analysis
- The political and social implications of changing energy sources
- The historical circumstances surrounding the growth and decline of energy technologies

Energy is both the cause and the solution to a vast array of society's problems. How has energy changed society in the past? How will new sources of energy change society in the future?

On March 14, 2007 (π day), the faculty approved a motion to offer these first two seminars. Just as with the approval of the WPI Plan, there was not universal support. Many faculty were concerned that the content covered could not be uniform because of the emphasis on project work. The credit for the first seminars would count toward distribution requirements but could not be defined as equivalent to any existing course. For example, the physics content of Power the World was certainly not the same as that covered in a traditional introductory mechanics course. The competition between covering content and providing context, engagement, and motivation for learning that content while developing skills that benefit the student is still debated.

In 2007, Feed the World students developed nine different projects. One group analyzed the cost and benefit of extending the Meals on Wheels program to Worcester residents ages 60 to 64 years. Another group studied the problem of food security in inner cities. Students in Power the World developed 13 different projects, including an energy cost analysis of green roofs and photovoltaics for a new building at WPI. Another group asked this controversial question: Is the United States responsible for air pollution in China?

Students who had completed GPS projects presented their work to the campus community in December, at the end of their first semester at WPI. Because we were so impressed with this work, it became the centerpiece for presentations to alumni, trustees, and open house events for prospective students.

Alumni have provided significant support for the GPS, many stating that they only wish that the GPS had been available when they were students. One alumnus, Eric Hahn, made a significant donation to support the first two years of the pilot program. Another alumnus, Fred Molinari, provided a significant gift to support a visiting scholars program. This program has connected the GPS students to innovators and entrepreneurs from around the world. For example, Martin Burt, CEO of Fundación Paraguaya and pioneer in microfinance and developer of the poverty stoplight program, provides projects for GPS students every year and has also helped WPI open a new project center in Paraguay. Through partnerships with the NGO Seven Hills, students developed a set of guidelines for the installation, maintenance, and use of a commercially available solar kit for charging mobile devices in rural Africa and explored use of bio-sand water filtration to reduce incidence of cholera in Haiti. Other projects have focused on bettering our local community, supporting local schools, food cooperatives, and women's shelters; the need for problem-solving is ubiquitous. (Visit www .wpi.edu/+firstyearprojects to see the full range of projects.)

At an open house event, one of the students who completed her project in Feed the World was asked by a parent, "What do you think is the most important thing you learned in your project work?" The student thought for a moment and answered, "I learned to ask a better question." Simply put, part of education is about getting the answers right, but it is just as important, and perhaps more difficult, to learn to ask a good question.

This fall, more than 300 first-year students, about a third of the class of 2021, enrolled in 1 of 7 different GPS seminars. The seminars, the themes and the approaches, continue to evolve. Challenging discussions continue regarding disciplinary credit and whether the program should be optional (as it now is) or become a requirement.

In Conclusion

At a meeting of engineering education experts in 2009, a panel was discussing the challenges facing the profession. After the presentations, the audience was invited to ask questions, and a student went to the microphone and asked, "Isn't the real problem that engineering students don't get to work on anything real until their senior year?" The panelists thought for a moment and then one answered, "Well, obviously, you have to have all of the theoretical background before you can work on anything practical."

Every mathematics student will recognize this as *proof by intimidation*: When you cannot really defend your claim, you state that it is "obvious" and assign the responsibility to the audience. This assumption was rejected when WPI was founded in 1865. The WPI Plan rejected that assumption again when it eliminated required courses and focused on learning through project work. The faculty who developed the GPS weren't sure what they could expect first-year students to do. Students have continued to exceed our expectations in their first-year projects every year.

PART ONE

MAKING THE CASE FOR
PROJECT-BASED LEARNING
IN THE FIRST YEAR

In part one, we set the stage by explaining the benefits of having students start their college career with project-based learning (PBL). We provide evidence of the value of using authentic projects early in the college experience rather than waiting until students are seniors before asking them to take on significant project work. The goal of these chapters is to convince you, and decision makers, that embarking on PBL in the first year is not only possible but also incredibly valuable. We provide guidance on mind-set and resources that make PBL an effective approach.

Chapter 1, "An Introduction to Project-Based Learning in the First Year," provides a broad overview of the rationale, benefits, and challenges of embarking on PBL. Grounded in the literature of teaching and learning, Boudreau and Wobbe make the case for the value of incorporating PBL in general, and our decade-plus experience is used to highlight the particular advantages to doing it in the first year.

As real-world projects rarely fit neatly within disciplinary boundaries, chapter 2, "The Value of a Transdisciplinary Approach," focuses on the challenges and benefits of project-based courses that transcend a single discipline. Boudreau and Rosbach provide rich examples to make a case for expanding beyond the traditional disciplinary boundaries—to have students see problems through a variety of disciplinary lenses, while never losing sight of the human context of the problem.

Chapter 3, "Institutional Support," discusses the ways that institutions can and should support initiatives in PBL to best set them up for success. PBL done most effectively is resource intensive, and in a resource-limited environment, justifying the additional needs can be difficult. Rulfs and Wobbe delineate the needs and also provide arguments for them.

Throughout this book we will provide both theoretical and practical guidance for various aspects of using PBL for first-year students. Many chapters end with a section called "Try This," which contains suggestions to spark your creativity to remodel your activities, assignments, and assessments to incorporate more project-like aspects in a way that works for you. Visit our companion website (www.wpi.edu/+firstyearprojects) for examples of student project work.

AN INTRODUCTION TO PROJECT-BASED LEARNING IN THE FIRST YEAR

Kristin Boudreau and Kristin Wobbe

Projects as vehicles for student-centered learning have a rich history in higher education, with considerable evidence demonstrating their value (Skorton & Bear, 2018; Thomas, 2000). The primary use of projects in higher education has been as a culminating, or capstone, activity where students demonstrate their mastery of knowledge and skills developed earlier. Our objective, on the other hand, is to convince you that projects, in particular interdisciplinary projects, can be just as valuable in the first year and provide a wealth of advantages to students who participate in them, including a richer, more intentional college experience; the development of important professional skills like communication and emotional intelligence; early opportunities for internships and more professional-level summer work; motivation for subsequent course work; and the building of both confidence and academic community.

The chapters in this book derive from our 11 years of experience teaching the Great Problems Seminars (GPS) at Worcester Polytechnic Institute (WPI), whose 47-year curriculum centers on project-based learning, which we will refer to here as PBL. The GPS is an interdisciplinary, project-based, first-year course cotaught by two faculty from different disciplines. We introduced this course after recognizing that WPI's first-year curriculum did not match the ambitions of the other 3 years and that our students missed the challenge of diving into PBL from their first weeks of college.

PBL can be hard emotionally, as well as intellectually and logistically. While some students will decide that PBL is not for them, others will develop the character traits that educational researchers know to be essential to academic, professional, and personal success. These traits include persistence through failure (grit), optimism, curiosity, gratitude, conscientiousness, and self-control (Bain, 2012; Duckworth, 2016; Tough, 2012). They are hard to develop in traditional courses, where faculty rarely address the emotional and psychological challenges of academic work. We have learned to confront these challenges openly and discuss them with our PBL students, because otherwise they will perhaps not recognize that ambiguity, unanswered (if not unanswerable) questions, and complexity are part of PBL and will help them develop into successful leaders and people. Of course, being honest about the challenges of teaching and the limits of a professor's expertise leaves faculty vulnerable in front of their students in a way that older models of collegiate pedagogy would find risky. And yet, the payoffs of doing this work can be profound.

As an important and extensive 2014 research study (Gallup–Purdue, 2014) revealed, a college graduate's overall sense of well-being and workplace engagement (the depth of involvement, enthusiasm, and commitment to one's work) greatly depends on two factors from the undergraduate experience: first, if they recall having had a professor—even just one—who cared about them personally, made them excited about learning, and encouraged them to pursue their hopes and dreams, and second, if they took up a research project that extended for at least one semester. Better yet is if they'd had some experience that allowed them to apply what they had learned in some practical way—in an internship or job or, as in the experiences of our GPS students, in a project that allowed them to use what they'd learned to help a sponsor or a specific community. And yet, only 3% of the college graduates surveyed reported that they had both experiences as undergraduates.

Education through project work can be difficult for faculty and students; however, benefits accrue also to the faculty who take on the challenge of project-based teaching. Faculty who participate have said, "I had more fun teaching [in this course] than I have had in years" and characterized the experience as rewarding and worthwhile. One even exclaimed, "It was fun. I loved working with these kids, and they were open and had crazy ideas, and they had dumb ideas and good ideas and I got to watch them grow and . . . they do a really good job."

Drawing on the examples of the more than 2,300 first-year students we have taught over more than 10 years teaching PBL to first-year students, we offer here some guidance on how you might develop your own first-year courses to include meaningful projects that will make a positive and long-term difference for your students. Although we include the research behind our claims, particularly in this first chapter as we make the case for the value of PBL and what perceived needs inspired PBL, we have chosen throughout this book to highlight our practice rather than the theory behind it: stories, examples, and materials to help you imagine how you might develop your own project-based courses or assignments. Our examples and anecdotes are taken from our own experiences as teachers and coteachers in a variety of courses, our conversations with each other as coteachers and during our annual weeklong faculty retreats for GPS teachers, in our experiences teaching in WPI's annual Institute on Project-Based Learning, and in our research and faculty development within the community of PBL teachers and researchers. Our goal is to inspire you and help you adopt PBL interventions, small or large. If you have never taught using projects before, try something small at first; you can always extend a project later. Chapter 4 has suggestions for reenvisioning the role of faculty as they venture into project-based learning.

We begin in this chapter by addressing the question of why an institution or faculty should invest in PBL. It's hard, it's time-consuming, and one cannot simply reuse lectures that have worked well in the past. PBL is dynamic, with the approach and often the content changing according to the students, their interests, their capacities, and their difficulties, as well as according to your local context. This chapter and the chapters that follow will begin by considering the question of "why," then move to explain "how" with challenges and benefits identified: approaches and examples that have worked for us and can be adopted and adapted by others. Above all, PBL should be conscious of its context and its participants and adjustable to those variables.

Why Use Projects in the First Year? To Motivate Students!

Educators understand the importance of motivation to student persistence and success: Only a student who cares about learning is likely to learn. However, not all highly motivated students are driven by the same aims, and the varieties of motivation can make a big difference in how well students learn. Some students are motivated simply to pass the course. Others want to perform extremely well and care most about grades; parental or instructor approval; or the award, internship, or job that might result from high performance in a course or a subject. These are all examples of extrinsic motivation, learning driven by the belief that success in the class will lead to some other goal. Extrinsic motivation often results in what Derek Bruff called "surface" or "strategic" learning—learning that, because it is valuable only to reach some other goal, is soon forgotten (Bruff, 2011). On the other hand, an intrinsically motivated student, driven by the desire to master a subject without much thought about grades or other rewards, is much more likely to learn the subject deeply rather than strategically, to be able to apply what has been learned to different contexts, to recall and use this learning after the course has ended, and to persist through difficulties (Bain, 2012; Bass & Elmendorf, n.d.; Lang, 2013).

The animating question behind this book: How do we move first-year students to this more rewarding kind of motivation? Drawing on our experiences teaching PBL to first-year college students, we hope to help you design and deliver your own PBL courses or activities for new college students. As you will see, well-constructed PBL experiences include many of the experiences that George Kuh and the National Survey of Student Engagement (NSSE) identify as "high-impact practices" because they contribute to enhanced student engagement, learning, and retention (Kuh, 2008). These practices can be life changing for students from many different backgrounds. And there is good news for those of you hoping to include them in your first-year courses: They can take many different forms, depending on your priorities and those of your institution. High-impact practices have these factors in common: They demand considerable time and effort from students (and, we must acknowledge, often also from faculty), they facilitate learning outside the classroom, they require meaningful interactions with faculty and other students, they encourage collaboration, and they provide substantive and frequent feedback.

To understand how these different practices support intrinsic motivation and student engagement, it is helpful to survey some of the groundbreaking research in educational psychology. The behaviorist theory of motivation holds that rewards (money, prizes) can effectively induce people to study and learn. However, Edward Deci and his collaborators have discovered that these incentives can actually destroy a person's motivation to work hard on a challenging and engaging project that leads to learning. Instead, they argued that basic human emotional needs are much more effective motivators. In their classic work on motivation, Deci and Flaste (1995, p. 71) identified the perceptions of both *competence* and *autonomy* as powerful motivators: "The strivings for competence and autonomy together—propelled by curiosity and interests—are . . . complementary growth forces that lead people to become increasingly accomplished and to go on learning throughout their lifetimes." Ryan and Deci (2000) later added a third human need, that of *relatedness* or personal connection. Finally, Derek Bruff (2011) added a fourth element, *purpose*. Camille Farrington and colleagues' 2012 research on adolescent learning supports these findings and affirms what people familiar with PBL have discovered about the process of learning with open-ended, challenging projects. In a conversation with Tough (2016), Farrington noted that moments of failure are the times when students are most susceptible to messages of encouragement from their teachers. Farrington argued that "academic perseverance" can be supported by a student mind-set consisting of four key beliefs (which correspond to the four principles of education): "I belong in this academic community," "My ability and competence grow with my effort," "I can succeed at this," and "This work has value for me" (cited in Tough, 2016, pp. 74–79).

The theorists of education who resonate the most with us begin with the axiom that everyone has the desire to be competent, autonomous, and related to others and to live for some purpose. The lesson for teachers is that if we give our students assignments that they believe can help them meet these four elemental human needs—for *competence, autonomy, relatedness,* and *purpose*—they will be much more likely to work hard in our courses, will be more engaged in the process, and will remember and be able to apply what they have learned throughout their lives. Teachers can leverage these four principles of education to enhance a student's intrinsic motivation. We will discuss each principle in turn, suggesting ways that you can put these theoretical discoveries to use in your first-year courses and illustrating the pedagogical theory with a representative PBL assignment.

Competence

Why. As we have seen, deep learning, or learning that will endure beyond the term of the assignment or the course, results from intrinsic motivation. Everyone wants to feel competent at something, to feel, as Paul Tough (2016) put it, that "this wasn't easy, but I did it" (p. 80). The challenge to instructors is to set assignments that are demanding but not impossible. Does this mean dumbing down the assignment? Not at all. As Ken Bain (2004) suggested, the best college teachers tell their students that they are setting a very high standard and that they believe their students can reach it. This high standard can be conveyed to the entire class; however, the confidence in the individual student must often be conveyed individually, especially in the case of students who do not have a lot of self-confidence. For underrepresented or at-risk students in particular, Bain noted that the combined approach of "set[ting] high standards and convey[ing] a strong trust in their students' abilities to meet them," along with promoting an environment of "intellectual excitement and curiosity rather than worry and doubt over 'making the grade'" (pp. 73–74), can have a powerful effect on overcoming stereotype threat and more general lack of self-confidence. Tough (2016) reported on the profound effect of a simple Post-it note written by an instructor: "I'm giving you these comments because I have very high expectations and I know that you can reach them" (p. 84).

How. Students need to rise to a challenge but at the same time believe that they are capable of reaching it. When we were disappointed with the results of our GPS students' first effort at a problem statement, instead of returning them with discouraging grades and comments, we told our students that we expected them to write strong problem statements that would set up their project reports. We told them that we wouldn't record a grade until they earned at least a B. Chisom's team (see Box 1.1) submitted multiple versions (each of which received feedback), and as they moved closer to their goal of real competency, they became increasingly excited and motivated. Lang (2013) said it well in *Cheating Lessons*, his book about how to discourage academic dishonesty: "Nothing says mastery—seriously, nothing at all—like telling a learner that they get to keep practicing and trying until they get it right" (p. 97).

Why. There are many benefits when we enable students to experience the kind of inquiry that helps them feel competent in some meaningful and genuine way. We have found in PBL that when students set out to find solutions to problems or answers to questions that their instructors haven't yet investigated, they often end by saying the experience was one of the most challenging and rewarding of their lives. As research has shown, one reason is simply that when students know they are answering a real problem, not one for which the instructor already has the answer, they are much more likely to work hard to resolution. This hard work helps to establish in students a habit of discipline that will serve them well throughout college and beyond. Moreover, it helps them learn some of the valuable skills and capacities that belong within general education requirements, a context in which students do not always give these skills much importance. Authentic questions and problems—for which there are multiple answers or not (yet) any answers at all—tend to be complex; if they were simple they would have already been solved. The solutions to these questions and problems also tend to be interdisciplinary, offering students opportunities to see the value of other disciplinary knowledge beyond their own major. We have seen, for instance, that while librarians and faculty often struggle to make students appreciate the importance of developing information literacy, students conducting research as part of their project-based work often dive into their research and critical reading, knowing that these are means to an end that interests them very much (Hanlan & Boudreau, 2014; Mathews, 2015). This is true as well of communication (whether on posters, in oral presentations, in classroom discussions, or in written reports and essays), the study of ethics, and other competencies identified with general education requirements.

How. Developing competency also depends on appropriate assessment, examinations of one kind or another that say something meaningful about

BOX 1.1
Chisom's Story

Hello Professor! I just wanted to say hi and hope that your term is so far fantastic (by fantastic I mean not so stressful because we're in WPI, stress is a norm). Anyway I hope this term is great for you. Thank you for the help you gave my team last term in GPS.

This was the e-mail we received from Chisom, a first-year student from Nigeria who had been in our GPS the previous semester. Chisom had been a quiet student; our interactions gave us very little insight into his personality or experiences. He had been part of an early, almost disastrous team whose dysfunctional behavior was so extreme that we two instructors decided to send the whole team together to our student counseling office, where they each explained their perspective and practiced listening and trying to hear the feelings of each other. The session helped the team pull together their project, but just barely. They didn't look at each other during their presentation, and they begged us to let them deliver it to us instructors in private, not in front of the class. (We agreed.) One student wore her baseball cap so low, we couldn't see her eyes.

We had been particularly anxious about Chisom, knowing how difficult it can be to recruit and then retain students from underrepresented populations into science, technology, engineering, and math (STEM) fields. What would his early experience on this team do to his interest in STEM and in PBL? In addition to Chisom, the team included a confident and outspoken woman and two other students who openly fought with her and resisted her efforts to lead the team. For his part, Chisom was quiet and tended to go along with the drift of things and to pull back and simply observe when conflict erupted. We took him aside several times during this trial to encourage him to speak up, to hold his ground, and to understand that the challenges of working with a very diverse and difficult team would make him stronger for the next team project. He always nodded but never opened up to us.

Then, in the second half of the course, Chisom formed a new team interested in education in the developing world. Together they researched African NGOs and developed a procedural intervention for an NGO working in sub-Saharan Africa to reform the public schools. This NGO had trained women to work as classroom facilitators, and many of these women were talented enough to advance into supervisory roles that required them to work in nearby villages. However, responsibilities to their own children prevented them from leaving their own villages,

BOX 1.1 (*Continued*)

contributing to the full extent they might, and enjoying the benefits of more responsibility and income. Chisom's team interviewed the NGO director via Skype multiple times and worked to propose a culturally appropriate system for child care that the director is now very enthusiastic about implementing.

In the process, each team was asked to write up a problem statement that described the problem, giving evidence of its existence, its cause, and its impacts. After we read the first draft of these problem statements—and because Chisom's team was interested in revising based on our comments—my colleague and I decided that to avoid discouraging our students as they dove into their projects, we would not grade them but would ask for revisions until each statement was worthy of a B grade. Chisom's team got closer and closer to this goal, tackling each successive draft with the excitement of a fortune seeker panning for gold. Finally, they hit pay dirt. Here was our e-mail to them:

> Wow. Beautiful. May we share this with the class? You folks have worked hard and done an impressive job here. Bravo!

The team worked effectively but not perfectly; over the course of the seven-week project, some teammates were available when others were not, and some were more comfortable following than leading, which meant there were periods when work didn't progress as it should have or one or another student found himself or herself working alone. But they became adept at communicating their concerns with each other and, at times, with us. In the end, their project was among the best of the WPI first-year class.

a student's intellectual or personal achievement. As Bain (2004) contended, exams and quizzes and grades "are powerful aspects of education that have an enormous influence on the entire enterprise of helping and encouraging students to learn" (p. 150) (see chapter 6 in this book for more on assessment). Because project assignments tend to be unconventional, faculty may be tempted not to assess them because assessment measures are less familiar. However, in spite of all we have said about intrinsic motivation, students need to know that their work is valued by their instructor. We recommend using assessment rubrics to identify the important components of a strong project for the instructor and students. With good rubrics, students can even be put in charge of their own assessment; for instance, we distribute score sheets to the class during team presentations and ask everyone to score the other teams.

Finally, as instructors seek to develop projects that help students realize their goal of competence, one very powerful instructor practice is to decrease the intimidation students feel in a classroom environment by being accessible to their students. Positive personal interaction between students and faculty has been found to result in positive effects on student achievement, particularly for underrepresented student populations (Anaya & Cole, 2001).

Autonomy

Why. Reflecting on his own time as a college student, Bain (2012) described a student who, in his spare time, went after the questions that most fascinated him. The challenge for teachers is to figure out how to make room in PBL for this kind of autonomy. Student investment in and control of the research questions they pursue is one of Bruff's (2011) principles of intrinsic motivation. It is not difficult to see how the very typical human desire for autonomy applies to the learning context. Although students without experience in PBL might struggle to identify a project of their own (given that their experiences in course assignments have been prescribed, more or less, by their instructors), PBL can give students the latitude to choose their own projects or the questions they will ask and the methods they will use to pursue them. While instructors can and should set the broad parameters—"Here is the problem you will address, the topic you will explore, the disciplinary content you will apply"—the best projects give students the autonomy to identify their own goals. With instructor guidance they can determine their project objectives and the activities they will conduct (a survey? a stakeholder analysis? a prototype?) to meet those objectives. Along the way, students apply principles they have already learned or stretch to learn new principles and skills as they dive into their project. In the process, applying theory to practice in some context or particular application they have chosen, they experience intrinsic motivation—interest in the project for its own sake—and thereby realize the value of what they are learning much more clearly than when they are learning principles outside of this particular context that they have chosen.

As Bain (2012) observed,

> People are more likely to take a deep approach to learning when they are trying to answer questions or solve problems that they regard as important, intriguing, or just beautiful, and they can do so without feeling like someone else controls their education. In most classes, however, students

usually aren't in charge of the questions, leaving an enormous gap between the realities of schooling and the conditions that promote deep approaches. Although we all can make a good case that teachers should control the questions simply because they know more and can imagine inquiries that their students will never otherwise consider, the structure nevertheless fosters strategic and surface thinking. (p. 44)

How. The following section describes a student project we designed for our GPS on food sustainability. As we will demonstrate throughout this book, authentic projects extend to fill one or more semesters, but shorter term opportunities are also possible. Open-ended, authentic problems designed to promote competence, autonomy, relatedness, and purpose can be of short or long duration, depending on one's desired learning outcomes. We will use a representative short-term assignment to demonstrate the connections between projects and student engagement.

The Ethnic Food Market Assignment

We developed this assignment with the goal of helping students understand food access, food choice, and hunger in a specific local setting. The assignment introduces students to the topic of food insecurity both intellectually and emotionally, so they can understand the conditions leading to poor nutrition while also empathizing with the people affected by it. (See Appendix 1.1 for the assignment and scoring guide.)

In this assignment, each student team is instructed to visit a different local food vendor. Each team is charged with spending no more than $90 to feed a family of four for one week. We chose these stores to represent the wide variety of food stores spread across our city, each located in a diverse neighborhood: a Hispanic market, an Asian (primarily Vietnamese) market, a convenience store, a suburban supermarket, a budget market, and a high-end organic market. The assignment presents the students with the logistical challenge of figuring out as a team how they are going to get to the store. Once there, they must decide which foods to "buy," then document their choices and analyze their weekly "purchase" to determine the per-person daily average of calories and the caloric breakdown of fat, carbohydrates, and protein. Students have one week to complete the assignment, which comes early in the first semester, when they are still unfamiliar with the campus neighborhood and, in most cases, are not familiar with each other, and many have never had primary responsibility for food shopping.

This assignment builds competency by presenting students with a multifaceted challenge they most likely have never confronted before. How will they get to the store? (We recommend they walk; all of the selected stores are within a two-mile radius of our primarily residential campus.) In venturing off campus, they are leaving their comfort zone at a time when they are just starting to become comfortable with their campus. Because they do so as a team, and because their professors are available for advice, they have support as they take on a new kind of responsibility.

The work of making personal decisions as a team is another unfamiliar activity for most students. In having to adhere to a tight budget and make choices that have important (if only theoretical) consequences for an imaginary family, they are forced to collaborate on a difficult decision; their $90 budget requires them to make sacrifices, and as a team they must decide what sacrifices to make. They must also divide the work of the analysis.

As this is the first group assignment of the course, all these activities are unfamiliar. Some activities are difficult: either logistically (organizing the field trip), emotionally (showing up in an unfamiliar place, being conspicuous in an unfamiliar environment, making difficult choices), or intellectually (doing some analytic work in the shop as they choose which groceries to buy and try to stay within budget, and again back on campus as they analyze the content of their choices). However, in their end-of-semester assessment, the students rank this assignment very highly, finding it not only "interesting" but also "worthwhile." They seem to recognize the value of taking on this set of unfamiliar challenges. In short, the assignment helps students develop feelings of competency, particularly with open-ended problems with multiple solutions and no one, clear answer.

This assignment also gives students autonomy to decide how they will approach the problem. While the broad parameters of the assignment are set—the market, the budget, the due date—students choose the timing of their shopping expedition. They also have complete choice of all foods in the market and know that their solution to the problem will, of necessity, be different from any solution presented by the other teams. They feel the challenge of complying with the budget restriction while supplying sufficient calories to their "family." The students have a number of different routes to find their best solution, and while they feel the stress of their constraints, they also enjoy the challenge of identifying creative solutions. Their restrictions are also different. While the food available in a convenience store is markedly different from what can be found in an organic market, the options in each case are sparse—poor nutritional selections or healthy and overpriced possibilities. The two teams sent to these shops have the most significant challenges and are most likely to need some reassurance that we recognize their difficult challenge. We tell them to do their best; some of life's problems do not have optimal solutions.

Relatedness

Why. The feeling of belonging to a community is an important factor in student engagement. Of course a supportive learning environment depends on a supportive teacher or adviser, but that is only one element. Learning environments that encourage peer relatedness are more likely to develop student engagement than those where students labor side by side but in isolation (Wakefield, 2016). Susan D. Blum (2016, p. 249) hypothesized that many students find nonacademic activities more absorbing than course work because these activities "are embodied," "are social," and "involve play." In contrast, traditional classrooms tend to overlook the emotional and embodied person by making students sit motionlessly, work seriously, and think in solitude for the duration of the class. Students, like all people, want to connect with others and share themselves with their communities (Benkler & Nissenbaum, 2006). When we look to the activities that motivate people to work voluntarily, we might find models of engagement that can help us think through course assignments. Collaborative activities that establish the classroom as a "community of practice"—a "shared domain of human endeavor" dedicated to "collective learning"—can set the tone for a supportive environment (Wenger-Trayner & Wenger-Trayner, 2015) that endures even through individual assignments. In addition, assignments that bring students into real or imaginative relatedness with other people can have a powerful motivating effect.

How. Consider again our ethnic market assignment, which throws students together for an unusual assignment that takes them off campus for perhaps the first time in their college experience. Of course they learn to rely on each other for support, most dramatically during their field trip adventure and then for the follow-up intellectual work they must do to complete the assignment. The assignment is embodied and social and allows for playfulness in the trip itself. In other words, there is room in this assignment for teams to have fun, learn about each other, and learn about their new community. And to the extent that the assignment makes students think about the difficult lives of some people living within just a few miles of them, it helps that they are able to do so in the company of other students.

Purpose

Why. In his study of "deep learners," Bain (2012) observed,

> Each step in that growth—success or failure—gave them marvelous new ideas about how they could become more productive and creative. They did not, however, just set out to become creative for its own sake.

That productive life had a purpose that drove their endeavors. They sought to grow and use their creativity in order to address some issue or achieve some goal that had become important to them. (p. 48)

How. Purpose is the fourth element of student engagement. When students see the value of their efforts beyond the grade, course credit, or diploma, they are much more likely to throw themselves into their academic work. Again, we turn to our GPS and ethnic market assignment. One advantage of these courses is that we organize them around important global challenges so that they are already inherently purposeful. Because they introduce PBL, moreover, the students are generally aware that the course topic and approach have some relationship and relevance to their lives or their futures. However, even such globally relevant subjects as food and water do involve theoretical considerations and could, without careful course design, deal primarily in the abstract. By sending students to food markets in their community, we deliberately make them confront the visceral issues surrounding food and its availability. We make this challenge real to our students by reminding them that while they are tasked with giving their families the healthiest food they can afford, they must also keep their children satisfied—keep them from crying of hunger at night, for example. In addition, students must think about cultural food preferences, nutrition, the economics of stores and of shopping, and the mobility challenges that make food deserts a reality for people who cannot afford cars.

For students who have never had to worry about planning meals, shopping for food, or living on a budget, these aspects alone are enlightening. The very concrete nature of walking through a market, identifying items, and making choices brings an unparalleled awareness of the reality of the issues. Students who have had these responsibilities may still struggle in markets that carry unfamiliar foods. The need to analyze the nutritional content of these same items again connects the abstract theory of nutrition to the mundane process of picking one item rather than another off the grocery shelves. Students feel this connection both intellectually and emotionally. In class, when the different student teams describe their shopping experiences and the diets they chose, the broad range of stories helps everyone realize and even empathize with the variety of experiences that different people have with food. The course takes on an aspect of reality rarely felt in a typical first-year curriculum.

While we discuss the results of the shopping assignment, some of our students are shocked to learn that there are families that depend heavily on the options offered by convenience stores, and they begin to conceptualize life without a car always at hand. In ways that watching a video or reading an article could not match, they become aware that their own experience with food—its identity, availability, and significance—is not universally shared. We work to reinforce this awareness by asking them to reflect individually on their experience with the following prompt:

> Describe the experience of trying to buy food for your family on a limited budget at your assigned grocery store. What feelings might you experience if you were really trying to buy food for your family at this grocery store? How is this similar or different from your own family's experience of shopping for food (or eating meals) when you were growing up? How does this link to one or more of your identities and/or your privilege statuses that you identified in the first exercise?

The responses from our students demonstrate their growing awareness of the disparity of experiences and access. Their reflections reveal levels of privilege. Delightfully, student responses also reveal that the assignment benefits the less-advantaged student for a change. The students who have struggled with these issues in their personal lives have already developed strategies and menus that make the assignment that much easier. This assignment and the subsequent reflection engage the students' emotions and their intellect, providing motivation for continuing to explore the issues surrounding food security and access. One of the best results, for us, is that students make these discoveries on their own, without our having to lecture about inequality of access. Instead, they discover it inductively and better understand the complexities and multiple dimensions of food insecurity. For the students, one outcome of this assignment is that they achieve the sense of purpose we hope they will develop, and it propels them through the rest of the course. They want to do something that will reduce inequities, achieve better food access, and result in more sustainable food systems, and so they have found a real purpose for the work they will undertake in our course.

Benefits

While increased student motivation benefits students at all levels, PBL in the first year provides a number of distinct benefits to those students, to faculty, and to educational institutions. For students, it offers the following advantages over traditional course work.

A Richer, More Intentional College Experience

When projects are based on authentic, real-world challenges, they almost always span more than one discipline and call on a variety of approaches and ways of thinking. Because an authentic project-based approach to learning is different from traditional assignments, it requires faculty to think about learning outcomes and design their assignments to meet those outcomes. Well-designed project assignments foster integrative learning, one of the "high-impact practices" identified by George Kuh (2008). For first-year students, this can be an effective awakening to the value that their general education classes hold—at a time when they can still make course selections to intentionally add or strengthen knowledge in areas outside their major. In the words of one GPS alum,

> My GPS, Power the World, focused on sustainability in the energy sector. Our class frequently delved into discussions about the way "green energy" is portrayed to the public. Conversations about the structure of arguments and identification of logical fallacies stuck with me, and I went on to take several classes in rhetorical theory to fulfill part of my Humanities and Arts requirement. As a mechanical engineering major, these studies gave me a unique perspective on how assumptions are made in science and engineering.

Purposeful Learning

Because PBL asks students to grapple with the complexities of real-world problems, students often find not only motivation but also purpose for their studies.

> The tremendous sense of accomplishment and the appreciation for both the joy and the pain of doing research obtained in the project made me realize what I truly wanted to do in college and rest of my career. I had never been so sure that researcher was exactly the career I wanted to take and mathematics was the science I wanted to explore.

> My GPS . . . got me interested in health and solving health problems. And the experience, the project I did in GPS, and particularly one guest speaker we had, always stayed with me. And now, thanks to all that, I am 1 month and 1 week away from graduating with my master's in public health, concentrating in epidemiology and global health. I don't think I would have realized that this is what I wanted to do if it wasn't for Heal the World.

Professional Skill Development

Regardless of major, most graduates of colleges and universities will find themselves better prepared for the next step in their lives if they have developed a set of professional skills, including writing, giving presentations, and working effectively on a team. Each of these can be a central component of any project-based class. Students from our classes have recognized the skills they have developed while working on their project, as evidenced by their own words.

> I am extremely glad that I took the opportunity to take a [GPS]. This class not only gave me a new perspective on the world and all of the challenges and problems it faces, but it taught me a lot about working with others. I wish I could say that my project team and I got along smoothly and perfectly, but that would stretch the truth. However, the bumps and curves that we faced in the road taught us a lot about each other, and helped us learn what does and does not work in a team setting. I have learned how to rely on others and trust them with responsibilities. I feel as though my capacity for patience and cooperation grew tremendously during this short timeframe. Hard work and collaboration with others leads to inspiration and positive results. I believe that teamwork is the key for success, whether it is on the scale of a college campus or in the world of international relationships.

> The whole experience was invaluable to me. My presentation, research, and teamwork skills improved immensely. More importantly, I learned how to think in different ways. I had to think of a system even when focusing on a certain aspect in that system. . . . That one class was invaluable to opening my eyes to the possibilities of new knowledge just from the way in which research is conducted or the perspective the world is seen.

Improved Competitiveness for Internships, Jobs, and Research Experiences

Because PBL involves many of the skills employers seek, we have found that our first-year students who participate in these courses are far more competitive for internships and Research Experience for Undergraduates (REU) programs. Generally, these opportunities are given to more advanced students—sometimes rising juniors, more often rising seniors. However, numerous students have reported that their ability to talk about their project work has led to offers as early as the summer following their first college year.

> This summer I will be researching as a part of the UMASS–REU program on wind energy, and I directly credit my acceptance into this REU program to the [GPS] research experience. I feel very privileged to be a WPI student and have the opportunity to engage in many teamwork projects and to be challenged by rigorous courses.

> I have an internship lined up for this summer and will be able to use the experiences I've already gained from project work in my GPS course to

excel there, then carry the experiences from the internship to my future at both WPI and beyond.

Confidence

Assessment of our first-year project program has repeatedly reminded us that one of the most easily identifiable outcomes of the program is an increase in student confidence. In student surveys and focus groups and in comments from instructors across campus, we hear that students who participated in the program have increased confidence in their abilities. In focus groups conducted a year after the experience, students attributed to their project experience the following skills:

- Assuming positions of leadership on a team
- Accepting critical feedback from others
- Having confidence to speak with individuals who are in positions of power
- Presenting oneself professionally

The student voices themselves relay the message far more powerfully.

> Now when we encounter a problem or project without any direction, we can feel confident in trusting our own judgment to approach it. This confidence is the most important thing that I'll take from this course, and something I'll be able to apply not only to future projects, but also to my employment and life after WPI.

> [GPS] was a great way to start my freshman year. I intend to go forward with a new set of ideals and role models, and a new set of goals. . . . I am grateful for the experience, and would love to do it all over again. IQPs, MQPs, summer projects, and global studies—I will be ready for you.

> Having survived this experience, I know that I can absolutely handle anything that can be thrown, unexpectedly, in my way. Whether it is academic or otherwise, I have learned that an impossible situation can be broken down into enough parts that it can be manageable and finished successfully.

Academic Community

Tinto (1993) argued that retention of first-year students is higher if the student becomes integrated both socially and academically into the academic culture. Project-based courses can do both to an extent difficult in many traditional courses.

Many students I know came out of this class with some sort of social network after the class. This network has extended throughout many people's classes, such that other courses benefit from this. I've heard people from the GPS discussing work being done in a totally different class, something I rarely hear anywhere else. The importance of such a network tends to be underplayed, and I feel this seminar excelled at creating this important part of a college experience.

In addition to all the experience and knowledge I gained, I also made friends that I will be able to keep for the next three and a half years. It was the only class where I was able to be with only freshmen, and therefore was able to meet people that were going through the same process of being a first-year student and will also continue the progress through WPI with me.

Challenges

The chapters that follow will explore this topic from different angles, considering the different challenges that complicate PBL. Here, we address a key challenge to the very idea of introducing PBL in the first year: the belief of some that these students are not yet ready and do not have sufficient foundational knowledge to undertake significant projects. This belief can come from faculty and sometimes from the students themselves. It is true that first-year student projects do not yield the same results as those from seniors, and they should not be expected to. Careful design, careful mentoring, and expressed confidence in the students will yield remarkable results all the same.

There may be many different reasons for embarking on a course or curriculum revision that considers projects in the first year. We certainly had our own, and as we have worked with these courses over the past 11 years, we have arrived at many more positive outcomes that we had never anticipated. To help you put the challenges of PBL into perspective, consider these words from a student, who describes his growth as emotional and intellectual:

> I feel this class helped shape me more than any other activity I have gotten involved in here at WPI. This class was a real challenge for me, and taught me the value of hard work, organization, and teamwork. I feel the experience of completing this project pushed me more than anything else I have done here to become a more responsible and professional person.

Given what this student and many others discover after completing a project in their first year of college, we believe that students should not wait for their final year to discover their capacity for the kind of intellectual and emotional growth that occurs in PBL. We encourage you to attempt the experiment and be amazed at what you can unleash when you give students the chance to show you what they are capable of.

ETHNIC FOOD MARKET ASSIGNMENT

Great Problems Seminar: Food Sustainability

A Term

Professor Stoddard and Professor Wobbe

Ethnic Markets/Food Costs

Targeted learning outcomes: teamwork, problem-solving, cultural awareness

Goals of this assignment: By the end of this assignment you will know a bit more about Worcester, and you will have a broader awareness of the constraints on food choices imposed by income, geographic location, and cultural preferences, as well as the impact on nutrition. (Plus you might have a greater appreciation for whomever it was in your family who did the shopping and meal prep in your household!)

You have been divided into groups and assigned 2 amounts of money, either $90 and $120 or $90 and $150. Each group has also been assigned a local market. Go to your assigned market and determine what you would buy to feed a family of 4 for a week if you had only $90. Then decide what you would do differently if you could spend the larger amount of money (either $120 or $150 depending on your group). Assume your cupboards and fridge are empty. You must buy *everything* they are going to eat or drink (except water) for that entire week, and you may spend no more than the amounts of money that you were assigned. *Your primary consideration is to keep your family from being hungry;* this means meeting the caloric needs of the family for the week.

1. Make a list of each item that you would buy, the amount, and the price. Try to keep this on one page.
2. You also need to calculate for both shopping lists (either from labels or your other resources) the totals for the number of calories and percentage

of calories from each category: fat, protein, and carbohydrates. Create a summary table that compares the daily per person averages of these for both the lesser and the greater amounts of money. Turn in only the summary table! Use the the following layout:

Category	$90 Budget		Bigger Budget	
	Cal/person	% Calories	Calories	% Calories
Carbohydrates				
Protein				
Fat				
Total				

3. Be prepared to give this information to the class on Friday, September 16.
4. Write a one-page (max) description of the process, answering the following questions:
   a. We would like a description of your market—the types of food, the size of the store, the presence of parking, the neighborhood. Learn a little more about your neighborhood here: www.city-data.com/nbmaps/neigh-Worcester-Massachusetts.html. Include information about the median income, ethnicity, and age of the residents of the area.
   b. How did you decide what to select?
   c. How well did you do in meeting the family's caloric needs? How nutritious is this diet?
   d. What effect did the larger budget have on the nutritional value of the foods you selected?

Grading

Items that will be turned in: NOTE: One per group!

1. List (25%): Food items should total the required amount of money. It should be clear how many of each item would have been purchased.
2. Table of total *per person average* calories, calories and percentage of calories from fat, protein, and carbohydrates for each diet:
   • Layout (15%): 5 columns, appearance, labels
   • Content (25%): required nutrients listed, all data present
3. Description (35%): Questions answered clearly, appropriate mechanics, demonstration of some creativity in approach to solving the problem.

2

THE VALUE OF A TRANSDISCIPLINARY APPROACH

Kristin Boudreau and Derren Rosbach

First-year college students arrive on campus excited, curious, and not yet shaped by the disciplinary cultures that will soon take hold. What better time to invite them into a course of study that is motivated by a human need rather than by disciplinary content? What better time to appeal to their desire to understand and shape the world around them? Or to guide them through the kind of intellectual inquiry proposed by the famous American biologist E. O. Wilson, who noted in 1999, "We are drowning in information while starving for wisdom. The world henceforth will be run by synthesizers, people able to put together the right information at the right time, think critically about it, and make important choices wisely" (Wilson, 1999, p. 294).

We guide students in synthetic, integrative learning in our first-year GPS, six-credit, semester-long courses taught by interdisciplinary faculty teams, typically one from a technical discipline (science or engineering) and one from a nontechnical discipline (humanities, social science, or business).

We dig in to problems that require an integrative approach to learning:

- *Reuse, Recover, Recycle*, an exploration of sustainability taught by a mechanical engineer and an English professor
- *Heal the World*, taught by a biologist and a management professor
- *The World's Water*, taught by a social scientist and an environmental engineer
- *Livable Cities*, taught by a biologist and a philosopher

- *Food Sustainability*, taught by a biochemist and a social scientist
- *Humanitarian Engineering Past and Present*, taught by a team of faculty from engineering, the humanities, and social science

In all these courses, students learn to approach a topic or problem from more than one discipline. Through readings, field trips, and various assignments, students learn how various disciplines think about a subject before they venture into their own heterogeneous teams to try to frame and solve a complex problem using whatever resources seem most appropriate to the problem.

Why a Transdisciplinary Approach Is So Valuable in the First Year

Why should universities take an integrative approach to first-year education, even as students are thinking about which major they will declare? Our GPS makes explicit in the first-year curriculum what many parents and people beyond academia have been thinking for some time: The traditional disciplinary organization of academia does not resemble the world beyond our university boundaries. The philosopher William James (1907/1981) said this emphatically more than a century ago: Compared to the "simple, clean, and noble" world of the philosophy classroom (one might replace *philosophy* with any other discipline), the world beyond the university is "multitudinous beyond imagination, tangled, muddy, painful and perplexed" (p. 4). The world beyond, we might say today, is a world of "wicked problems" (Rittel & Webber, 1973, p. 160) and "Grand Challenges" (NAE Grand Challenges for Engineering, www.engineeringchallenges.org), where what James (1907/1981) called the "purity and dignity" (p. 4) of isolated disciplinary knowledge does not exist.

Rather than inviting students into this complex world only in their later college years, we choose to introduce them to problem-based learning immediately, as one of the first courses they will take in college. We want to help our students from their very earliest days in college as they learn to become what the Association of American Colleges & Universities (Association of American Colleges & Universities [AAC&U], 2002, p. xi) called "intentional learners," people who take an active role in their education rather than thoughtlessly meeting major and university requirements. Although students will, of course, specialize as they enter their major, they must also learn to "become intentional learners who can adapt to new environments, integrate knowledge from different sources, and continue learning throughout their lives."

This integrative learning—and, in particular, the transdisciplinary approach we describe later—is valuable for both technical fields (STEM) and nontechnical fields (the humanities, business, and social sciences).

The Transdisciplinary Approach

It may be helpful to explain transdisciplinarity by considering the most familiar alternative pedagogical approaches that integrate disciplines. In a *multidisciplinary approach*, different disciplinary perspectives are incorporated in an investigation, but always in the exclusive service of the home discipline. A literature professor may draw on Freudian psychoanalysis when teaching a novel by Henry James, for instance. An *interdisciplinary approach* alternates between two different disciplinary lenses, each retaining its own methods and concepts even as the disciplines unite to answer a question. One might imagine a course on medical narrative taught by an interdisciplinary team from literary studies and psychology. As students read texts—for example, Breuer and Freud's 1895 collection *On Hysteria* and Charlotte Bronte's 1847 novel *Jane Eyre*—their professors each model their own disciplinary training to make sense of the texts; students thereby learn the methods of two different disciplines as they explore the history and culture of hysteria before turning to modern-day cases of conversion disorder. A *transdisciplinary approach* differs from both these other models in aiming at the unity of knowledge beyond disciplines with the goal of understanding the world in its messy complexity. In transdisciplinary thought, disciplinary experts come together, all of them working collaboratively to understand the problem and consider different approaches to solving it. In this way, they create new knowledge that differs from the knowledge produced by any one discipline. If disciplinary training leads to particular ways of thinking that are intelligible within but not always beyond disciplines, then transdisciplinary thinking is a deliberate way of moving beyond the limits and blind spots of these different epistemologies. A transdisciplinary approach to mental illness might include a team from literary studies, cognitive science, psychology, and social work, all of whom work to learn something about the disciplinary methods of the others so they not only contribute their own knowledge but also develop new knowledge that could not be developed from within any one discipline.

Any intellectual inquiry that focuses on a "wicked problem" or "grand challenge" is likely to take a transdisciplinary approach, if the main purpose is to understand the problem in its fullest complexity and then solve it. In our GPS, we begin with a wicked problem—something complex enough that it has not yet been solved in its entirety but where innovative, interesting, and inspiring partial solutions and approaches do exist. We choose topics we think will engage our students. One of our former presidents liked to tell graduates that their world, unfortunately, "again needs rebuilding." We aim to inspire our students to do this work as early as their first semester in college, empowering them with the feelings of autonomy, purpose, relatedness, and competence that help develop strong motivation (see chapter 1 in this volume for the scholarship behind student engagement). Like our former president who urged new graduates to "set no modest goals" because, quoting our most famous alumnus, "the dream of yesterday is the hope of today and the reality of tomorrow" (Goddard, 1904), we choose topics of broad interest for young people, giving them enough latitude to define manageable problems and set attainable goals within those grand challenges. As we discussed in chapter 1, these projects do indeed inspire students to go beyond the requirements of the class assignment, motivating them to find internships, form organizations, and identify research related to their project work.

Since 2000, the Accreditation Board for Engineering and Technology (ABET) has required engineering institutions to prepare their students to be more than mere technicians who follow the instructions of a boss. Rather, ABET recognizes that the world needs engineers who can exercise their own judgment and moral autonomy not only in solving given problems but also in defining them at the outset and in challenging assumptions about problem definitions. In addition to teaching technical skills (being able to apply STEM principles, design and conduct experiments, analyze data, and so on), ABET calls on engineering schools to teach students how to understand their ethical responsibilities, communicate effectively, engage in lifelong learning, and "understand the impact of engineering solutions in a global and societal context" (ABET, 2017). These skills are equally valuable for scientists, who increasingly are being called on to communicate their findings with the public and to understand the context in which scientific understanding is received (or rejected). These skills cannot be taught exclusively in STEM courses but must draw on the expertise of humanists and social scientists. In addition, students engaging in an integrative or transdisciplinary learning environment will be more prepared to work with experts from various disciplines in the future. A scientist who comes to understand and recognize the importance of a humanist perspective is more likely to value and be positioned to collaborate across various disciplines in the future.

Isolated disciplinary approaches make just as little sense within the humanities as within STEM. Today, humanities scholars searching for ways to deepen and expand the public role of the humanities are turning to the problem-based approach that organizes so much of STEM education, taking their place on transdisciplinary teams that include STEM professionals. These include projects like University of California, Los Angeles's (n.d.) Urban Humanities

Initiative, aimed at "more fully comprehend[ing] the space of our collective life" and exploring "the lived spaces of dynamic proximities, cultural hybridities, and networked interconnections." Programs like this one bring together the humanities, environmental design, and computer science to understand the dynamic relationships in urban space. In the words of the National Humanities Alliance and the Federation of State Humanities Councils (2017), "Increasingly, humanists are working to ensure that scholarship, pedagogy, public programs, and preservation play a key role in addressing complex issues of public concern. Cutting-edge scholarship has engendered productive public conversation on divisive issues." The movement within the humanities is away from isolated, single disciplinary work toward questions and problems that are "multitudinous, . . . tangled, . . . and perplexed" (James, 1907/1981, p. 4).

To be sure, integrative learning is part of the old liberal arts ideal, emphasizing "broad knowledge of the wider world (e.g., science, culture, and society) as well as in-depth achievement in a specific field of interest" (AAC&U, n.d.-b). However, the old approach to integrative learning is inadequate to the growing pressure of disciplinary specialization. In former days, and today still on many college campuses, integrative learning is supposed to take place in the interplay between general education and major courses. Under this system, students choose from a menu of courses in the sciences, humanities, mathematics, and social sciences, often before embarking on their major course work, and sometimes after specializing within their major. However, changes in higher education have impaired this general education ideal in many cases. After World War II, driven partly by competition for federal research funding, scientific and technical fields became more specialized. Disciplinary specialization now saturates higher education, including nontechnical fields and including, distressingly, many general education courses (National Academies 2018, p. 27). As a result, general education does not always reflect the integrative mission of general education and its proponents, most notably the AAC&U. A recent consensus report by the National Academies of Sciences, Engineering, and Medicine puts the case this way: "As general education lost ground to specialization over the past century, it has often taken the form of superficial exposure to a smattering of disciplinary approaches whose relationships and relevance to one another are rarely made clear to students" (p. 29). Because students often need help making connections between domains and applying the knowledge learned in one discipline to the context of another, general education requirements only rarely lead to deep and authentic integrative learning. When the faculty teaching the different courses are not in dialogue with one another, it is hard to imagine any but the most curious and motivated students being able to make meaningful connections. For another, many students are not deeply interested when they enter the classroom of a required general education course. If they are not motivated extrinsically to do well in the course, or intrinsically by their interest in the subject matter, it may be difficult for them to perceive the value of the course in relation to other courses they may be taking and particularly in relation to their major field of study. WPI's 10-year-old experiment with transdisciplinary, project-based courses in the first year has convinced us that one effective means of delivering truly integrative educational experiences is through transdisciplinary approaches to PBL (see Box 2.1).

BOX 2.1
Course Projects Can Inspire Continued Efforts by Students

Students in the GPS program have been inspired to start a club on campus to continue their work. In 2008 several GPS students, including Anna Chase, started the club Industry's Humanitarian Support Alliance NGO (IHSAN) because of their work with that organization in their project. This later became the Global Humanitarian Alliance (GHA). GHA currently has 95 WPI student members. They are involved in both international and local projects: Dengue Project in Paraguay, Save a Child in India, and Worcester-based efforts to help educate refugee children and harvest crops to fight food injustice. GHA was awarded WPI's Best Club of the Year (2015) and Best Program of the Year (2016) for #beAware.

Transcending the Limits of Disciplinary Knowledge

While most of our institutions are organized in ways that separate people from different disciplines—with the greatest institutional impediments separating science from humanities from business from engineering—a transdisciplinary approach can overcome those artificial boundaries and "the mismatch between knowledge production in academia and in real-life problems" (Hyun, 2011, p. 9). A course or assignment that takes a deliberately transdisciplinary approach participates in "the science and art of discovering bridges, interconnectedness, and interdependence among different areas of knowledge (hard, social, and applied sciences). It concerns possibilities in the natural and social ecology of human living in a socially responsible way to respond to and deal with emergent human and natural problems" (Hyun, 2011, p. 9).

When we approach a topic from the vantage point of more than one discipline, we open up possibilities for exploration and understanding that a single discipline cannot offer. Often this approach requires us to invent new course assignments. In Food Sustainability, for instance, we wanted students to understand the concept of food deserts—not just intellectually but also emotionally. What does it feel like to live in a neighborhood where affordable, high-quality, fresh food is not available? What kinds of trade-offs are necessary? Of course, readings about food deserts helped students understand the concept, but we also wanted them to develop some direct experience with the challenges of food deserts in order to comprehend some of the many factors responsible for malnutrition and poor health. A literary approach might help students develop empathy for people who go hungry, while a biochemical approach could help them see what nutrients are necessary to keep the body healthy. An economic or sociological approach could help them understand the economic factors responsible for putting certain kinds of grocery stores in certain communities. Each approach has its strengths, but none will give students a full understanding of the problem. Rather, we developed a pair of structured assignments that began with students themselves: What do you eat? How many calories and what nutrients do you consume? How much energy—time, calories, fuel—does it take to bring you and your food together? What might be different if you had no access to a dining hall, an automobile, a mother who cooks for you, the money to order a pizza? Then we asked them to walk in the shoes of someone else: Dividing them into teams, we gave each of them a budget, assigned them to a particular market, and told them to investigate that market and decide what to buy for an imagined family of four (see Appendix 1.1). This shopping trip was to provide food for one week. Their criteria—or design requirements—were to keep their children from going hungry, to provide them with nutritious meals, and as a very last desirable (a luxury) to give them a treat of some kind. Students learned how difficult it is to meet these requirements when one's budget is tight and mobility is limited. Readings in economics allowed us to introduce the concept of elasticity, so students could think about what extras they might buy if their budget increased. Would they buy more of the starchy staples, or something more nutritious like meat or fresh vegetables? If they were inclined to buy something nutritious, did they live near a market that had such goods available?

This assignment forces students to be both analytical and reflective, to take account of quantitative values (nutritional content, cost, distance between shopping and housing) and qualitative values (Which foods are most appealing? Culturally familiar? What does it feel like to be restricted to processed food? How might that feel to someone raised on fresh food? Is it fair that some people in your city have access to a wide variety of foods, while others do not?). It calls on practical resources (how to work within the constraints of budget and mobility), as well as imagination (What alternatives to the local convenience store might be possible?). Moreover, by putting students in the shoes of the stakeholders who experience the problem of limited access to food, we encourage them to understand the problem as it really exists, beyond the arbitrary boundaries of disciplinary expertise. A field trip is not necessary for a transdisciplinary assignment: Websites such as those maintained by the Centers for Disease Control and Prevention, the U.S. Department of Agriculture, and the United Nations Food and Agriculture Organization offer a wealth of information that can be used to develop an experiential, transdisciplinary project assignment. Other GPS courses, like The World's Water and Power the World, include similar activities where students track and reflect on their personal use of water or energy and the impacts of this consumption on society. The key is to identify an authentic problem or challenge and draw on resources that do not limit users to a single disciplinary perspective.

Using a Transdisciplinary Approach for First-Year Project-Based Courses

Although not all PBL is *problem based*, WPI's focus on global problems in its GPS program results in a necessarily transdisciplinary approach. Faculty use a complex global problem to shape the process of student learning and to guide student projects. As seen in our assignment about food deserts, the needs of communities and the realities of their circumstances transcend disciplines and require students to learn about the different aspects of a challenge and to explore possible solutions. They then work to develop new knowledge by finding and practicing new and unfamiliar methods of analysis.

WPI's GPS program consists of project-based courses that engage first-year students in authentic learning, current events, societal problems, and human needs. Each seminar focuses on an important global problem and works with students to develop a project that addresses one small piece of the broader global problem. The goal of Food Sustainability, for instance, is not for students to solve the world's hunger problem but rather to identify a specific, contextualized food challenge (e.g., one particular community's struggle with food deserts, maternal milk supplies, or diabetes and obesity; project posters viewable at www.wpi.edu/+firstyearprojects) and develop a solution or reduce the scope of the problem. By focusing on global problems and challenging students to define and address some particular problem, these courses help meet the challenge that Brundiers, Wiek, and Redman (2010) identified:

> Because incoming students are usually unfamiliar with the concepts and practices of real-world learning, they need to be introduced to those models, methods, and tools. This could be done through integrating an introduction to real-world learning paradigms into a regular course, such as an undergraduate methods course or the general introductory course for freshmen. (p. 320)

We meet the transdisciplinary challenge by offering our seminar as a six-credit course taught by two faculty members from different disciplines who are present and active in all class meetings. This course carries three credits for the home discipline of each instructor. Thus, Power the World, a seminar focusing on energy, taught by a philosopher and a social scientist/environmental engineer, carries three humanities credits and three social science credits. Students spend the first half of the course exploring the nature and extent of the problem and searching for a piece of the problem that they can address. In the first part, they confront the problem from a number of disciplines, but especially those represented by the two faculty. In the process, they embark on a number of low-stakes assignments that introduce them to open-ended research questions and the necessity of drawing from a range of disciplines and ways of thinking. For instance, students complete a personal energy use log and reflection activity that challenges them to think about their own part within the landscape of global energy. They also explore the various types of fuel used for energy production, answering questions about the origins and uses of particular renewable and nonrenewable energy sources (e.g., solar or oil) in relation to the social, economic, and environmental impacts of these types of energy production. They also do some team-based academic research on these sources, teaching a class about their findings. All of these assignments are designed to incrementally progress from basic to more advanced learning opportunities that introduce students to the scope of the problem from different perspectives and prepare them for the development of their own projects (Pfeifer & Rosbach, 2016) (see Box 2.2).

Of course, a transdisciplinary approach does not need to involve a complete course, let alone a six-credit course. We can imagine two faculty from different disciplines scheduling complementary courses to meet at the same time; a single curricular unit might bring both classes and faculty together for a transdisciplinary project. In any case, your course design should begin with an open-ended, authentic challenge or problem complex enough to draw on more than one kind of disciplinary knowledge. An *authentic* problem is a problem that has significance beyond the walls of the classroom and whose solution is not already known by scholars in the field. In the case of our GPS program, we want to give students a full semester experience with a grand challenge, moving them from exploration in the first half of the semester to team formation, problem definition, and project design in the second.

Start modestly: All you need to begin are two faculty from different disciplines who are willing to spend some time together designing an assignment, sharing class time, and taking the risk that comes from moving beyond familiar territory. Start with a problem of some kind: maybe an injustice in your neighborhood or in the national news; maybe a question you don't know the answer to; maybe a place whose history is unknown. Talk over the dimensions

BOX 2.2
Scaffolding the Transdisciplinary Approach

Students must discern, evaluate, integrate, and apply the important facts that exist across multiple disciplinary environments based on their relevance to the specific problem, place, and people with whom they are working. An example of a first, low-stakes assignment we use in Power the World is as follows: Students begin by exploring the various types of fuel used for energy production. They are prompted to answer questions about the origins and uses of particular renewable and nonrenewable energy sources, such as solar or oil, in relation to the social, economic, and environmental impacts of these types of energy production. Then they must do some team-based academic research on these sources, give a short presentation to the wider class about what they learned, and write a research essay. Complementary assignments include a personal energy use log and reflection; a research notebook, a research workshop with our research librarian (with whom students work closely for the duration of the course); diversity training with the director of our office of multicultural affairs; and a larger, more open-ended, team-based assignment on global energy issues. In aggregate, these experiences are designed to incrementally progress from basic to more advanced learning opportunities and from local to global challenges. All students are challenged to reflect on their own impact on their local environment, on the campus, and on the global consequences of their lifestyle choices.

of the problem with your colleague, try to get at its many facets. Then design an assignment that invites students to explore those facets, identify a challenge, and solve it. The more you experiment with transdisciplinary, collaborative teaching, the more likely you are to want to include projects in every course.

While the ideal is to coteach these courses, it is possible to imagine ways that a transdisciplinary experience can be created by a single teacher. To begin, some instructors already work in interdisciplinary fields and can to some extent provide disciplinary integration. Furthermore, as discussed elsewhere in this book, partners can be used at different stages of the course to broaden disciplinary perspectives. Assignments, activities, guest lectures, and collaboration with external partners or project sponsors can lead to a more transdisciplinary course and project.

An additional option is to collaborate across courses. For example, a few courses could examine multiple aspects of a common problem like climate change. A biology course could be paired with a social science or humanities course like economics or history. Crosscutting assignments or joint activities could be used to encourage students to learn and apply multiple ways of examining the common problem. This type of collaboration could even go a step further and create a shared authentic project that unites the various courses. For example, courses in economics, biology, and philosophy could work together on addressing the problem of food waste on campus. Each would contribute to a shared understanding of the different aspect of the problem and more effective solution. The biology students could study processes of decomposition, the economics students could examine market and financial aspects, while the philosophy students focus on ethical issues surrounding food waste.

The Challenges of a Transdisciplinary Approach

A transdisciplinary approach offers different challenges to the groups that experience it and the larger environment in which it takes place.

For Students

Because faculty are also learning, students quickly understand that there are no clear answers to transdisciplinary problems or a single and limited body of knowledge to be learned. The ambiguity of these open-ended problems, where knowledge has no boundaries and the faculty "experts" are also learning, can be very difficult for students. One advantage of exposing first-year students to a transdisciplinary approach is that they are to some extent "undisciplined." They have not yet developed a narrow disciplinary way of thinking.

For Faculty

True collaboration requires a significant investment of time. Most obviously, the work to develop a course or assignment in collaboration requires time to meet and talk through a developing idea (see chapter 5 for more on team teaching). A truly transdisciplinary project or assignment requires that multiple disciplinary experts learn something about new disciplines and work together to create new knowledge. When transdisciplinary course work includes community partners—experts to help teach a class (see Box 2.3), sponsor a project, or contribute to an assignment—the work of coordinating these partnerships becomes an additional obligation (see chapter 8 for more on working with sponsors). This kind of work cannot be rushed and, of course, it takes time away from other responsibilities, including scholarship, which in many institutions is the primary basis for faculty recognition. Moreover, collaboration can be hard, calling on people at times to make difficult compromises. For faculty whose primary work has always been solitary and independent, these new pedagogical relationships can be a struggle.

BOX 2.3
Assignment on Contacting Experts

One way some of our courses supplement the expertise of the faculty is to have students contact outside experts. In one assignment, students are required to identify, contact, and interview at least three experts in a field who will help them better understand the challenges and possible solutions of the problem they are addressing. Many times, these are other academics at the same institution, but students can also consult experts at other universities, corporations, or nonprofits. Students then must develop questions and conduct interviews with these experts. Through this assignment students get a much broader view of the complexity of a particular problem: what is known about the problem and—more important—what is not known. The assignment also provides opportunities for students to develop skills in interviewing, professional communication, and data analysis.

For Campus

As Rossing and Lavitt (2016) noted, "Institutions impose the demands of collaborative work on an environment designed to support and reward individualistic work" (p. 3). The traditional structures (academic departments, discipline-based courses, professional support, and faculty reward systems) discourage transdisciplinary teaching. And because faculty are presumed to be experts in their disciplines, colleges can be reluctant to recognize or reward the time faculty spend developing themselves so they can be better teachers. As Ramalay (2016) observed,

> The new collaborative problem-solving approaches developed by communities outside of academia are often incompatible with the culture and organization of higher education institutions. It can be challenging to draw upon the resources of an academic community in order to contribute to community-based collaborations. (p. 36)

To support transdisciplinary teaching, most universities will need to work hard to understand the different inputs and outcomes of transdisciplinary teaching and to support this teaching, often with new standards and processes (see chapter 3 for more on this).

The Benefits of a Transdisciplinary Approach

With a clear view of the challenges ahead, those who embrace transdisciplinary teaching should also prepare for dramatic benefits—again, for various stakeholders of a transdisciplinary approach.

For Students

One of the most important student benefits is the strong gain in student engagement that derives from the authenticity of PBL. Stolk and Martello (2015) noted that within engineering education, contextualized learning, which puts "human contexts at the center" of technical content, helps students see the societal value of what they are learning, helps them develop feelings of relatedness to the work they are studying, and leads to measurable improvement in student motivation and lifelong learning skills. While this disciplinary integration is effective for all students, it offers particular benefits to women. "Improving cross-disciplinary connections between technical studies and societal contexts may help spark the type of student engagement that leads to long-term growth" (Stolk & Martello, 2015, p. 434). This quasi-religious description of a course by one of our former students illustrates the deep motivation that can be harnessed in PBL: "The GPS experience isn't like anything I've ever done," explained Jacob Aki. "It's not a class in an ordinary sense. In fact, I feel it has more in common with a vocation. It's a call to do something real and tangible, which [in academia] is an all too rare occurrence."

Moreover, when the representatives of their disciplines honestly address the limits of disciplinary thinking and model exploratory, transdisciplinary thinking, students are able to see into the black box of intellectual inquiry. For many students, and particularly for first-generation college students, academic study can seem like a secret society with indiscernible rules. When faculty address the value and limits of what one discipline can bring to a question, they empower students to think about knowledge as contextual and available for human ends. Students thereby learn to prioritize the questions they want to answer over disciplinary conventions, and they learn to take an active role in intellectual inquiry. Rarely do first-year courses enter into the question of what constitutes knowledge. Discovering their own agency in intellectual inquiry can empower students to take an active role in designing their own curriculum and their assignments for any single course.

Finally, a transdisciplinary approach can have a significant impact on a student's career prospects. According to Linda Katehi (2015), an engineer and former chancellor of UC Davis,

> Leading information-based companies will always need bright young engineers and other technical experts to solve problems. But they need more people who know how to think across boundaries, integrate information, identify social and cultural trends, acquire data in support of their ideas, crunch it, and present it in a clear and compelling way.

For Faculty

Once we understand the benefits of integrative, transdisciplinary learning for students, it is hard to overlook these same benefits for faculty. Transdisciplinary teaching connects faculty with experts from other disciplines as they address meaningful problems. As faculty model "co-constructed, decompartmentalized, shared, and applied knowledge" (Rossing & Lavitt, 2016) for their students, they simultaneously take part in this same knowledge production and can draw on their new understanding and relationships as they seek research funding or join community-based research teams.

At the same time, faculty share the best of all the disciplines that engage them. The reciprocal gains of working alongside a professor from a different discipline can be hard to overstate. In many cases, being exposed to different pedagogies can be transformative. At the very least, the relationships forged in a transdisciplinary classroom can be rejuvenating, fun, and professionally satisfying.

For Campus

An institution with successful models of transdisciplinary teaching can be transformed in valuable ways. Like our classes, which start with a meaningful and complicated problem, college campuses also aim at a challenging problem: how to educate students to ensure an adequate stewardship of the future—not only for the individual student but also for the world the student inhabits. This is a *wicked problem*, and one that universities have the resources to address. What happens in a transdisciplinary classroom can be a model for what happens on campus, and the faculty who teach these classes can be leaders in their communities. Ramaley (2016) observed that to

> prepare a differently educated citizenry and to play meaningful roles in new forms of community-building, colleges and universities must model informed and collaborative ways of learning and working within their own institutional contexts as well as through their interactions with the broader society of which they are an integral part. (pp. 41–42)

If, as Ramaley (2016) noted, colleges "have been slowly embracing a culture of engagement that supports the new kinds of relationships and collaborations that will be needed to address the 'big questions' and challenges that shape our era," then transdisciplinary teaching can help accelerate and strengthen that process. Faculty who teach in courses like the ones we are describing can lead with "new forms of improvisational expertise, a kind of process expertise that knows prudently how to experiment with never-before-tried relationships, means of communication, and ways of interacting that will help people develop solutions that build upon and surpass the wisdom of today's experts" (Heifetz, Grashow, & Linsky, 2009, pp. 2–3). Finally, the campus environment is stronger when faculty learn how to work together across organizational lines, drawing on insights from many disciplinary and community perspectives. The faculty alliances formed through transdisciplinary teaching can demonstrate the successes that are possible when faculty from both sides of Snow's (1959/1998) "Two Cultures" divide lay aside their identities as individual departments and disciplines protecting their own interests and come together to form a shared educational community.

Try This

1. *Think about some of your academic or nonacademic friends from different disciplines.* If you were to sit down with one or two of them for a cup of coffee to discuss a "grand challenge," whom would you choose, and what challenge would you discuss? Try it: Invite one or two people to join you to identify and explore a challenge. Take turns describing how your distinct disciplines might approach the challenge: What questions would you ask, what resources would you bring, and where would you go for additional information or understanding? Ask questions of each other so you learn about these different approaches, which you may have thought you understood—you may be surprised to learn what you don't know. Finally, lay out a provisional student assignment that draws on these different perspectives, and try it out in one or more of your classes.

2. *Identify transdisciplinary projects using your own local context.* When thinking about projects to pitch your students, consider the following:
   - Students (what they already know and are interested in)
   - Local resources (organizations that might need help, local history or green spaces)
   - Faculty (those you know from other disciplines)

Putting these disparate parts together, think about a single assignment you might propose to students in two very different classes. It might be a citizen science experiment that connects science students with media or art students to document the experiment or writing students to seek a funding agency and write a grant proposal. It might be a historic preservation project bringing together students from history, engineering, art, writing, or sociology. It might focus on a literary classic, asking students to recreate some scene, for instance, taking ecology, philosophy, literature, and art students to retrace Thoreau's boat trip on the Concord and Merrimack Rivers.

3

INSTITUTIONAL SUPPORT

Jill Rulfs and Kristin Wobbe

Because Jill is a good "utility player" in her department and often fills in to teach courses when other people can't, her department head was initially reticent to let her be involved in teaching in our GPS series. But when the university president mentioned that departments that had faculty members participating in the GPS would be given an advantage in the faculty hiring process, her department head's mind suddenly changed. Institutional support can and does make a difference!

What does it take to drive successful curricular change? At WPI we knew for many years that our first-year curriculum left our students frustrated with the similarities to high school, the lack of project opportunities (we sell ourselves as a project-rich school), and the fact that the first-year students were demonstrably less engaged in their work than our upper-class students. We spent many committee years worrying, discussing, and proposing solutions and finally decided to experiment with an interdisciplinary, team-taught, project-based class for our first-year students, called the Great Problems Seminars.

This book arose from that experiment. One of the keys to the success and longevity of that experiment was sufficient institutional support. That support took many forms, some requiring funds, many requiring some creativity—and some support is cheap and easy. This chapter identifies those areas that we found to be significant drivers of our successful venture into a curricular change that has lasted over a decade. In this chapter we begin with a focus on the reasons institutions should support initiatives to introduce PBL in the first year; then suggest a number of areas in which institutional support can be critical, including faculty development and broader programmatic support; and finish with the institutional challenges and benefits of adding PBL.

Why Commit Institutional Resources to PBL in the First Year?

There is no question that a successful venture into PBL will require extra—extra effort, extra time, extra funding. But we point out in this section that the yields in student learning, preparation for accreditation, and fodder for institutional promotion can make the investment worthwhile.

Demonstrates a Commitment to Student Learning

While PBL presents many challenges at the institutional level, some of which will be discussed here, it also provides an opportunity to show the university's commitment to making student learning a priority. As brick-and-mortar institutions face increasing competition from online options and public debate about the value of a university education, the ability to demonstrate an institution's focus on student-centered learning is critical to the perception of value and to student retention (Kuh, 2008; Tinto, 2010). One way to do this is to offer innovative undergraduate programs that address personal and societal responsibility, knowledge construction beyond content, and development of life skills to address real-world problems. These are some of the value-added aspects of undergraduate education that online courses generally do not provide.

Yields Material for Institutional Promotion

In recent years, institutions of higher education are dedicating increasing attention and resources to marketing and branding to enhance the school's reputation and visibility. Students in our GPS program have provided great fodder for our marketing efforts and are often showcased on our university website. PBL can yield deliverables that are well suited to public presentations—posters, robots, plans, stories. Our program concludes with a public poster session that provides wonderful material for both photography and videography. At this event, the students are dressed for success, are proud of their work, and have something to show. They can tell stories that demonstrate the skills and abilities they have acquired. If some of the projects have sponsors, they can provide endorsements of the student work. Your marketing team will find these more interesting and powerful examples of the kinds of work that students at your institution do. This is important for your external reputation and it can strengthen morale and enthusiasm for the program internally.

A few years ago Jill had the pleasure of advising a project team in her GPS course that was subsequently featured in a *New York Times* article

(Drew, 2011) talking about its GPS project on herd immunity. That kind of national coverage from such a respected outlet not only was great as a marketing tool but also gave the students a chance to realize how important the work they were doing was and how innovative this approach to learning is.

> I talked about my GPS project at my interview for veterinary school. Even though it was a freshman year project, it was something I felt was unique to me that reflected who I am. I was really proud of the work and, of course, the recognition it, and I, got in the popular press.

. . . And Yields Material for Institutional Accreditation

Project work combines content learning with skills building and can easily provide students with competencies that employers of our students value (National Association of Colleges and Employers, 2016). These include collaboration, communication, problem-solving, and critical thinking skills (see chapter 10 for more detail). In addition, they provide institutions with evidence of progress toward institutional learning outcomes. All universities are faced with the need to provide accreditation bodies with data supporting their claims. Well-designed assessment from these courses can provide data on outcomes such as information literacy, global and cultural competence, civic engagement, and ethical decision-making that can be difficult to demonstrate in other more traditional disciplinary-based courses.

How Can Institutions Support PBL?

The place to start with institutional support is with the individual faculty who will be on the front lines of this work. We will explore the obvious need for faculty development and more, including rethinking faculty assessment metrics, recognizing the scholarship of teaching and learning, and recognizing their effort to try this new approach and the value it brings to the program and the institution.

Supporting Faculty

Faculty development. To realize the benefits, the institution must provide support for faculty at the university administrative and departmental levels. For faculty not used to teaching in nontraditional formats, there is a learning curve that accompanies the paradigm shift to PBL. Working with peers on campus who are also experimenting with PBL can be very helpful. Most campuses also have a Teaching and Learning Center where there are sure to be resources to assist faculty initiating a PBL approach.

One mechanism that has proved enormously beneficial to the long-term success of the program is our GPS Summer Institute. Participating faculty are paid a small stipend and are provided with lunch. For a week of mornings shortly after commencement, all GPS faculty meet as a group, and through this we have developed a community of practice (Wenger-Trayner & Wenger-Trayner, 2015). During these mornings, we discuss our project-based courses, experiments we tried that were either spectacular successes or spectacular failures. We share assignments, frustrations, and accomplishments. In these morning sessions we have developed a core set of learning outcomes and associated rubrics. We have had guest speakers help us with shared problems; for example, our Counseling Center staff on team issues, an assessment expert on how to help students create useful surveys. Each of the topics has been useful, but the main benefit has been the generation of a sense of community and shared purpose. Through these mornings (and paid-for lunches), faculty have recovered a renewed sense of joy in the art of teaching.

Recognition of teaching as scholarly work. Providing opportunities for faculty to attend conferences and workshops of organizations, such as the Association of American Colleges & Universities and Project Kaleidoscope (PKAL), is also very helpful. These meetings provide the faculty with opportunities to present course design, delivery, and assessment as evidence of scholarly work. The time and effort to develop and evaluate these courses is often more work than might be required for a more standard course. Generally there are no standard texts or published course outlines to rely on for project-based courses. Finding creative, active-learning-based approaches to delivering content from even one or sometimes two often diverse disciplines while also supporting the embedded skills-based learning requires significant investment of time by faculty members. Faculty recognition at the institutional level for this effort is also important. On-campus presentations sponsored by our university's Teaching and Learning Center can help assert the importance of this kind of educational initiative to colleagues and administrators and legitimize the time and effort required of faculty participants.

Faculty assessment metrics. As the number of these nontraditional courses increases, institutions must also determine how to evaluate them using "nontraditional" metrics. Institutional research offices can provide data to allow norming of scores on teaching evaluations from these courses rather than just including them in the data pooled from courses across the university. Student learning gains will be very different in a project-based GPS compared to a traditional calculus course, and student reactions to these courses may also be more diverse. The value of this specific set of institutional research data is also critical to ongoing course and program improvement, allowing evaluation of faculty and topic-specific approaches. Joint meetings of the course instructors provide critical opportunities for faculty to share approaches, as well as review the assessment data to determine the success of a variety of approaches in meeting learning outcomes. At the faculty level, these normed evaluations are also important for teaching portfolios, annual reviews, and the like, where metrics are often used to evaluate teaching quality with often significant consequences relative to tenure and promotion.

Supporting participation. Recognition of a faculty member's willingness to participate in these courses is essential at both the institutional level and the department level. As noted in the opening vignette, evidence that the institution at its highest administrative levels supports and values the effort required by these courses can be critical to allowing participation. A letter in this regard from the chief academic officer is also a valuable artifact for a teaching portfolio. One of the key levers to early acceptance of our experimental program was the frequent public praise given to participating faculty and students. We were recognized for our courage and rewarded for the successes of the students and the programs. The best thing about this kind of support is that it is easy and it is FREE!

Valuing the approach. From the faculty perspective, trying this different kind of course can be difficult, especially for junior faculty looking to demonstrate their value both as teachers and as departmental contributors. Many senior faculty often devalue this "newfangled" approach to education and may be quite vocal and negative in their comments. This—despite the well-documented evidence that this mode of teaching requires more of the instructor's time and increased levels of individual mentoring—often encompasses broader advising as students begin to rethink their personal goals as a result of the project work they choose. It seems evident that introducing the kind of learning inherent in these courses would provide value to other faculty as students progress through the university curriculum. At our institution, where PBL is included across the curriculum, the value of students' bringing skills related to project-based team learning as they progress onto other courses cannot be understated. The students themselves are explicit about the value they have received in these kinds of courses.

> GPS helped kickstart my career by showing me what it is like to work for several months in a group to start and finish a major project. This project will help me throughout my career, not only in my resume, but using what I learned in working with others to build my leadership and teamwork skills.

Now when I receive a project, I know what I have to do, and I know that it is never anything too large or difficult. At the beginning . . . I thought that what they expected was too much for one term. It was not, and now when I am handed a project I never think it is too much; I look at it and think this is doable. This project-oriented curriculum also drew me to WPI, since I knew I would be able to get my hands "dirty" and not just learn in a classroom.

I completed a [GPS] my first semester of work here, which introduced me to the [PBL] WPI is famous for. It taught me about some of the current world issues that need solving, and what I can do to help. I learned about the leadership necessary to develop a project, and the fact that I can make a difference. This experience showed me that I don't want to be a cog in a machine of progress; I want to be leading the progress.

Expanding the Instructional Team

Beyond ensuring that there are well-supported and trained faculty to deliver project-based courses, we would encourage you to think more broadly about the instructional team. There are additional resources that can be leveraged to increase student learning, the professionalism and impact of the student projects, and the success of your program.

Student leaders. For classes that have more than 24 students, we have provided support in the form of upper-class student leaders (peer learning assistants, or PLAs), typically at a ratio of 12 to 15 students to 1 PLA. PLAs can greatly improve chances for an enjoyable outcome. The PLA role is varied but can be divided into two major categories: resources for faculty and resources for students. As key resources for faculty, they can grade some assignments, typically the more quantitative or less writing-intensive ones. They can test-drive new assignments. For assignments that involve open-ended problem-solving, having a PLA try them first can be invaluable for gauging the difficulty and time involved in completing the assignment, both of which can be difficult for faculty to determine. They can provide feedback on how the class is going from the student perspective and even suggestions for improving class structures and assignments.

The role of the PLA in supporting first-year students is even more significant. Most first-year students are unfamiliar with the kind of open-ended assignments typical in PBL and are anxious about revealing their lack of understanding to the faculty. They more readily turn to the PLAs for help with interpreting the complex directions and for guidance about the expected products of their work. The PLAs can even review the student work prior to submission.

Perhaps a PLA's most important contribution is helping students navigate team dynamics. As will be discussed in chapters 11 and 12, team dynamics can be the largest hurdle to successful completion of team-based projects. Students are often reluctant to discuss problems in meetings with teammates and faculty—there is a strong, if misguided, concern about "ratting out" their teammates who may not be living up to expectations. They are far more willing to discuss team issues with a PLA, and the PLAs are trained to help the students deal with the issues in a fair and productive way. This is an important part of the learning process, and one that is delivered, in our experience, far better by student peers.

PLAs are generally recruited from the students who have had a similar classroom experience and can be compensated either by pay or by credit. Our PLAs are paid slightly above minimum wage and work approximately 8 to 10 hours a week. They attend the class and have office hours, respond to e-mails from students, and perform tasks as assigned by the faculty. It is important to have weekly meetings with the PLA team where the group can review the prior week and prepare for the week to come. These weekly meetings can be run by the PLAs as well.

Before the course begins, however, it is important to give the PLAs training to prepare them to deal with issues they may face. No matter what roles the PLAs are going to be asked to fill, they should be educated about FERPA (Family Educational Rights and Privacy Act) and its implications. PLAs will no doubt have access to student performance information that will need to be kept confidential. A set of scenarios that can be used to guide training and discussion of FERPA issues is found in Appendix 3.1.

Team dynamics issues will almost certainly be a key area where students will seek PLA support. The PLAs will need guidance on how to guide the students through their challenges. We've found that acting out scenarios is one of the best forms of preparation for this. Several of our most common team dynamic issues are represented in the scenarios found in Appendix 3.1. Further valuable resources for both PLAs and faculty guiding student teams are chapters 11 and 12 and *Team Writing* by Joanna Wolfe (2010). *Team Writing* contains supports for students around writing and provides great instruction on producing team charters, setting group expectations, and navigating difficult situations. Finally, PLAs should be educated about the benefits and issues surrounding diversity. See chapter 11 for more information about the challenges and benefits of having diverse teams.

Instructional librarians. In chapter 7 we discuss the value of working with librarians, typically a research or instruction librarian or perhaps a librarian dedicated to first-year courses. In our program, we designate a specific research and instruction librarian as the "personal librarian" for the course. That librarian attends class several times during the course to deliver key information at strategic intervals timed to coincide with the need to know. As the project begins, we also encourage our project teams to meet with their librarian for a consultation. Students are intrigued by the idea of a personal librarian and are more likely to approach this person than an unknown librarian when they need some assistance. Asking the students to set up a consultation within a given window of time both optimizes the librarian's time and makes sure the students get the necessary research tools at the right time in the project. These consultations are where the most learning happens, and the students are unfailingly enthusiastic about their meeting because of the search strategies they have developed with the librarian's help and with the wealth and variety of information they now have access to (see Box 3.1).

As the class librarian is part of the instructional team, it is very useful for him or her to be included in an early planning meeting. Once the librarian understands the class and project objectives, he or she can know best how to support the instructors and students and devise appropriate activities. It is helpful for the librarian to have access to any course management sites and be able to post resources, suggestions, reminders, and so on.

One librarian can serve as the personal librarian to several courses simultaneously. This, of course, is additional workload for the librarian but perhaps is one of the best ways to advance information literacy on campus. As students learn how to navigate in an information-rich environment in a first-year, project-based class, they can carry that learning forward and might need less support later.

In addition to library staff, access to citation software simplifies and improves student use of reference materials. We encourage providing access to one or more of the current citation software packages.

Academic technology professionals. These experts can provide support for a number of project-related activities, such as creating effective visual displays (e.g., PowerPoint slides and posters), videos, and other digital artifacts. Student projects frequently require and/or benefit from the creation of digital elements, such as videos, infographics, or online surveys. Creating these elements can engage students to an extent that writing a paper simply

BOX 3.1
Students Value Working With Librarians

Asked to creatively express an aspect of the course they found memorable, one of our project teams wrote a song about their research librarian. The lyrics included all of the many skills they had acquired and alluded to their intention to seek her help and advice in the future. Perhaps fittingly, it was set to the tune of "My Girl."

does not. In a world that increasingly relies on visual and video information, incorporating activities that demand that the students gain not only familiarity but also proficiency can improve postgraduation outcomes for the student. However, video storyboarding, equipment use, and editing are skills less frequently found in faculty, and technical staff can fill that void. Done well, these elements can have value beyond the classroom, serving as artifacts of student learning in ePortfolios and program accomplishments in accreditation reviews.

Assessment Support

As with any curricular change, assessment should be considered from the beginning of the planning stage. Learning outcomes for the project, course, or program should be identified as the first step in development—these can be content or skills based. Select a method to determine to what extent the learning outcomes have been attained. A simple way to do this is to ask the students themselves. We routinely ask students in our program to assess their progress toward our seven learning outcomes at the end of the course. While self-reported progress is sometimes seen as less than best evidence, surely it is significant if the students themselves don't believe they have made progress on learning outcomes.

For a more independent evaluation, project deliverables can be assessed for evidence of accomplishment of outcomes. Rubrics facilitate this evaluation. The Association of American Colleges & Universities has produced a number of rubrics that can be used to evaluate a broad range of learning outcomes (VALUE rubrics), as well as some resources on how to use them (Rhodes, 2010). The process is time intensive and probably most easily done over the summer, requiring summer pay for those willing to participate. However, there is much value in undertaking this type of assessment, as it can yield significantly better insights. Don't be surprised if initial results are less than an overwhelming success. These methods are new to both faculty and students and take some adjustment time. As faculty modify assignments and the course in response to the assessment data, improvements should follow.

Support for Team Teaching

Forming the partnerships. If your PBL involves team teaching, as ours does, there are additional issues that need attention. The first is forming the pairs. One best if the partners find each other, but that is not often the way it has worked for us. The most important elements for success of the partnership are that both faculty members are willing to work with each other, that they have a high interest in the subject of the course, and that each sees what he or she can contribute. However, that's not enough. The faculty must be fairly flexible and accommodating because the two must also agree on grading schemes, classroom management issues, number and complexity of assignments, and so on. (See chapter 5 for more tips on successful team teaching.) Though we have had experience with random pairing of faculty volunteers (in this case, the fact that they were volunteers was significant), generally we have the two meet to share their vision for the course before we commit them to working together. An IDEA paper on team teaching by Kathryn Plank (2013) is a very useful resource. We've also developed a set of scenarios the partners can use to discuss issues that might arise during the course so they can have some idea of how they would like to deal with them. These are found in Appendix 3.2.

Faculty workload. This is a key issue for administrators around team teaching. The temptation is to consider a team-taught course as one course divided between two faculty members, with each instructor credited with half a course and half the credits delivered. However, team teaching a project-based course is not half the work; it is actually significantly more work than teaching a class by yourself. All decisions must be joint decisions; negotiating assignments, materials, and leadership of activities all take more time and more effort. Thus, we believe that each faculty member should be considered as taking on a full class load, and ideally the total credit hours delivered should accrue to both faculty, though this latter suggestion is something we have not managed at our institution. Considering a team-taught course as only half a course when calculating faculty loading is likely to lead to faculty burnout and a decline in interest in participating faculty. We have found, though, that faculty in these classes can handle more than the usual number of students. So we have team taught classes of up to 60 students, which for many schools would be double the normal class size.

Institutional Challenges and Benefits

Transformation in education requires risks in order to reap rewards. Here we present some of the benefits and challenges we have identified in our process of introducing PBL into our first-year curriculum.

Benefits

Engaging in PBL in the first year provides benefits that accrue to the community, the students, and the faculty.

Community building. One perhaps unanticipated benefit is the development of a stronger sense of campus community. As students work on their projects, they often have to reach out to people and offices they might never have experienced, giving them a broader sense of what your institution has to offer. Furthermore, students working together on projects can form strong relationships with each other, and in these classrooms a sense of camaraderie develops during the course.

On our campus, the faculty who engage in PBL have formed a community of practice through our summer week of meetings (the GPS Summer Institute; see the previous Supporting Faculty section). The connections between faculty in this community reach beyond disciplinary and even division boundaries. When there is team teaching, particularly if the coinstructors come from different departments, the ties forged between these instructors can also help link disparate parts of the campus (see Box 3.2).

New perspectives on teaching. Teaching project-based courses can also provide new insights on the process of teaching and learning. It necessarily changes the role of faculty, as described in chapter 4. Faculty must focus on student-generated knowledge (see Box 3.2). This new focus then spills over into teaching in their other courses.

BOX 3.2
Quotes From Faculty Focus Groups on the Impact of PBL Courses

On community building: "I'm definitely more connected. I know people, I can talk to them, I lend books to them."

On perspectives on teaching: "These classes help me because I am more involved, more engaged, more interactive with the students, which helps them [because] . . . I can give them more feedback."

"I [now] worry much more about [whether] I have a relationship with the students where I can sit down and [ask], 'Well, what do you wanna do, and how are we gonna get there, and what don't you know, and how can we help you find it?' and not 'You know, this isn't the right way to do this.'"

On team teaching: "The opportunity to work with another faculty member from a different discipline was marvelously enlightening. . . . It's been a huge learning experience for me."

"Certainly being in a classroom with another professor from a different discipline has opened my eyes to different ways of teaching. . . . Because [of this experience] I've become more experimental in my individually taught courses in things like incorporating different styles of assignments, thinking about having students do more of the teaching than I've done in the past."

Student learning. As delineated in chapter 1, there have been significant findings that PBL, like other high-impact practices, provides opportunities for deep and engaged learning and is particularly significant for women and underrepresented minorities. Institutions that desire better outcomes for these students should consider moving to this or another high-impact practice. The first year of college can frequently appear to students to be far removed from real-world issues, hence unrelated to preparation for that real world. In contrast, PBL is firmly grounded in reality, and solving problems is an identifiable skill of value. Furthermore, engaging in projects in the first year can show students where they need to deepen their own knowledge and skill base, while they still have time to build that into their college experience.

Challenges

Though the benefits of PBL in the first year are numerous and of great value, there are certainly significant challenges associated with it.

The numbers game. PBL requires significant amounts of student support from faculty and/or peers. It would be difficult to do with large numbers of students and few faculty. We have tried exceeding 60 students per 2 faculty on several occasions, and each time we have concluded that 60 is about as high as works well with 2 faculty. Perhaps with more senior support—grad assistants, for example—it could work, but certainly something would be lost, as the faculty would have more difficulty working with all the students in the room.

The high-touch delivery can raise questions of efficiency. And, of course, having one faculty member delivering lectures to a hall filled with hundreds of students will be more "efficient" in terms of credits/full-time equivalents; however, value is measured in many other ways as well. In which system will students feel more connected to faculty and the institution? Which system will better retain women and underrepresented minorities? Which system will generate more prospective student interest? Which system will generate more artifacts of learning for accreditation? Which system will generate more community engagement and civic-minded graduates? Which system is likely to generate more student interest in further education? Which system will alumni remember more fondly? When the long view is taken, PBL is a clear winner.

Probationary faculty participation. When these courses were first envisioned at our institution, the underlying assumption was that they would be ideal opportunities for senior faculty to make unique and valuable teaching contributions based on their long experience and their secure positions in the academic hierarchy. As it has turned out, the tenured faculty represent half of those involved in teaching these courses. Pretenure, tenure-track faculty often have been advised to put their efforts elsewhere until their positions are more secure. In the evolution of our GPS curriculum, we have now engaged a cohort of continuing non-tenure-track teaching professors who are hired expressly with the understanding they will engage in GPS delivery. How or whether to shift this distribution is not clear. In our experience the people who chose to accept appointments as teaching professors, whose focus is entirely on teaching and learning, are dedicated professionals who serve the program remarkably well. But from an institutional perspective, this creates a visible divide that may reinforce the views and attitudes of the more traditional faculty.

Adjunct faculty participation. Successful project-based courses require faculty who have time and training. This kind of teaching demands faculty time outside of class and benefits from repetition and the ability to interact with other faculty engaged in similar kinds of teaching. Faculty development is essential. The use of part-time adjunct faculty who have significant additional teaching responsibilities is therefore difficult, but possible if there is a structure that provides the time for training and perhaps even mentoring relationships.

Paradigm shift from lecturing. Much has been published, both in popular press and in the literature, about the relative values of lecture and active learning (e.g., Freeman et al., 2014; Paul, 2015). Yet, lectures still seem to be the dominant form of instruction on college campuses. It is difficult to shift faculty from this traditional form. In our experience, celebrating those willing to move to different forms of pedagogy is more useful than chastising those who remain committed to their lecture notes. Faculty who do move to PBL are often the best ambassadors for this type of teaching. They find it stimulating, ever changing, and rewarding in the relationships they form with the students and in the excitement of the students as they solve their problems. It is best to work with your coalition of the willing, praise their successes, support their needs, and set high standards. Not everyone is well suited for this kind of teaching, and it is a mistake to think that everyone can do it.

Classrooms. Project-based courses can take place in a variety of classrooms, but this kind of teaching is best supported by rooms with moveable tables and chairs. Group work is central, and the ability of students to seat themselves in conversational groupings is very helpful. We have done this in theater-style classrooms, but it is awkward. Our favorite rooms have flat floors and moveable tables that easily accommodate groups of four or five.

Interdisciplinary or team-taught courses. Particular issues arise for courses that are interdisciplinary or do not lie directly within a single department. From a departmental point of view, faculty teaching in these programs may be viewed as contributing less or not at all to the discipline-specific courses that compose a departmental curriculum. When the institution compiles department teaching metrics, it is often unclear where and when these courses should be included. One specific example of potential barriers to participation is that at our institution, when courses are team taught, faculty are recognized as each delivering half of the student credit hours for the course, even though both are in the classroom with all of the students at every class meeting. This can cause concern at the department level.

Conclusion

In his 2013 book *College (un)Bound: The Future of Higher Education and What It Means for Students*, Jeffrey Selingo wrote, "College students need real-world experiences that will help them connect concepts they learn in class to everyday problems" (p. 184). In his examples of colleges with programs that do this well, he included WPI and specifically the GPSs. What better investment can an institution make than in "strategies and programs that prove the value of their degree in the years ahead" (Selingo, 2013, p. 184)?

Perhaps from a more sanguine and less self-serving viewpoint, it is our experience that PBL is an incredibly powerful form of pedagogy with benefits for students, faculty, and institutions. Students engage better, learn valuable transferable skills, and absorb content in a more meaningful and long-lasting way. Faculty gain new perspectives on teaching and enjoy more meaningful interactions with their students. Institutions can leverage all these gains for institutional promotion and programmatic assessment. However, to reap these benefits, the institution must also commit resources to support the faculty and the program. These span a range from no- or low-cost changes in assessment metrics and attitudes to more significant commitments such as professional development, teaching assistance (TA or PLA), and administrative support. While no amount of institutional support can guarantee success, long-lasting and impactful curricular change is unlikely without institutional support and encouragement. We've found our commitment to PBL in the first year to be rewarding in ways we hadn't anticipated, as well as in ways we had. We encourage you to see what adoption of PBL can do for you and your students.

Try This

1. *When you are ready to incorporate PBL into your program, send out a broad invitation to all faculty to find those interested in participating in a pilot.* In the invitation, ask that they identify a possible topic (or have them select one from a list you generate) and then let them know that there will be a selection process. This ensures that you will be working with willing faculty and creates the sense that it is an honor (and it is!) to be one of the explorers of this new ground, while leaving control in your hands. Then be sure to recognize the participating faculty often—and publicly.

2. *Once you have a group of faculty engaged in PBL, empower them to identify new topics, to suggest other faculty to recruit, and to solve the problems that arise.* Treat them as we have recommended you treat the students. Motivate them by recognizing their needs for *competence, autonomy, relatedness,* and *purpose* (see chapter 1).

TRAINING MATERIALS FOR PEER LEARNING ASSISTANTS

Facilitating Group Work: Real-World

Scenarios

(created by Natalie Farny, Worcester Polytechnic Institute)

For the scenario your group is assigned, discuss the following questions and be prepared to report out to the whole group:

1. What problems is this group encountering?
2. What should the PLA do, and/or how could the situation have been avoided?

Group 1

You approach a group that is particularly quiet. One student is checking his Facebook page. Another is texting. Two are sitting together talking about an assignment for another class. You ask, "How are you guys doing over here?" The texter replies, "We agreed to meet outside of class to work on this later."

Group 2

You receive an e-mail from a student in the course. This student complains to you that one member of the group rarely comes to class, and when he does come he is not prepared for the group work. The portions of the group report he has written are very poor, and other group members have to rewrite them. This slacker is a nice guy, and this student does not want to get this group member in trouble with the professor, but she is tired of doing all of the slacker's work.

Group 3

You notice a particularly vociferous group in one corner of the room, and you approach the group to see what's going on. One member is clearly agitated with the other group members and insists that her way of completing the problem is just as valid as another way explained by the professor. The other group members disagree and are attempting to explain to her why her solution is not valid, but the agitated student continues (louder and louder) to refute them, saying, "You must be stupid if you can't see why this is right!"

Group 4

You approach a group that is working hard and seems to be collaborating well together. However, as you listen in on their conversation, you realize they are completely on the wrong track and are giving each other false information.

Ethical and Legal Responsibilities: Real-World

Scenarios

(created by Natalie Farny, Worcester Polytechnic Institute)

For the scenario that your group is assigned, discuss the following questions and be prepared to report out to the whole group:

1. What are the ethical and/or legal issue(s), if any?
2. What should the PLA do, and/or how could the situation have been avoided?

Group 1

While grading homework assignments, I came across several similar write-ups by students that contained the exact same mistake. Then I noticed that same mistake was in the solutions manual. (The professor had given me the solutions manual.) The professor made clear on the first day of class and in the syllabus that collaboration on homework is permitted since it's helpful for learning, but that each student must write his or her own solutions independently, without copying from others. The professor didn't say anything directly about not using solutions available online.

Group 2

One term I was assigned to assist with grading an upper level course that I had taken the previous year. I don't think any of the other PLAs or TAs in the department had taken the course. Right before the course started, I discovered that one of my apartment roommates was going to be a student in the course.

Group 3

I was returning graded homework during a conference section, and a student got really upset about his grade in front of the whole class. He went off on a tirade filled with swears, complaining that the grading was unfair and that too many points were taken off for really small mistakes.

Group 4

When I was returning graded homework during a conference section, a student came up to me and said, "Andrew Miller is my roommate. He couldn't come today but asked me to pick up his homework."

TEAM TEACHING VIGNETTES

1. Coinstructors See the Subject Differently, and That's Okay

John and Carol have agreed to teach a project-based course that addresses the problem—money. They think that money, in spite of not having an intrinsic use value like food, water, or power, is nevertheless a worldwide problem because it assigns value to—and thus our capacity to acquire or dispose of—much that matters in life.

John teaches literature in the Humanities and Arts Department where his scholarship focuses on narratives of the oppressed and underrepresented, with special attention to the portrayal of poverty. *Les Misérables* (Hugo, 1862) and most of Dickens's work are among his favorite texts. Carol is a tax policy expert in the School of Business, where she studies the impact of federal and state revenue programs on small enterprises. Her father started a Main Street hardware store in the 1950s that is now part of a regional franchise and currently managed by her brother.

After an initial get-to-know-you conversation, John and Carol begin to discuss their course. They talk about the academic calendar, enrollment, and the kinds of things they'd like to do with students and what has worked for them. In the course of the discussion, many of their preferences are offered as suggestions; both are keen to respect one another and to find points of agreement, to participate in building an intellectual rapport and common ground for practice. Nevertheless, they both notice distinct differences in their notions of money and can sense the need to restrain themselves at times in response to each other's comments. They realize that the differences can be used as a positive tension for the class, making it possible for students to see in action how different points of view can be juxtaposed and can interact to benefit understanding, but they also realize that they'll have to give up, to some extent, the last say that faculty so often treasure when they teach a course of their own.

2. Learning Outcomes and Data-Driven Instruction

John and Carol want to see whether the use of quantitative feedback can help them better understand what students learn in the class. They start by examining a chart supplied by instructors from Food Sustainability. In this chart (see Figure A3.2), the Food Sustainability instructors looked at how students scored the 7 learning outcomes identified for the project-based course. Specifically, midway through the course, and again at the end, the students quantified the change in their ability in terms of a scale, 1 to 5.

Figure A3.2. Assessment results.

Seven Instructor-Supplied Questions

Food Sustainability

As a result of the work for this class, I am significantly more able to do the following:

1. Work effectively on a team
2. Identify and use information from a variety of sources
3. Produce clear, effective, evidence-based writing
4. Prepare and deliver engaging and effective presentations
5. Identify approaches to solving complex, open-ended problems
6. Describe the causes and consequences of the central global issue (food and hunger) from a variety of perspectives such as economic, political, historical, technical, and cultural
7. Be aware of the differences in experiences of the global issues by peoples from different cultures, regions, and economic status

Question	Midsemester Average (*n*)	End of Semester Average (*n*)	Δ
1	4.3 (41)	4.5 (34)	0.2
2	4.1 (41)	4.4 (35)	0.3
3	3.9 (41)	4.4 (34)	0.5
4	4.1 (41)	4.6 (35)	0.5
5	4.1 (40)	4.5 (36)	0.4
6	4.3 (41)	4.4 (36)	0.1
7	4.4 (37)	4.5 (32)	0.1

John and Carol learned from the Food Sustainability instructors that they used the results at midterm to help focus and emphasize the teaching for the rest of the course. In particular, the Food Sustainability instructors deliberately spent more time, and pencil lead, talking about good writing, extensively responding to student writing, and showing students examples from their own assignments of better and worse grammar and style. In addition, the focus on preparation for good presentations manifested as a significant increase (nearly every class period) in public feedback from students and coaching from instructors on each team's oral presentation and poster effectiveness.

John and Carol immediately notice the half-point improvement in outcomes three and four. They also note the relatively small changes with regard to outcomes six and seven. The Food Sustainability instructors agreed that the latter outcomes, though implicit, never received the kind of explicit emphasis that promoted the improvement seen in outcomes three and four. John and Carol realize that assessments such as these are terribly qualitative for all their numerical veneer, but they acknowledge that the changes are large enough to suggest that deliberate emphasis within a course can show up on the learning meter. It's worth a try, then, to determine what they'd like to measure, to establish a baseline, and to have a go at testing the effectiveness of their instruction.

3. How Much Clarity?

John and Carol have heard a lot about clarity and expectations from other instructors of project-based courses in the first year. It seems that students complain that these are hard because the students don't know what the professors want. If you want me to solve a problem, what, exactly, is the problem? Where, exactly, can I find examples of how to solve the problem? What am I supposed to get out the reading? If I'm supposed to think independently, how come I feel like my ideas aren't well received? I got good writing grades in high school, but the expectation at WPI is different, so how do you want me to write? How come there doesn't seem to be a right answer or even one that is better than the others?

John and Carol realize that some of this complaint is the typical learner grousing that comes from the strain of having to intellectually dig in. No pain, no gain kind of thing. But they also know that learning usually takes place more productively when the learning goal is clear, when there are examples of good work (writing, for example, or an award-winning poster), when the implicit is made explicit. They know that sometimes faculty don't provide this kind of clarity because it "gives away too much," it holds the students' hands, it doesn't test the learners' ability to work hard. There's some truth in that. On the other hand, maybe faculty don't provide clear expectations and examples because the faculty themselves aren't really clear or haven't taken time to generate illustrative models. John and Carol agree this may be the case because it's a lot of work to specify what faculty want so that all the students in the class understand. In any case, to whatever degree John and Carol decide to make explicit what they want from students and how to do it, they realize that they must know precisely what students should know and be able to do as a result of each and every activity of the course. If a chapter is assigned, what is the student to come away with? If there is a writing assignment, what characterizes good writing? If there is to be a video presentation, what should the student have as a result of the viewing? This commitment is part of John and Carol's rejection of the professorial excuse: "I taught it; they just didn't learn it."

4. To Sponsor Projects or Not?

John and Carol have heard that some instructors solicit sponsors for student projects, whereas others do not. Leaving aside the logistics of finding sponsors at the moment, John and Carol discuss the pros and cons of project sponsorship. (See chapter 8 for more on sponsored projects.)

Clearly, sponsored projects give students a great starting point for research and development. With a sponsored project (a) the need is identified; (b) the client is known; and, in many cases, (c) the sponsor will provide support, both material and informational. The latter may be especially important when the project requires expertise that the instructors do not have but the client/sponsor might. Such focus and support will give the students more time to develop and test solutions and therefore "get further along" on their project in the relatively limited time available in a semester. This progress will surely show in the final presentations, final papers, and, ultimately, the level of expertness gained by the students. This approach closely parallels many graduate research programs where the student is given a problem by the senior researcher and learns the habits of mind and techniques for work in the field by trying to solve the problem. It avoids the waste of time that may take place as a graduate student "searches" for a problem to solve.

On the other hand, asking students to identify a need before refining a problem statement and working on solutions puts much more emphasis on the open-endedness of research and innovation. Students must struggle with the uncertainty of trying to find something worth solving, of false starts and "cluelessness." Making one's psychological way through this nebulous situation can be very taxing, but when it is clarified, the sense of accomplishment and subsequent confidence are enormous. Typically, this approach leads to a much larger range of project quality, some being extraordinary and others modest, even mediocre. Concomitantly, the kind of learning that takes place varies a lot. Those who discover and address a need in a truly innovative way make great strides, whereas those who never dissipate the fog often experience little except frustration. Furthermore, the success of many teams ends up being a function of the expertise of the GPS instructors, because they can more effectively coach the progress of teams who are engaged in familiar content areas.

Carol and John realize that the sponsor versus not-sponsor issue is really a question of educational philosophy and of the level of motivation and achievement of the students. They talk a lot about what they think should be the educational aims, the learning goals of their course, and the intellectual and emotional experience of first-year students. What do we most want our students to know and be able to do as a result of our course? Of what are students in these courses capable?

All vignettes were authored by Rob Traver, WPI.

PART TWO

PREPARING FOR PROJECT-
BASED LEARNING

I n this section we include a number of aspects of PBL that you should
consider while in the planning phase. Tools, examples, and approaches
are provided to facilitate the switch from more traditional content delivery to PBL. The goals of this section are to help you think through some of
the changes needed to make PBL as effective as possible. We provide examples and scenarios that bring PBL to life.

The switch from more traditional pedagogies to PBL requires a change
in mind-set for faculty and in how the learning is designed. Chapter 4,
"Reenvisioning the Role of Faculty," helps you rethink your role as the
instructor of a project-based course—from leader to fellow learner. Project-
based learning asks the students to take some control and asks faculty to cede
some control, an initially uncomfortable position but one that Pfeifer and
Spanagel show has many rewards.

If PBL is at its most powerful when it transcends disciplinary boundaries, this can become more explicit when students are exposed to more than
one way of viewing the problems. Team teaching is perhaps the best way to
ensure that students are exposed in meaningful ways to the multiple lenses
from which problems can be viewed and the value of incorporating the differing viewpoints. Chapter 5, "Team Teaching: Dialogic Duets," focuses on
team teaching in project-based courses, and Nikitina and Apelian provide
tips and suggestions for forming productive and effective team-teaching
pairs.

Chapter 6, "Assessment of Project-Based Learning in the First Year,"
reframes assessment of project-based work as educative. Traver and Ziino

Plotke provide guidelines on using models, practice, and feedback to improve student deliverables and processes and make the case for educating also the stakeholders who are not students.

As most, if not all, projects require that students effectively find and use information to complete a project, chapter 7, "Supporting Project-Based Learning With Librarians and Information Literacy," describes working with librarians to incorporate information literacy skill building in project-based courses (bonus: working with librarians is also fun!). Bakermans and Ziino Plotke provide specific activities and exercises to help faculty and librarians get started.

Project ideas can come from a variety of sources, but Nikitina and Apelian demonstrate in chapter 8, "Sponsored Projects: Learning With a Sense of Urgency and Agency," that working with problems provided by outside organizations can be especially compelling for students and faculty alike. They provide guidance on how to identify potential project sponsors and then how you can set appropriate expectations for both the sponsors and the students about the project process and potential deliverables.

Many chapters end with a section called "Try This," which contains suggestions and prompts to help you incorporate PBL into your classroom. Visit our companion website (www.wpi.edu/+fi rstyearprojects) for examples of student project work.

4

REENVISIONING THE
ROLE OF FACULTY

Geoff Pfeifer and David Spanagel

Project-based instruction can put instructors into unusual situations. As those who teach using project-based approaches know, the role one plays as a faculty member in this style of classroom can be quite different from the role played by faculty in a more traditional classroom environment. Geoff Pfeifer encountered this the first time he cotaught a project-based class. They were well into their project work, and student teams were giving presentations on their progress. As one of the more troubled teams walked up to give its presentation, Geoff knew something was really wrong:

> It had been apparent for a while that this team of three was struggling with their project and their team dynamics, but they hadn't taken us up on our gentle offers for help and had barely spoken to us about the problems they were having. When they got to the front of the room, all their troubles seemed to come to a head. Even their body language and positioning betrayed their problems. Two students stood on one side of the room, and one stood far away from the others. As they began to give their presentation, I could see the one student becoming more and more agitated. When it came time for him to give his part of the presentation, he stopped, looked at his teammates, and blurted out, along with a few expletives, that he hated them. The room fell silent, and in the discomfort the students took their seats. My coinstructor and I looked at each other, not really knowing how to respond, as neither of us had experienced such a public breakdown of a student team.
>
> We moved on to the next presentation but ended class early so we could have a discussion with our problem team about what had happened. In this discussion we listened to the students—about their frustrations with one another and their project—and asked questions and offered suggestions

that might help them through these difficulties. The team ultimately came together and ended up producing a good project (and liking each other!) but not without teaching me a lot about what it is to be a faculty member in this type of environment. In this situation (and many since) I had to be a good listener and a counselor, among other various roles that we take up when teaching in this way.

This chapter focuses on some of these roles and the ways they present both challenges and exciting opportunities for faculty.

Going Beyond the Traditional "Instructor as Subject Matter Expert"

Why. Anyone employed as a member of a college faculty must demonstrate adequate professional preparation to conduct research and/or teaching within a specific content area. This is a given. Traditional models of faculty evaluation reinforce the importance of this fundamental core of subject matter expertise by predicating rewards structures of job security and promotion on some constellation of assessments of the faculty member's performance in teaching, research, and service capacities.

Researchers who study the demands placed on college professors, however, have long argued that command of knowledge within one's own narrowly defined research specialty provides an insufficient skills base for effective college teaching:

> Faculty must be able to design and deliver a set of experiences to the learner such that, if the learner engages the experiences, there is a high probability learning will occur. In addition, the faculty member must validly and reliably assess the learner's progress so as to both enhance the learning process and, ultimately, certify that learning has in fact occurred. The areas of Instructional Design, Instructional Delivery, and Instructional Assessment are professional endeavors in and of themselves (doctorates are offered in all areas). Thus, at least four different arenas of professional performance are required of the college professor. (Arreola, Theall, & Aleamoni, 2003, p. 2)

PBL provides an extremely fruitful opportunity for college professors to develop teaching capabilities outside the comfort zone of their own subject matter expertise. In addition to providing knowledge and academic skills, some other features that define a project-based approach to teaching and learning are that projects focus on authentic and complex real-world problems or issues, that there is "student voice and choice" in how and what ways they work on the problem, and that products of the projects are in some way public (Buck Institute, n.d.). Problems that display real-world complexity are notoriously difficult to contain within any disciplinary boundaries; students working collaboratively on teams and on such open-ended problems do not behave in the same way that students working individually do. Therefore, the role of the faculty member who seeks to provide useful background knowledge—and then advise student projects on such multidisciplinary challenges—must necessarily engage in a serious manner with a variety of methods and subject matter details that may have been as previously unfamiliar to the instructor as any aspect of the course content may be to its students.

For instance, in one of our first-year project-based courses, students are asked to work on issues that surround the interlocking problems of climate change, land use, and biodiversity. Working on and teaching about these complex issues requires some knowledge of biology, history, public policy, economics, environmental and human ethics, political theory and science, and so forth. No one faculty member teaching such a course can have expertise in all these areas, and so learning becomes a collaborative process in which students and faculty work together. It even becomes natural to invite additional experts to give class presentations, such as research and instructional librarians, academic technology professionals, scientists in the field, and community members and political activists who can illustrate the important contextual issues, all to build a common language and knowledge base from which student-led projects emerge. As a philosophy professor, Geoff has found it a completely rewarding experience:

> I have felt free to experiment with a variety of methods/assignments and often find that I am learning right along with my students in ways that hark back to my grad school experience. Teaching in the project-based environment has also allowed for the acquisition of knowledge outside my discipline, and this has had an impact not only on the ways I teach in the GPS courses but also in my more traditional philosophy courses. I find that I can speak to issues of climate change, land-use change, and biodiversity as they present themselves in my philosophy courses in ways that I could not have before teaching in this environment. As we work to build a skill base for the students around these complex issues, the faculty skill base expands at the same time.

Reinvent and Augment Your Repertoire of Instructional Approaches

Why. We have found that codeveloping and coteaching project-based courses can provide rich learning opportunities to observe, absorb, experiment, and model distinctive teaching ideas with a colleague. However, because few campuses offer regular chances to work so closely with a colleague from a different discipline, this section focuses on how an individual instructor can acquire the skills needed to begin teaching outside his or her comfort zone even without the benefit of a coinstructor. All you need is the willingness to take that first big step into the unknown and let the students come along with you.

How? Teacher Behaving as "Fellow Student"

David Spanagel began his college teaching career as an instructor of mathematics and computer science at the tender age of 23:

> I embarked on this calling as a college professor on the slender basis of having completed the requirements of an undergraduate math major, and then obtaining a master's degree in mathematics education. My first teaching position called on me to offer a lot of remedial instruction to entering college students, but during my second semester of teaching, the department head offered me his favorite upper-level course to teach while he was on sabbatical: Non-Euclidean Geometry. I had never even studied that aspect of math in my own previous education, so it was a giant leap outside my comfort zone. Nevertheless, I enthusiastically accepted this challenge (and privately reveled in the marvelous degree of trust that it represented) but also realized immediately that I would have to embrace a different attitude toward my teaching in order to be able to survive the term.
>
> What transpired between me and the dozen or so students placed under my charge absolutely redefined who I was as a professor and radically altered my entire approach to teaching. Since I did not already possess a secure mastery over the subject matter, I proceeded to work through the material in the suggested textbook alongside rather than "above" my students. I stayed about a week ahead of the class as I tried to do all the homework questions following each chapter, and I chose assignments based on problems I was figuring out how to solve at the same time. I could not, and therefore did not try to, hide the fact that this was new material for me as well as for them. Instead, we shared the challenge of working together to come to deeper shared understandings of how geometrical structures and theorems work when you set aside Euclid's parallel postulate and try to see the universe through either the ingenious hyperbolic geometry independently developed in the nineteenth century by both Janos Bolyai and Nicolai Ivanovich Lobachevsky or the elliptical geometry system put forward by their contemporary Bernhard Riemann. In other words, I challenged my students to see me as a fellow mathematical novice, leading them through the unfamiliar material by dint of sheer curiosity, fascination, and the inevitable hard work. They learned as much as (I suspect) they ever did about

the properties of those different systems, but, more important, my students saw the magic of authentic mathematical thinking when it has to operate without the safety net of the professor's expertise. I won't say it wasn't messy at times, but I will say that it crystallized my confidence as a teacher, and I have never looked back.

I eventually returned to graduate school to train to become a historian of science, but the life lesson I gained as a novice math teacher has served me well ever since. My best teaching always involves "learning out loud," and I try to take advantage of every reasonable opportunity to incorporate fresh source materials into my courses so that I can recapture that sense of shared discovery with my students in whatever classes I am responsible for.

How? Teacher as Facilitator and Cognitive Coach

A facilitator brings out the knowledge and ingenuity already possessed by the group members to assist them in making collective decisions effectively. A coach emphasizes that the obstacles to success are external to the team and cultivates the skills and capabilities of a group's members so they can work together to overcome such challenges. The point of either of these different ways of casting the role of the teacher is to introduce a shared experience (perhaps novelty as well) for both instructor and student, in which a "democratizing" situation can radically alter the experience of both teaching and learning. By emphasizing the collaborative dimension of problem investigation and by working together through the actual content challenges of proposing and testing a solution approach, students and instructors gain opportunities to break away from stultifying patterns of hierarchy, obedience, and "taskmastership" that can typify a traditional classroom. In their role as course designer, faculty members now become less responsible for imparting expert knowledge (though some of this still happens) and more responsible for thinking about ways in which they can assist students in their own pursuit of knowledge through the effective design of the learning environment.

Project-centered instruction requires creating an environment in which students are given more control and responsibility over what types of knowledge they pursue (in the context of the topic of the course and/or project). Though the prospect of handing over control and responsibility to students for what knowledge they should pursue can be a daunting one for faculty, its accomplishment clearly does empower student learners. We have found, for example, that letting student teams choose the topics of their projects (with help in narrowing and focusing) leads to better student engagement in the process of learning. Furthermore, faculty engage in learning about the project and problem alongside the students. In this way, the role of the faculty member becomes one of consultant, or what Steinemann (2003) called a "cognitive coach" (p. 218), someone who helps students clarify their questions. An effective cognitive coach challenges students to think carefully about how they might pursue their self-chosen topics but does not provide answers. Rather, the instructor acting as cognitive coach encourages students to think about their project or problem in different ways, to brainstorm potential solutions and avenues for research, and to see the problems presented in the project in new ways.

For instance, Geoff was helping a team that was looking at the problem of indoor air pollution caused by cook stoves in the developing world. The students had an interest in solar cookers as a replacement for the inefficient, polluting, wood-fired cook stoves, and they were researching different models and the experiences of NGOs that had been working with communities in implementing solar cook stoves. The team kept finding that community adoption of these solar cook stoves was not really happening and that NGOs struggled with getting communities to move to this form of stove for a variety of reasons. The students were disappointed by their findings and were feeling frustrated. Geoff suggested they make or buy a simple solar cooker kit that many NGOs were promoting and try using it themselves to see if they could determine what the issues were. They did this and found many problems, such as lack of real heat, very slow cook times, and the need for constant monitoring. The team realized that available solar stove options are simply ineffective as replacements because of these and other reasons (and that this is why so many NGOs struggle to get communities to switch to these types of stoves).

The students were concerned that they had wasted time and still did not have a solution to their problem, and because the term was coming to a close, they were worried about finishing with a grade-worthy project. Geoff backed them up a bit and helped them see that they did, in fact, have a project and that they had learned a lot about their chosen topic—just not what they thought they'd learn. They learned that solar cookers, at least in their current state, were poor replacements for the traditional cook stoves used in many developing communities. They ended up shifting their project focus slightly and argued that if NGOs and others really wanted to help with this problem, they needed to shift their focus away from solar cookers or come up with a better design that would be as cost-effective.

Cognitive coaching can play out in many ways, but here it played out in helping the student team see how it is that good research can lead a project in an unexpected yet still successful direction. We should not be too committed to one specific way of understanding a given issue before doing the research required to gain a fuller understanding. Whether the outcome of this shift in pedagogy is scary and disappointing or rich and liberating (for everyone involved) depends critically on the enthusiasm that the instructor brings to work that frankly goes even beyond the realms of instructional design, instructional delivery, and instructional assessment. Effective project-based *teaching* requires the instructor to share in the experience of project-based *learning* on an equal footing with the students, at least some of the time.

The Reward for Relinquishing Total "Control"

Fortunately, embracing these alternatives to traditional modes of didactic instructional design can strengthen and reinforce the kinds of active learning modes that educational researchers at all levels have been urging teachers to favor. Frank Thoms (2010) summarized these findings about "how people learn" by organizing them into a hierarchy of effectiveness. In his casual display of suggestive findings from educational research, widely used but often disappointing means of internalizing information cluster together above a horizon, whereas more effective participatory modes of deeply engaging student learning cluster below the horizon (see Figure 4.1).

Students who see professors operating only within their own carefully defined areas of expertise are likely to magnify the distance between themselves and the level of achievement that they seek in any given field. It may well seem as if one "must already know" the answer before one has any chance of finding a solution to any tough problem (Schoenfeld, 1992, p. 359). Conversely, students whose professors model the authentic struggle

Figure 4.1. "How People Learn."

People learn . . .

- 10% of what they READ
- 20% of what they HEAR
- 30% of what they SEE
- 40% of what they both SEE and HEAR

- 70% of what they SAY
- 80% of what they EXPERIENCE
- 90% of what they SAY and DO
- 95% of what they TEACH

Note. Adapted from *Teaching From the Middle of the Room: Inviting Students to Learn* (p. 54), by F. Thoms, 2010, Lowell, MA: Stetson Press.

to understand a novel problem situation learn the following extremely valuable lessons: (a) Real problems actually do require hard work and persistence, and (b) there are many ways to gain traction on a challenging problem besides knowing in advance what the optimal solution approach ought to be. Professors may, after all, be novices to a new field, but they almost certainly have acquired a wealth of heuristic tools that enable them to make progress through inquiry even in the absence of subject matter expertise. By modeling or suggesting some effective problem-solving heuristics (e.g., reframing the question, breaking a complex problem into simpler subtasks, examining extreme cases, and/or looking at specific cases to identify significant problem and domain features or patterns), the project-based instructor can equip students with a repertoire of valuable skills that will complement and strengthen their own acquisition of subject matter expertise in whatever field of study they may pursue (Schoenfeld, 1985, pp. 23, 109, 191).

One further challenge that sometimes gets raised in relation to project-based approaches claims that one has to sacrifice content in allowing students more control over the classroom. We have found ways of combating this problem (see chapter 10 for a more detailed description). In short, the most effective of these is careful assignment design in the early stages of the course prior to (and during) the project process. Assignments that ask students to do the work of researching and reporting out on the content that you would ordinarily lecture on are an effective way of both keeping the course content heavy and teaching skills (e.g., good research and good presentation) early on that will serve the students well during their projects. We tend to prefer that these assignments also be done in teams, as collaboration helps build vital teamwork skills that will also be useful in the projects. These types of assignments are beneficial not only for students in the ways described earlier but also for faculty insofar as they can induce student-initiated opportunities for faculty to share aspects of their own expertise without having to make the case for its relevance (a burden often provoked by traditional modes of instruction).

How? An Example of an Early Assignment That Combines Content Material and Skills Development

Geoff employs this assignment regularly in his cotaught course on energy issues (titled Power the World). The assignment is called the "Energy Source Types Project," and it is given out on the first day of the class. This is an assignment in which we break students into teams of three or four and give them a particular energy "source" such as natural gas, wind, solar, and so on and ask them to do some research into the source as a team, write a team research report, and present their findings in a jigsaw-style presentation (where one student from each team meets with others as the "expert" on their particular source and teaches them about it). For this assignment, because it is a first "project" and requires specific types of information to be gathered, we give the teams a list of questions to answer in their research. This is much more structured and like a more traditional paper assignment with a set of prompts, except that the teams are doing this prior to having read anything about these sources or hearing any lectures covering them (the team is generating the content).

We usually pair this assignment with a visit from a research and instruction librarian who gives a presentation on how to do good research that is directly tied to this assignment (see chapter 7 for more on the benefits of bringing librarians into the classroom). When the teams come back together and present in the jigsaw style, we are able to augment their presentations with knowledge that we have. Students get content via student-led learning, with the instructors there to help clarify when necessary; they also get experience doing research, working as a team, presenting, and so on—all skills they will need in the more open-ended projects that they will choose and work on later in the class. We also do some debriefing in the form of individually written project reflections at the end of this project where the students write about what it was like to work on the team, how their research went, what skills they thought they learned, and where they needed to improve. This helps them begin to think about their problem-solving approaches in real time.

The impact of authentically modeling problem-solving approaches may be just as profound and life changing for college instructors. The result of this kind of open-ended, inquiry-driven teaching mode can directly lead to increased capability in those metaprofessional areas of teaching excellence: instructional design, instructional delivery, and instructional assessment. Teaching outside one's comfort zone and being forced to think and perform in the absence of a deep reservoir of subject matter knowledge brings fresh awareness and respect to the challenges of learning as a novice to a new field. Armed with the experiential insights, and perhaps a reawakened sense of humility and enthusiasm for the transformative power of active learning, the project-based course instructor is better positioned to reassess the course design, delivery, and assessment modes that pervade all the other teaching that he or she carries out from term to term.

Conclusion

Effective teaching in the PBL environment places a variety of demands on the instructor. Students are being asked not only to master specific disciplinary subject matter knowledge but also to practice and develop research approaches and problem-solving skills that have the potential to work across disciplinary domains. Naturally, a traditional top-down or formulaic instructional approach is *not* well suited to support problem-centered investigations, especially where "the problem" comes from the real world and therefore tends to spawn a wider variety of learning tasks and less predictable challenges. While taking on the more creative and elusive dimensions of project-based instruction can destabilize the familiar and reassuring expert and authority roles that both students and instructors typically brought to college classrooms of the past, and while the nature of the work of crafting a different faculty role can be quite labor intensive, not to mention "scary" at times, the rewards of making all those investments and of taking that big risk are myriad. The students have a greater chance of actually acquiring both the knowledge and the skills they need to gain traction on the problems that face them, and the instructors themselves stand to gain new knowledge (which is intrinsically rewarding) and cultivate a broader repertoire of teaching tools (which can be professionally rewarding).

Try This

1. *Demonstrate astute heuristic strategies for making progress on a difficult task even in the absence of some key domain-specific knowledge or expertise.* Concoct and present a problem or issue for investigation relevant to the class topic but for which no simple, algorithmic solution approach will suffice. Think out loud in front of your students or, better yet, lead an interactive class discussion in which various approaches to the task are proposed, examined, or tried out (at least partially) and then compared and evaluated for their promise in terms of the value of the strategy employed. In this manner show your students that practitioners in your field do not give up just because they lack immediate means to obtain an answer; they explore the problem and use "tricks of the trade" to try to gain a better handle on it.

2. *Act like Socrates, refusing to "answer" questions.* When covering course material familiar to the students, try teaching a whole class meeting in which you solicit student discussion and questions about the material but refrain from actually providing any direct responses or new information that might supply answers. Instead, respond to their questions with questions of your own—ones designed to help guide *how* they proceed. See how far you can get them to explore the issues and difficulties involved by applying their own knowledge and sharing key pieces of information among themselves. Try to coach the students through their collective deliberations by helping them ascertain the relevance of the various pieces of information that they attempt to introduce into consideration.

5

TEAM TEACHING

Dialogic Duets

Svetlana Nikitina and Diran Apelian

Vignette: Was the Industrial Revolution a Mistake?

Our class of 50-some students is astir. They have just finished reading a chapter in *Cradle to Cradle* (McDonough & Braungart, 2009), which proposed that "there were fundamental flaws in the Industrial Revolution's design" (p. 26). Could it be that this turning point in history was not such a great thing after all? It set the cradle-to-grave cycle in motion in all industrialized economies and eventually led to global warming and many other problems we have now. Yet, wasn't it the greatest thing ever?!

One member of the teaching team, Svetlana Nikitina, who teaches literature, gets up to discuss the reading. Her question to the class cuts to the chase: "Was the Industrial Revolution a mistake? Did human civilization take a wrong turn at that historic juncture?" This is a shocking proposition for future technologists and engineers who see themselves as the major beneficiaries of the era. It is a radical position for Diran Apelian, the other member of our teaching team, whose work and research as a mechanical engineer builds on the foundations and the innovations that resulted from the Industrial Revolution.

Everyone's mind is trying to reconcile the great technological achievements with oceans of waste, social dislocation, and horrific health effects. "Wasn't it a major technological breakthrough?" asks Diran. "Wasn't it the cause of social hardship for all the displaced and disenfranchised?" asks Svetlana, pointing to how skeptical poets and artists of the time were of this "march of progress." Everybody is beginning to wonder if the price of "progress" wasn't too high in environmental and public health terms. Everyone in the room, the teaching team included, is contemplating the other side of the industrialization coin—the shiny and the darker sides both.

In this chapter we describe why we team teach, how we collaboratively deliver both sides of the coin, and what benefits and challenges it presents for the campus community, its students, and its faculty.

Why Do We Team Teach?

All our seminars are offered by two WPI faculty members, typically representing *the two cultures,* as C.P. Snow (1959/1998) defined them: the sciences and the humanities/social sciences. Navigation of the chasm between the two cultures is at the heart of our teaching model because all great problems of the world demand holistic approaches, and faculty need to demonstrate the art of connection-making to students. Bringing faculty members together to teach as a duo demands more institutional resources, more coordination, and more personal stretching. So, why do it? What is the value added by teaching collaborations to campuses, faculty, and students?

Value Added for the Campus Community

Team teaching returns academia to its original mission of unifying rather than segregating knowledge around the central issues of society. GPS and the team-teaching paradigm are WPI's efforts to connect distant knowledge shores and to bring members of the "two cultures" and the whole campus community together to replicate the complex connections that exist in the real world. Team teaching and collaborative execution of the joint curriculum offers tighter collegiality than departmental ties and research partnerships. Working together in this case serves not just the professional interests of an individual faculty member but also a communal goal of education through dialogic exploration of new disciplines and engagement with the process of learning itself.

Our collaboration in team teaching The Grand Challenges seminar is an example of this. Our joint teaching helped stitch together the campus fabric both in terms of connecting us socially and professionally and in terms of connecting our respective departments and disciplines, engineering and the humanities. A community of two, we quickly became a community of many through a teaching collaboration. Our contact list, as well as the joint curriculum, became quickly populated with guest speakers and sponsors from the Museum of Russian Icons, the Chemical and Environmental Engineering departments, the Global Studies program, industry leaders, library staff, and facilities managers, to mention a few. This expanding network of connections has a direct institutional value. Team teaching strengthens interdepartmental ties, brings community members closer together, allows voices from the outside to be heard, and provides professional development opportunities for us as we learn from each other and acquire new pedagogical, research, and even disciplinary insights. Our voices, sometimes complementing and sometimes clashing with each other, always leave students in a state of generative cognitive expansion and creative dissonance. As a result, both faculty and students become part of a much larger and richer community than they inhabited before.

Value Added for Faculty

The teaching duos result in a disciplinary convergence, a wider network of social connections, a richer pedagogy, and a more inclusive dialogic mindset. Our (Svetlana and Diran's) pairing was a stroke of chance. Our academic experiences, research interests, and disciplinary affiliations were vastly different. We came from different worlds in almost every sense of the word. Diran has served as WPI's provost; he also founded the Metal Processing Institute. He is WPI's only member of the National Academy of Engineering, and he is a senior faculty member with an endowed chair. He is a strong voice in the governance of our school. He is also part of the department (mechanical engineering) that is very central to WPI's mission and profile. Svetlana was a very junior and expendable non-tenure-track faculty member in the humanities and arts department, which—although large and well respected—is not the academic cornerstone of this engineering school. The disparity in our administrative standing was stark, as was the chasm between our disciplines: mechanical engineering and comparative literature.

At the onset, we wondered if the disparity of our respective backgrounds would be challenging or uncomfortable. However, we quickly learned to be comfortable with being uncomfortable. The personal space we established and the trust we developed allowed us to take risks and to improvise in the classroom, with many of the seminar discussions (like the one described in the vignette at the start of this chapter) flowing free and unscripted. We realized that we learn the most when we are in discourse with colleagues with whom we do not have as much in common as scholars and professionals. In our team teaching, we embodied the joy of learning from different perspectives, and this resonated well with the class.

The teaching partnership that seemed almost impossible in theory took little time and effort to establish in practice, and it remains strong to this day. Having multicultural and multilingual personal backgrounds gave us a sense of appreciation of differences and mental flexibility to accommodate each other's differing perspectives. The way we teach now, even when teaching solo, is more community oriented in the sense that we involve more voices, more disciplinary approaches—and we always seek out alternative perspectives. Our own collegiality and mutual respect sends a message to students that every input is valuable and should be attended to.

Combining knowledge to create new knowledge takes courage, vulnerability, and extra effort. It also generates excitement, shakes you out of the epistemological rut, and puts you right back on the uncharted path of discovery. We both relish the idea of learning from each other while guiding the students to do the same. Sometimes this dialogue works by adding on to each other's ideas, while other times we question each other's perspectives (The Industrial Revolution—a positive or a negative development?). Still, other times, we incorporate each other's views and integrate different perspectives in one presentation. Diran, for example, will bring legal and policy considerations into the discussion of how to improve resource recovery. Svetlana adds technical facts about smelting points and furnace design in her historic overview of the role of metals in shaping our civilization. This collaboration results in new lines of research, a wider network of connections, lots of new learning, and a richer pedagogy for both members of the teaching team.

Value Added for Students

Students see the value of team-taught seminars in the variety of disciplinary approaches they get to experience, in the wider reach of different learning styles by faculty, and in the access gained from the start to a professional community inside and outside academia.

Students enrolled in our seminar are exposed to both technical and humanistic knowledge through readings, discussions, and class assignments. Because the two faculty members represent different "cultures," they bring with them different pedagogical approaches and appeal to a wider variety of learning styles among students. A wider assortment of assessment tools (essay, multiple choice, quantitative, qualitative analysis) taps into more students' strengths and provides more opportunities to excel. Students who are not quantitatively minded, for example, could reveal their talents in a position essay, while those who are particularly good with charts and analysis could find exam questions that will give them a chance to shine. Though students generally do not come out of our seminar as experts in mechanical engineering or literary criticism, what they firmly internalize through our class discussions and assignments is that there are different ways to approach problems and phenomena (math equation, poem, drawing, lab report) and that all these forms of knowledge have intrinsic value and distinctive structure. Learning for them becomes a fluid process of incorporating different modes of inquiry that have their own focus, internal logic, and tool kit. Students enjoy access to more people inside and outside the classroom because it allows them to discover their own interests, define their own disciplinary leanings, and find a variety of methods in which they can learn and express themselves.

Forming a Partnership: What to Look for in a Teaching Partner

Effective team teaching requires a strong partnership between two faculty members. Here are some suggestions on what to look for in a teaching partner:

- Open-minded curiosity about things outside of disciplinary pursuits (world events, trends in different industries, wide-ranging hobbies, multicultural interests, inclusive reading lists)
- Ability to remain in a learning mode (admit ignorance, be enthusiastic to bridge gaps in knowledge, maintain avid curiosity, invite help)
- Comfort with a level playing field (no pulling rank or authority when it comes to exploring new areas of knowledge)
- Comfort with unfamiliar topics and different ways of doing things
- Ability to embrace and enjoy difference and ambiguity
- Comfort with improvisation

These qualities are springboards that allow the collaboration and trust to develop and produce the teaching synergy necessary for joint instruction. This synergy is partly derived from the mind-set of the participants and partly from the effort of coordination, sharing, and learning from each other, as described next.

How Do We Collaborate?

Team teaching can take many forms. Perry and Stewart (2005) suggest thinking about them as "a continuum" from low-collaboration arrangements to highest levels of collaboration where courses are "co-planned, co-taught and evaluated by a pair" of instructors who "share all aspects of the course, including instructional time" and where "teachers trade off lead and supporting teaching roles as they orchestrate instruction" (p. 564).

Similarly, Sandholtz (2000) identified the following types of team teaching: (a) two or more teachers loosely sharing responsibilities; (b) team planning but individual instruction; and (c) joint planning, instruction, and evaluation of learning experiences. Each of these cooperative modes has its uses and strengths. The looser modes (the first and second) of collaboration afford more freedom to faculty members to present their perspectives with disciplinary rigor and personal conviction. The tighter mode (the third) of collaboration requires the most adaptation, dialogue, and give-and-take; faculty spend more time working out a plan of joint action and coordinating its execution in the classroom. The success of this model heavily depends on personal trust and openness to learning. Our team-teaching effort tends toward higher levels of integration rather than a division-of-labor approach. The "great problem" acts as a centripetal force that calls for synthesis of multiple voices and perspectives and a much more synchronized joint action. By design, both members of our teaching team are present in the classroom, both plan the curriculum and choose textbooks, and both invest time and effort into advising and evaluating students' work. Different stages of course development and delivery call for specific collaborative activities (summarized next), and anyone interested in implementing this approach could see how the different disciplinary modes of thinking are consistently brought together at each juncture.

The tighter forms of collaboration demand more time and effort from faculty who need to expose themselves to new forms of knowledge and to coordinate actions. This approach adds new layers of concern and complexity to the issue as opposed to breaking it into neat silos of inquiry. The advantage of this approach is that different forms of knowledge are not mechanically superimposed on each other but synthesized to elucidate the problem and find a fitting solution. The time and effort expended by the faculty is justified by students' growing awareness that complex problems require synergistic approaches that cannot be packaged in disciplinary foil or easily acquired from experts.

Developing Teaching Synergy

Teaching synergy is bolstered by overcoming both the division of labor and the division of time between the collaborators. It is also supported by careful selection of complementary course materials and by the integrative assessment strategies devised by the teaching pair.

Use of Class Time

During our presentations of new material, we offer students a mix of classroom activities that includes the discussion of big societal issues (food, mobility, etc.), along with an overview of technical parameters. The technical-engineering part of a lecture on battery recycling, for example, includes policy or public health considerations regulating battery technology. Likewise, a historical review of metal mastery through the ages includes technical facts about the melting points of metals and details about the furnace structure. Class may also start with a technical exposé (by Diran) and end up with a debate or discussion of its cultural meanings and implications (by Svetlana). Interweaving of perspectives happens both when we present our own disciplinary data and when we present material that lies outside of our disciplines (e.g., public health or policy issues). To make sure that interweaving or integration happens, we touch base *weekly* during the term. In addition, we hold a planning session during the summer, in which we map out the entire course and brainstorm guest presentations and field trips. We also meet regularly with our student assistants to get their feedback on the course progress.

Selection of Course Materials
To represent different disciplinary perspectives on the topic, we offer our students a variety of readings and study materials. We discuss our personal choices of sources during the summer meeting and typically arrive at a textbook that represents an inspirational social review of the issue (e.g., *Cradle to Cradle* for our Recycling or Sustainability seminar) supplemented by technical reference material constantly updated on our course site. Thus, our course materials include items that either of us would add from different areas of inquiry and representing different genres of discourse—from statistical data, reference material and databases, popular media clips, research papers, social science articles, links to TED Talks, and policy statements, in addition to a core reading. Both the quantitative and the qualitative aspects of the topic area are covered through this combination of resources for students.

Assessment
Assessment tools in team-taught classes represent a mix of disciplinary preferences and approaches. Our assignments and take-home exams include qualitative open-ended essay questions (see Appendix 5.1) as well as quantitative multiple-choice or targeted questions demanding specific knowledge of the relevant facts (see Appendix 5.2). Each of us contributes questions that will urge the students to learn the basic facts and to reflect on social trends and policies. As our exam questions demonstrate, students have to bring together personal reflection, technical knowledge, and social analysis.

Students' project work is also evaluated with a keen eye on how the teams are balancing their technical research with sensitivity to the social, cultural, or economic contexts. As we do that, we have to stretch ourselves in new directions and learn to read expository essays or futuristic poems (Diran) or correct statistical calculations (Svetlana) with full appreciation of the significance of the effort involved. Final deliverables—poster, presentation, report—have to present both quantitative and qualitative arguments, as students are evaluated on their integration of these perspectives.

What students discover as a result of this continuous effort to combine humanistic, societal, and technological aspects is that knowledge could be constructed on different complementary foundations. While engineering and technical data are important, the students learn that the data must be anchored in the human needs and economic conditions. We divide class time to allow for debate and delivery of technical and societal perspectives, and we evaluate the students' performance in class and in projects using a mix of narrative and quantitative tools. Each point of integration demands extra attention to the missing half of the argument, appreciation for another's perspective, and continued learning from each other.

Our summary suggestions on how to develop pedagogical synergy with your teaching partner include the following:

- Agree on the big ideas and general direction, but give each other space in the details.
- Embrace lifelong learning and admit to incompleteness of knowledge in any discipline.
- Coordinate actions but trust the process; don't overmanage the relationship.
- Acknowledge your partner as a valuable contributor to the elucidation of the problem, even when that contribution looks very different from yours.
- Celebrate each other's successes—professional, pedagogical, personal.
- Write a paper together—you will both learn a lot!
- Go to each other's professional conferences and venues and enjoy feeling like a novice.
- Show students your dialogic mind-set—your respect for difference, openness to a variety of disciplinary perspectives, relish of new knowledge.
- Give each other credit for new insights that result from the collaboration.
- Keep the dialogue going—share ideas, readings, professional work. You'll be surprised how much you'll see through a new pair of eyes.

Challenges of Team Teaching

Team teaching presents an investment for both the institutions and the individuals concerned. Its individual challenges are many, even in the case of a perfect personal chemistry among participants. Each of them has to have mental flexibility or a dialogic mind-set to appreciate the intellectual and pedagogical stretching team teaching involves. Combining disciplinary perspectives and different teaching styles also presents a challenge of coordination and accommodation that requires investment of time and effort by the teaching partners.

Developing a Dialogic Mind-Set

Bringing two faculty members together in one classroom for the entire semester is a big commitment on the part of an academic institution. Besides administrative and structural challenges (described in chapter 3), the challenges of aligning disciplinary knowledge and reconciling teaching and personal styles are no less formidable.

In the absence of overlapping research interests, personal chemistry between teaching partners becomes essential. It relies on the intangibles: personal compatibility, mutual respect, and open-mindedness. While the serendipity of personal chemistry is hard to predict, some factors seem to be reliable markers of a duo's success: openness to explore, willingness to embrace differences, and determination to remain in a learning mode. Fundamental to successful team teaching is respect for your teammate and complete trust in his or her ability to manage the learning journey.

Open-mindedness, inclusivity, and commitment to remain learners are the keys to success of most of our partnerships. Ours is a testimony to that. Our academic positions and disciplinary fields were vastly different when we met 10 years ago—and they still are today. Yet, our relationship has never been hierarchical or difficult. We have respect and open fascination for each other's areas of study, and we are both open to learn from each other and to make curricular changes in response to the changing times. We support each other's globetrotting and cultural exploration, and our seminar—by mutual inclination—is most welcoming to new voices (new speakers, sponsors, advisers) and to international students who push our thinking in new directions.

We also set up opportunities for students to learn from guest speakers whose work may demonstrate different approaches to the same issue. A good example of this is bringing David Spencer (CEO of Waste to Energy Corp.) and Martin Burt (social entrepreneur and director of the Paraguayan nonprofit Fundación Paraguaya) for two consecutive lectures. Spencer presents a business perspective on recycling bent on extracting value and profit from the recovered materials. Students learn from him about the business challenges different materials present, new and emerging sortation technologies, intrusive regulations, and environmental initiatives that often interfere (rather than help) with resource recovery. Burt, on the other hand, is an activist for social justice in Paraguay and around the world. For him, recovery of value from materials is a way to lift people out of poverty and detoxify their environment. Having these two perspectives back-to-back is an opportunity for us to have a rich conversation with students about the attributes of each insight and the importance of seeing both sides of the recycling coin.

Authoritative ownership of the discipline or approach is put aside in favor of collective learning and search for solutions. "Aren't we all outsiders?" Diran asks about our colleagues, meaning that we all are explorers of new disciplinary territories forging ahead with few maps in hand. "I would not distinguish from outsiders or insiders," he explains, meaning that nobody is on the "in" when it comes to traveling through uncharted lands—everyone is a novice and an adventurer. The point is to get the job done, to solve the real problem, and to have a real learning experience along with the students. Everybody shares in the journey. When everyone tackles the real problems, artificial boundaries and power lines fall off, and the input of all contributors is equalized and valorized. This may provide a clue to why rank, tenure, and disciplinary prestige have never been a factor in our teaching partnership. But such leveling is not a given for every teaching pair. Had our partnership been composed of different individuals, a more hierarchical and less dialogic relationship could have emerged. Such a relationship could lead to subordination of ideas and of people presenting them, producing much less synergy in the end.

We try to model "a community of learners" by having the two of us operate in a fluid dialogic mode. In literary theory, the term *dialogic imagination* is used to describe a situation when different people (characters in a novel) speak in "a multitude of bounded verbal-ideological and social belief systems" (Bakhtin, Holquist, & Emerson, 2014, p. 288). Dialogic or polyphonic mind-set is the attitude of acceptance of difference that refrains from subjugation of other voices and celebrates complexity, counterpoint, and openness to change.

This kind of mind-set is the foundation for successful team teaching. For example, we demonstrated our dialogic mind-set when discussing the historic event of the Industrial Revolution with students. The challenge of evaluating it, we explained, is to look not just at this event's outcomes (more speed, more power, etc.) but also at its environmental premise (anything goes, nature will absorb all) and economic assumptions (ever-expanding production and consumption). Also, should the impacts be measured in more than speed and power? What about health effects, social dislocation, and climate change? They are significant outcomes also! Our strategy (supported by the reading of *Cradle to Cradle*) has been to show the students how incomplete one view on the Industrial Revolution (as a technological salvation for human race) could be when challenged by a consideration of the entirety of its impacts and costs.

To be prepared to challenge each other and the students with a variety of perspectives, instructors in team-teaching contexts "must make the shift from being 'experts' to being 'expert learners' and share in the 'process of intellectual discovery'" (Wentworth & Davis, 2002, p. 23). This explorer attitude (discussed in detail in chapter 4) helps us with "negotiation of rapids" of disciplinary, departmental, and personal differences. The challenge of being always on the journey and ready to admit a lack of a road map is a chance to act as impromptu "guides" for each other and the students. The improvisational nature of team teaching builds on trust, dialogic mind-set, and belief in the journey itself. While those qualities could be elusive and hard to seek out, they are important to identify and build pedagogical synergies on. These are our recommendations for developing a dialogic mind-set:

- Stay curious, open-minded, and always learning.
- Refrain from value judgment when it comes to different forms of knowledge.
- Admit ignorance and offer expertise.
- Abandon the position of omniscience or superiority when it comes to a disciplinary insight.
- Stay alive to changes in social and technological landscapes and respond to them fluidly.
- Endorse differences, supporting different approaches to problem-solving.

Despite the administrative, disciplinary, pedagogical, and cognitive challenges of team teaching, its benefits for teachers, students, and the campus as a whole are rich and long lasting. As it unifies knowledge, it also builds a community of inquiry and civic engagement for faculty and students, which is the ultimate mission of any educational endeavor.

Combining Disciplinary Knowledge

Different academic tribes and cultures do not naturally mix, as academe is built on the vigilant delineation and preservation of disciplinary boundaries, which exasperated C.P. Snow (1959/1998) in his time. No matter how competent you feel in your own field, working with someone from a different discipline immediately exposes you to the vast store of knowledge you have no grasp of. Team teaching reveals the profound gaps in your knowledge as you come out of your disciplinary shelter and plead guilty to ignorance.

Why is water holy and sacred in all of the world's mythologies? What makes it a symbol of transcendence? These are not the questions a mechanical engineer asks as a matter of course. What is the melting point of copper? This question is not of any particular interest to a humanist. It is all too natural for the science faculty to view the humanistic questions as too abstract or vacuous and for the humanities and social science faculty to despair of seeing endless data points presented by their science-minded counterparts. In team teaching, the challenge is not only to make accommodations for each other but also to get excited about the other line of inquiry and go on a journey of exploration with the students. "Explore your differences . . . and show integration," suggested Plank (2012, p. 4), drawing on the extensive research on team teaching. To team teach, we ought to learn some of each other's disciplinary ABCs, stretch our teaching preferences, and demonstrate that reaching out to the other discipline is a trip worth taking.

Here are some guidelines for combining disciplinary knowledge:

- Discuss epistemological differences openly without smoothing them over or brushing them aside.
- Put aside disciplinary bias toward a more quantitative or qualitative mode and develop curiosity to look at the problem through a different lens.
- Demonstrate explicitly how approaches could differ and recognize the intrinsic value of each disciplinary tool kit.
- Reveal limitations and blind spots of different approaches and learn to bridge gaps in personal and disciplinary knowledge.

Combining Teaching Styles

Faculty who join forces in teaching often bring to the table different teaching styles. These styles are rooted in their research areas, personal preferences, and subject matter. Teamwork demands that those objective and subjective differences undergo scrutiny and adaptation for the joint venture to be successful. Gaytan (2010) pointed out that synergies emerge when instructors "adapt instructional strategies and overall course planning to suit a highly collaborative approach" (p. 83). For example, when science faculty are partnered with humanists, the humanities faculty need to shift away from their preferred method of interpretive analysis to embrace a more applied and hands-on mode of teaching: workshops, projects, and multiple-choice questions. This proactive, rather than contemplative, pedagogy could be both stimulating and frustrating to the humanities faculty. One has to learn to transition quickly from *why* to *how* and deal with the fact that deep exploration of the issue—its philosophical assumptions, cultural practices, and ethical implications—may not seem sufficient. The science faculty, on the other hand, may have to learn the value of time spent on what they perceive is a protracted debate about worldviews and ethics and be patient in their desire to move to solutions much sooner than their humanist counterparts.

Combining experimental procedures with discussions of historical antecedents and philosophical assumptions is challenging. We have to decide when to bring in ethical or technical insights and how to connect them with integrity and respect for each. The way we tackle this challenge is to allow time at the beginning of the class to frame the human significance of the issue, then follow that with the discussion of current technologies, and finish up with the discussion of social or policy implications. Alternatively, both instructors could interweave the perspectives of each other. For example, Diran will talk about policy issues, while Svetlana will use technical facts as points for reflection. To explain why China did not emerge as a leader of the Industrial Revolution in the eighteenth century, one has to consider its technical mastery of iron and furnace development. But this is not enough. Using this fact as a crucial starting point, one needs to proceed to the discussion of the social climate for innovation in a highly hierarchical Confucian society, which provides an essential insight to understanding the missed opportunity.

Combining a variety of teaching strategies—lab experiments, survey data, journaling, reflective writing, calculation, and historical overviews—is both a pedagogical challenge of coordination and an opportunity to reach more students with a variety of learning styles. To give students even more opportunities to find their own way through the course and express their knowledge in their preferred format, we have experimented with asking students to design their own exam and then take it. Students have to demonstrate their active thinking and learning about the subject, as well as their metathinking about what constitutes essential course content. They need to prioritize and own the material in ways they were never trusted to do before. To offer such an exam, we had to be secure in our own belief in the students' emerging critical thinking and in their ability to take stock of their learning.

The result was that the students spent a lot more time investigating the material and critically assessing it while making sure they could demonstrate mastery in whatever form they could devise. Their own learning style was engaged, as was their intellectual compass that guided them to the most important concepts and organizing ideas. Our goal was to launch students on the path of critical inquiry where the process was more important than the product.

Here are some suggestions for combining teaching styles:

- Accept the fact that different pedagogical methods stem from personal, epistemological, and historical differences that should be accepted.
- Learn enough about the other discipline to understand ways of the construction and assessment of knowledge to know where your teaching partner is coming from.
- Treat pedagogical differences with curiosity and enthusiasm rather than as a target for correction.
- Try your hand at a different pedagogical method (e.g., essay, equation, poetry) and seek help from your partner in navigating new terrains.
- Give your teaching partner all the help and support he or she needs in navigating your material and methods of presenting it.
- Swap graded assignments to learn from each other's comments.
- Include a variety of assignment types and give each other and the students opportunities to self-express in different ways.
- Incorporate (where possible) elements of your partner's pedagogy in your own teaching and note the richness of insight he or she contributes.
- Give your partner credit for introducing you to different approaches to teaching and show how it added to your teaching and assessment skills.

Benefits of Team Teaching

Team teaching is a personal, a disciplinary, and an institutional stretching exercise. It unsettles one's epistemological preferences and demands a lot of pedagogical coordination. It asks the instructors to model mental flexibility to students and to go on a learning journey with them. What does this personal and professional commitment yield in return? Why is it worth pursuing?

Benefits for Campus: Team Teaching Fosters Connections

Team teaching in GPS creates many circles of connections that tie together colleagues, departments, and communities on campus and beyond. Teaching together, collaborating on a book or article, attending summer training sessions, and reaching out to sponsors knit the academic fabric together. These connections support the campus culture of inclusion and foster a holistic learning community. They create a community in which students and teachers are not only present in the classroom with their intellectual abilities, but as individuals with different experiences and backgrounds. Mutual respect, honesty, willingness to explore issues, open-mindedness, and a genuine concern for learning are key principles that remain important. (Hanusch, Obijiofor, & Volcic, 2009, p. 73)

The teaching team models how to respect not only each other's disciplines but also each other's minds. By being inclusive of all epistemological inputs, we demonstrate inclusivity and respect for difference. When we bring many voices together in our classroom, the message students get is that all of them are valuable tools for addressing the great societal challenge.

Benefits for Students: Team Teaching Enhances Learning

Students benefit by exposure to a variety of teaching and learning styles that team teaching offers. Gaytan (2010) cited "the development of dynamic, interactive learning environments; creation of a model for facilitating the teaching of critical thinking within or across disciplines; and establishment of new research ventures and partnerships among faculty" (pp. 82–83) as the direct outcome of collaborative teaching.

Some students are naturally more at ease with quantitative or technical approaches, while others relish a qualitative inquiry. In our team-taught seminar, all students get to see the value of both, embodied in the humanist–scientist teaching partnership. Teaching teams create "a learning environment in which students can explore multiple perspectives and ways of knowing" (Plank, 2012, p. 5) modeled by their instructors. The result is "enhanced student learning" (p. 5), as students get to see different facets of the same problem (recycling as a challenging business of extracting value versus recycling as a form of environmental activism) and are left to reflect on the difference and complementarity of these approaches.

Benefits for Faculty: Team Teaching Enriches Pedagogy and Spurs Professional Development

Team teaching, according to Plank (2012), presents the opportunity "to teach in a different way, and to learn in a different way" (p. 1). As collaborations mature and develop, new interests emerge, and teaching partners, previously unconnected in their research fields, find meeting places in areas outside or on the borders of their disciplines. Pedagogy, sustainable development, and ethics have generated joint research and writing opportunities for many members of our teaching teams.

Team teaching transforms how we teach our own disciplines. Svetlana, for example, has introduced aspects of technology in her literature courses.

In a course on American literature and the environment, she supplements the reading of Thoreau and Emerson with contemporary expository writings that add factual and technical elements to the investigation of the classics. She does not hesitate to quantify the issues before engaging students in the interpretive meaning-making. Diran, on his end, adds socioeconomic considerations to the technological perspective he presents to students. Those considerations are typically seen as extraneous to the engineering lectures but are important to the implementation of solutions in the real world. Designing with an end in mind and with sensitivity to the needs of human and other species has made engineering a more complex and inclusive field for Diran. Giving first-year students the opportunity to immerse themselves in authentic problems facing society allows them to develop an understanding of the human condition, which will make them fulfilled individuals and professionals.

As a result of the combined teaching approaches, students experience a much broader range of learning tools, from journaling and lab reporting to surveying and interviewing. They also undergo a thorough workout in all forms of communications, from elevator pitches to poster production, report writing, and quantitative data analysis.

Team teaching is a recognized form of professional development, claimed Sandholtz (2000), and it has definitely pushed our professional and educational lives in new directions. How often does a mechanical engineering professor get to read and assess futuristic essays and poetic work? How often does a literature professor get to calculate human-energy-generating capacity and compare it to horsepower? Those assignments extended our teaching tool kits and got us both to try something new. Shibley (2006) asserted, "Collaborative teaching holds the promise of continued learning about interesting subject matter with engaged colleagues" (p. 271). This presents "a transformative, exhilarating experience" (p. 271) for all teaching partners. Plank (2012) confirmed that team teaching as "a unique and powerful form of professional development, leading to gains in both scholarly knowledge and teaching skills" (p. 5).

Perry and Stewart (2005) noted that team instructors "grow as teachers through effective partnership" (p. 573). Extensive communication with students and the teaching partners, these researchers claimed, make coinstructors "more creative and insightful" with "increased reflection and personal growth" (p. 573) being the result. The process of critical self-assessment and personal growth is the hallmark of such efforts because one is always reflected in the eyes of another. Perry and Stewart found that "effective team teaching is fundamentally a reflective process" (p. 573), as reflection relies on interpersonal and intrapersonal communication. "The benefits of having a sounding board for reflecting on teaching decisions" (Perry & Stewart, 2005, p. 573) have been present at every stage of the team-teaching experience as "any form of collaboration forces you to articulate your own assumptions and thought process" (p. 573). We look not only at the other side of the Industrial Revolution's coin—the social and the technical impacts— but also inside ourselves and reassess the nature of inquiry itself. The presence of another pushes the duo "to go deeper" and "to build something bigger than you could have built on your own" (Lester & Evans, 2009, p. 373).

Conclusion

While solo teaching could be insular, in team-taught classrooms faculty members are more like rivers connecting colleague to colleague, teacher to student, department to department, and the entire college to the real world. Just as rivers level out peaks and valleys, so does the dialogic democracy of our partnerships make rank and privilege irrelevant to the task of finding our way through new terrain together. Harmony or unison of voices is not the goal here. In fact, polyphony and disciplinary counterpoint often bring about more fireworks and unexpected insights than does monologic instruction. New research ideas are born; students realize that no singular point of view is privileged or complete when it comes to addressing the world's greatest challenges. Through such teaching partnerships, college campuses establish true bridges of consilience and collegiality that allow them to make major headway toward overcoming the chasms among disciplines, cultures, and structural barriers. The work of unification and connection-making is more easily done when you work closely with someone who helps connect you to a lifeline of contacts, services, and knowledge sources. Teaching together means receiving continuous stimuli to self-correct and to venture into new research territories on a daily basis. Team teaching is teaching with more tools, more appreciation for difference of opinion, and more respect for different modes of inquiry. Intellectual charity and consideration granted by each teaching partner to the other serve as the foundation for seeing multiple sides of each coin—the dark, the shiny—every single time.

SAMPLE INTERDISCIPLINARY ASSIGNMENT

It was early in the morning on September 3, 3018 . . .

Building on the views of human interactions with nature developed in *Cradle to Cradle* (McDonough & Braungart, 2009) and in class, please develop your vision of the future of our planet a thousand years from now, in 3018. Make this world come alive for your reader in all its details—sounds, shapes, smells, speeds, and life forms! Is this the world you would like to live in? Is this the world you are happy for the children of your children to inhabit? Do you see 3018 as the time of exquisite technical sophistication or of desperate survival? Is humanity able to sustain itself and thrive? Does it self-annihilate and perish? Is it barely able to hang on through some desperate technological or societal measures? Both optimistic and pessimistic visions are valid as long as you are able to tell a convincing and detailed story. What is the state of technology? How is food produced and distributed? What is public health like? Are people happy? Where and how do they live? You may choose to write this as a piece of science fiction, a letter to your great-great-granddaughter, an extended poem, a piece of investigative reporting, or a detective story. You could write it from the perspective of an extraterrestrial visitor, a *Homo sapien*, or a plant or animal (if any of these are still around in 3018!). The point is for you to *try on* this future time and reflect on whether anything could be done to build a better foundation for a viable future for our species on this planet—by you, by all of us, here in 2018!

SAMPLE INTERDISCIPLINARY EXAM

1. If you could rewrite history, what would you have done differently in the process of industrialization? What would "an effective" Industrial Revolution look like? *One paragraph.*
2. What is the biggest challenge that we face regarding materials' use?
3. What general historic trends could be observed in the use of materials by humans?
4. List major types of materials and their basic properties and production challenges. *Make a table to organize your research.*
5. What about the process of metal production that makes metals' recovery after use particularly imperative?
6. Which product enjoys the highest recycling rates in our society and why?
7. What is the key difference between natural and industrial systems?
8. Why is it essential to recapture and recycle critical materials?
9. In what way is the fate of the *Titanic* the symbol of the Industrial Revolution?
10. Name at least three essential uses for rare earth metals.

ASSESSMENT OF PROJECT-BASED LEARNING IN THE FIRST YEAR

Rob Traver and Rebecca Ziino Plotke

As seen throughout this book, projects are both processes and products. Projects develop in phases (or at least in fits and starts), typically engage teams of students, and deliver interim and final products. Projects are iterative and always interpersonal. They show their worth in outcomes that are written, oral, visual, and even behavioral. In this way, students who undertake projects are involved in something very much like the preparation and delivery of a performance (musical, theatrical, or athletic) where knowledge, skills, and attitudes improve over time, where shared understanding and competence—even excellence—emerge.

To guide this growth, assessment must do more than evaluate. It must educate. And to do this, it must align with the iterative nature of projects. It must discern and promote the progress of the team and the individuals that compose it by offering models of good work; time to practice; and regular, tailored feedback. Furthermore, it must try to realize that a learner's intellectual growth includes social, even emotional, well-being. In other words, assessment must work *alongside* and *with the team* to help it do well. Assessment, in this way, serves learning. It is assessment that educates. Call it educative assessment. Perhaps an extended vignette can help.

A Vignette

A project team of three students and a professor in a one-hour weekly meeting:

"Adrienne, Barbara, Chris: How are you today? I'm looking forward to our discussion of your team's work this week. What have you got?"

"Well, here's our agenda. Like last time, it lists our accomplishments, notes what we still have to do, and ends with some questions and issues we think we need to tackle next week. We also have a draft of the methodology section of our proposal you asked for."

"Thanks, Adrienne. I can see you're chairing today's meeting. Looks like a lot got done. We may not have time for it all; so what do you think is most important? Let's start there."

"Well . . ." [Adrienne glances toward her teammates to check that it's okay for her to go ahead.] "we talked with the project sponsor recently."

"Good choice. In the end, it's the sponsor we're trying to help. Now tell me, who made that call?" [Chris gives a confirming look to the professor.] *"Chris, you did. Great. How'd it go?"*

"It was really helpful. I learned a lot more, and I shared it with the team, about what exactly they want. It's a little different from what you told us. And that made things confusing at first. But now I think we've got it."

"Yes, the target always finds a way to move. So tell me, specifically, what did the sponsor say?"

"She said she wants us to focus on getting data using social media. She says that she and her staff are not as savvy with social media as . . . well, as she thinks we are, so we decided not to interview students in person in the campus center and just use social media."

"Is that what you agreed to?"

"Yes, that's what she said she wanted us to do."

"Okay, but did you discuss the advantages and disadvantages with her of social media versus in-person interviews?"

"Well, we kinda went with her request. I mean, she's the sponsor, we thought we should do what she wants."

"Okay, I think that's great that you affirmed your sponsor's request. It's really important that you build a good working relationship, and the last thing you want to do is appear difficult. But I worry that you may have lost a chance to get at some information that might be useful to your project. So here's what I want you, Adrienne, and Barbara to do. Take a minute among yourselves and give me some thought on two things. First, what are the strengths and weaknesses of the survey via social media compared to in-person? Second, if you were to go back to your sponsor, how would you present a suggestion that you do both kinds of surveys?"

About five minutes pass, time for the team to discuss both items. The team provides a good list of pros and cons for each method, how they might complement one another, and how this combination of surveys will serve the needs of the sponsor better than the single social media survey. They talk about how they will present this revision to the sponsor in the next phone call.

> *"Okay, let's go with that. Let's see what happens. . . . And now I want to change the focus. I want to look at that methodology draft. Barbara, you've been a little quiet today; why don't you take the lead. Read me the first paragraph, please. [The paragraph is read.] Okay, tell me what you and your teammates were trying to do in that paragraph."*
>
> "Well, we wanted to introduce our plan for the methodology of the project. We want people to know how we are going to collect information that our sponsor can use to improve their service. So we started with telling people in the first sentence that we will use social media to ask the kinds of questions that the sponsor needs to answer. Of course, that will change now that we've decided to do both surveys, but we didn't know that when we wrote the draft."

> *"Yes, I understand that, that's fine. But let's take a look at what you have here. Here's your first sentence: 'The project team will implement a survey that utilizes social media such as Facebook, Twitter, etc. to gather data that will be used to help the sponsor decide what changes they want to make in their services so they can increase sales and improve customer satisfaction.' I like the idea. You are trying to tell your readers how you will proceed and why you chose this methodology in relation to the project goals. It's a good effort, but there is really too much going on, and you've got the cart before the horse. What I mean is that you're way into the details of your methodology—the specific kind of survey technique—before your reader has a chance to consider, with you, what your methodology goal is. And your rationale is too global at this point in the paper; it should be based in the need for certain kinds of information and how to get it. So, let's rewrite this first sentence so that it frames the choice of methodology in terms of the kind of information you must gather for the project. Then it becomes more logical when you tell the readers what kind of methodology you've chosen. Let's write a sentence, and to help you get going, let's start with this phrase: 'The methodology section describes and explains the kind of information . . .'"*

The team works on rewriting the sentence, thinking about both the purpose and strategy of the first sentence and the wording that will present these in a clear and economical way. The instructor mostly listens but provides prompts and suggestions along the way. At the end, the team is reminded that there are several examples of methodology sections written by students available in the course resources' folder and that these can serve as models for how to organize and write this part of their proposal.

"It looks like time is about up. In the last few minutes, can you walk me through your plans for next week? What are your action items?"

Adrienne summarizes:

"We're still going to call the sponsor to follow up, but we'll include the outcome of our talk today. It does make sense to use more than one methodology, so we'll explain why we think so. And, of course, we'll revise the methodology section, rewrite the first paragraph, and use that to guide the organization of the rest of the section. We'll revise the timeline for the project, too, since it's going to take more time to do the different methods."

"All right, guys. Good session. You came prepared. You did your homework. We looked at some of the key parts of the project. Overall, you found the target moved and that revision is key to good work. Welcome to the real world. Things appear to be on track. Have fun."

What does this vignette reveal about assessment? Assessment for PBL approaches teaching and learning differently than most university classrooms. The difference is an ongoing relationship between teacher and learner that is more extensive, supportive, iterative, interdependent, and mutually reflective than usual. In this approach, traditional evaluation instruments—rubrics, tests, and classroom participation, for example—are not isolated but serve as checkpoints in a timely, integrated, interpersonal, more robust, and ultimately authentic response to the learners' efforts to produce real, consequential outcomes. The result is that assessment itself becomes educational. This chapter will describe the idea and delivery of such educative assessment by examining the reasons for such an approach and by providing a framework for its implementation. Challenges to educative assessment will be discussed at the end. The benefits for such assessment appear throughout.

Why Assess This Way?

There are several reasons an educative assessment approach needs to be employed to promote excellence and equity in PBL.

Inexperience

The primary concern is inexperience. First-years know little about project work. With only a typical high school education, they are not equipped to problem-solve in open-ended situations. Their experience with teamwork varies widely, ranging from no team experience (at least in an academic setting) to teamwork where the student played all the roles while everyone else watched or even checked out. Little capability results.

Similar to the lack of experience, first-years, unfortunately but understandably, are accustomed to prepackaged problems—math exercises at the end of the chapter, history debates with known outcomes, preprocessed science demonstrations like litmus paper indicators. When problems aren't packaged, the first-year has little idea what numbers to collect and what calculations to make, who and how to interview, what text is credible, which tool to take from the box. Therefore, assessment needs to work alongside in a timely manner with specific interventions.

Confidence

University professors and deans; established upperclassmen; and outside sponsors such as company directors, government officials, or military personnel can intimidate even the best-prepared 18-year-old (Palmer, 2007). How *do* four first-year students push back on a math department head who says their efforts to survey students and faculty in order to inventory their views on unpopular calculus courses are unnecessary? Educative assessment stays abreast of these challenges and can help students learn to assert themselves in productive ways, not the least of which is to get help.

Tailored and Timely

Educative assessment can provide the details necessary to discern individual growth, in addition to the progress of the team, by providing a structure for timely, regular review and feedback. Faculty and mentors who work alongside students while they undertake their project—interacting, deciding, planning, writing, building—can develop informed views of the strengths, weaknesses, contributions, resistance, and dynamics of each team member. This makes it easier to answer standard questions, such as "Does the person who speaks little really not know what is going on?" "Does another contribute infrequently but offer high-value remarks?" "Does the acclaimed leader really lead, or is he or she just the nicest person to work with?" "Is there someone left out who needs to be shepherded into the mainstream?" "Is someone riding coattails?" These and many other determinations about individual understanding, effort, and contribution need firsthand and periodic observation to evaluate and guide the student to appropriate responses.

Rapport

Assessment of the kind presented here improves interpersonal regard. It increases rapport and, through this, greater opportunity for lasting influence, not only from teacher to student but also the other way around. Students whose personalities and intellect do not immediately light up a classroom can go unnoticed. Regular meetings with teams allow the introverts, the timid students, to be heard, engaged, enjoyed, or at least acknowledged. Students whose personalities restrict others, and sometimes themselves, can be coached toward more productive styles. In turn, students show more of themselves to faculty, bringing into the open experiences that will enrich the team and strengthen the project.

Greater Fairness of Fit Between Effort and Product

It is disheartening to watch a team flounder in the delivery of final products when everything that preceded was managed adequately. Effectively written reports and engaging oral presentation are not the automatic outcome of hard work, organized meetings, team-dynamic problem-solving, good working relations with sponsors and clients, or a can-do response to multiple setbacks.

Educative assessment is necessary for project work because projects are iterative. For example, as in the opening vignette, the goal of the work changes midway. As many students will say, "If you tell me what you want me to do, I'll try really hard to do it. But if you keep changing what you want me to do, well, that's not fair." Trouble is, the world moves, and project targets move with it. Even if students are told to be ready for changes, it won't be long after a few of those shifts that the team becomes fed up. Educative assessment, on the other hand, makes it possible to discuss the frustration so that it turns to understanding, understanding to expectation, expectation to strategy, and strategy to success to the point where a weekly meeting opens with a team who introduces its agenda with this kind of mental outlook: "Well, the target moved again this week, but we suspected that, so here is what we did. We think it will work but wanted to check with you before we give it a try."

The late Grant Wiggins, a pioneer of the study of authentic project assessment, articulated well the rationale for the kind of assessment that is needed for project work:

> Assessment should be deliberately designed to improve and educate student performance, not merely to audit it as most school tests currently

do. Regardless of their technical soundness, audit tests (typically indirect multiple-choice or short-answer tests, be they national or teacher-designed) cannot serve the chief "clients" of assessment, the students, because these tests are inherently incapable of giving students the access to models and the feedback that are central to all real learning. Nor can these typical tests help teachers to improve their own performance. Because each major test is a one-shot effort, and because much secrecy surrounds these questions and test scoring, conventional approaches to testing cannot provide what we most need in our schools: a way to help students systematically *self-correct* their own performance. (Wiggins, 1998, p. 362)

In the end, educative assessment welcomes the learner's discomfort with ambiguity, setbacks, competing views, and messiness, because this is the look and sound, Dewey's (1997) "felt difficulty" (p. 72), of real problem-solving, of real growth.

How Can Educators Assess Using Educative Assessment?

For educative assessment to work, there must be well-defined aims and means. *Aims* include the following: (a) the production of deliverables, such as reports, posters, and presentations (e.g., see www.wpi.edu/+firstyearprojects); (b) the enhancement of team processes, such as improved group dynamics, effective meetings, and successful project management; and (c) the understanding of stakeholders and audiences, such as advisers, sponsors, and external judges. *Means* include the following (a) presentation of models and examples that supply explicit illustrations of what is valued; (b) practice in the form of opportunities to demonstrate and improve understanding and agency through drafts, exercises, iterations, prototypes, rehearsals, and traditional quizzes and tests; and (c) feedback that is formal and informal, oral, written, tailored, and appropriately timed (Tomlinson, 2011). This section examines each of the aims in terms of each of the means. Table 6.1 illustrates the key points.

Presentation of Models and Examples as Illustrations of Good Work

Assessment works best when there are models for deliverables, processes, and stakeholders. Modeling is necessary because it illustrates the values and sets the standards and criteria for assessment of the instructor and the course.

1. *Models of deliverables.* Students learn the characteristics of good work by examining it. If students in PBL courses look at concrete examples of designed objects—such as videos, websites, portfolios,

TABLE 6.1
Key Points in How to Use Educative Assessment

		AIMS of PBL ASSESSMENT		
		DELIVERABLES	*PROCESSES*	*STAKEHOLDERS*
MEANS for PBL ASSESSMENT	MODELS	Videos, websites, portfolios, AV presentations, writing, drawing Examples of these at both professional and student levels, rubrics, interim or partial examples to emphasize iteration	Team work, coaching by instructor, adviser Videos of student teams, rubrics and manuals, panel discussions, team charters	Expectations and examples of student work Rubrics, poster criteria, discussion with experienced judges, advisers, or sponsors
	PRACTICE	Writing, presenting and critiquing, meetings In-class writing exercises, presentation rehearsals, prototype tests, traditional testing for knowledge	Team-building workshops, active listening exercises, drafts of papers	Respond to papers, respond to presentations, coach team meetings, discuss rubrics and their applications with judges and sponsors, master class on advising
	FEEDBACK	Tell what works and why, what doesn't work and why, and how to fix it Be explicit and specific	Same as feedback for deliverables	Tell advisers, judges, and sponsors how they're doing and what they can do to help the students

audio-visual presentations, writing, drawings, or any other medium of deliverable—they can learn the essential features. Rubrics are excellent means to articulate the criteria and performance level of these essential features. It is paramount for expectations to appear in specific, descriptive terms, preferably illustrated by appropriate, concrete examples (some from our courses can be found at www.wpi .edu/+firstyearprojects).

2. *Models of processes.* Exemplars of good teamwork provide students with images and criteria of what works well. These examples can be videos of

students working together, as well as written guides, such as rubrics, and oral presentations from other students who have participated in teams. A lot can be shown with team charters, peer evaluation checklists, agendas, notes, and action items selected from effective student team meetings and with panel discussions with successful teams.

There are many video examples of teams in action and, sometimes more useful, teams in *inaction*. As prompts for team review and discussion, Wolfe (2010) presented several examples, in print and online, of dysfunctional undergraduate project teams. Less dynamic, but still valuable, can be illustrations of good team processes that emerge from panel presentations among members of former teams who discuss team roles and dynamics. Students pay a lot of attention to the successes and failures of their peers (Traver, 2016). In addition to traditional rubrics, team charters allow for explicit, guided assessment. A team charter states the responsibilities of the team members at the outset of the project in terms of meetings, attendance, late work, unfulfilled obligations, and resolving differences (Wolfe, 2010; see examples in Appendices 10.1, 11.3, and 12.3). First-year students frequently compare team charters to roommate agreements, and the comparison may promote understanding and use.

3. *Models for stakeholders.* Models and exemplars work well for project sponsors, new advisers, and judges. By examining the expectations and examples given to students, such as presentation rubrics or poster criteria, these experts can more accurately and reliably assess student work. A review of expectations and assessment techniques is necessary even for experts who have been invited to examine student work. For example, graduate students, research professors, and field-based experts who have agreed to review and judge a first-year poster presentation will need to be reminded that the students are probably making their first formal presentation. The students are not content experts, and they're not polished professionals. They may not think as quickly on their feet. The impossibly difficult question "Have you thought about this?" or an attitude where "I'm going to demolish your methodology to demonstrate that you haven't begun to apprehend the complexity of this problem" rarely helps. More seasoned and pedagogically aware colleagues can alleviate these *mis-educative* encounters by sharing ways they challenge first-year students without humiliating them. The discussion of one or two examples can be particularly beneficial. With these, many professionals can review and calibrate their expectations quickly.

Opportunities to Practice

The importance of assessment through multiple modes allows the faculty, instructors, mentors, and staff who work with first-year students to assess all components of project work, including transitional stages or "practice" work.

1. *Practice of deliverables.* A common example is *writing.* Even a single draft that precedes a final product can help. In-class exercises, where students write short pieces for one another or the class, can develop attitudes, hone skills, and solidify knowledge. One form of assessment for this type of practice is peer editing. By using the same criteria, such as appears in a rubric or model piece, peer editing provides the kind of structured feedback that will be given in the final stages of assessment.

   Another component of project work that can be practiced is *presenting.* Teams can practice oral presentation skills through short presentations of sections of their projects and evaluate posture, voice projection, and eye contact. Outside the traditional deliverables of classwork, there are "soft skills" such as writing professional- or business-style e-mails, making confident and articulate phone calls, or even tying a tie or selecting a wardrobe for a presentation.

   Traditional assessment such as *quizzes* and *tests* play a much smaller role in PBL, but they promote knowledge that will be key to successful initiatives. For example, do students know the statistics that are needed to analyze quantitative survey data? Are students aware of the regulations and ordinances of a town or city that will affect their plan to build a small structure, modify a park, or solicit for a new public service? Can students interpret a blueprint or topographic map? How much facility in a language other than English will be needed to interview nonnative speakers? All of these and many others will profit from review—a kind of practice—before the student goes on to demonstrate proficiency.

2. *Practice of processes.* Assessment of the different aspects of a project should include drafts, revisions, and iterations. These do not, however, have to be formal. For example, team building exercises that assess active-listening skills such as taking turns, giving and receiving critique, and recording useful notes can be staged along the way. Mental habits and skills that need regular practice—such as information literacy, reading and interpreting charts and graphs, written analysis, or rigorous comparisons of evidence and inference—should be practiced routinely as well. It is especially effective when students present their interim work to their peers.

For example, in one first-year project course, students submit a written draft, usually a short, one-page report or analysis, to a PLA (or undergraduate teaching assistant) for review. The PLA returns the draft quickly (within one to two days), and the student rewrites the draft. The rewrite, along with the first draft and the accompanying comments from the PLA, is then submitted to the course instructor. The instructor responds to and scores the paper (within four to five days). The student again rewrites the draft, and a final paper is submitted. At the same time, a second assignment is submitted to the PLA. In this way, students are simultaneously generating and revising two assignments. Through this work, students invariably see their writing improve and their projects become clearer. When such a writing-is-learned-through-practice culture takes hold in the classroom, student attitude toward writing changes from "it's a task with subjective, even arbitrary, either-you-get-it-or-you-don't scoring" to "it's a skill with reasonable and manageable criteria that can be mastered" and, most important, "it's worth learning."

3. *Practice for stakeholders.* To ensure a positive assessment culture, instructors must themselves undertake and practice assessment. They must regularly read and respond to student papers, contribute to student dry runs of presentations, and attend team meetings from time to time—in other words, model the habits of mind and skills that they want students to use. With this committed participation, instructors develop a repertoire of examples and cases that inform their future efforts.

Other stakeholders, such as sponsors and judges, also improve with review and revision. It is worth the effort to examine with sponsors and judges what they expect from student teams and how they might interact with them. And it is worth the time to consider with these same sponsors and judges how students have responded to their requests and revisions. Not least among the benefits of this kind of review is that sponsors and judges get better at helping students think about how to respond to people who serve in assessment roles, whether clients, supervisors, bosses, evaluators, or others who have a stake in the delivery and consequences of their projects.

Overall, these iterations represent the ongoing, thoughtful inquiry of ends–means adjustment that constitutes reflective practice.

Feedback

Feedback is integral to assessment because feedback drives improvement. Feedback is most effective when it is timely, specific, and ongoing.

1. *Feedback on deliverables*. It is not difficult to provide feedback in regard to deliverables. The basic rule says to specify (a) what worked and what was done well and worth continuing to do and (b) what didn't work and needs review and modification. In addition, and this is crucial, the students and the team need specific guidance for how to change things. The specifics can relate to anything—sentence structure in writing, schedule of activities in a Gantt chart, question order in a survey, criteria of an engineering design matrix, storyboard order for a demonstration video, or credibility of source material. But the suggestions must be specific. "Mute the orange and blue or try another combination" is better than "the color contrast is too strong"; "You're trying to explain subtraction to 10-year-olds, so remove the sophisticated math terms such as *minuend* and *subtrahend* and replace them with *top number* and *bottom number*"; "You need a prepared agenda before each meeting" gives more guidance than "team meetings need to be better organized." An extraordinary example of student feedback appears in the video *Austin's Butterfly*, where fourth graders diplomatically provide explicit feedback to a first grader who offers a series of drafts of a butterfly drawing (EL Education, 2012).

   When this kind of specific feedback is supplied, the effect can be significant and creates a foundation for evaluation at the end of the project. For example, a final grade can take into account how well students incorporated the faculty guidance.

   There is a caution, however. Too much specificity can overwhelm, especially if the specifics relate to several different issues or problems in the team's work. If these are addressed all at once, the team often will not make as much progress as when a couple of the difficulties are addressed in smaller clusters and practiced and mastered, and then the remaining challenges come up for review (Higgins, Hartley, & Skelton, 2001).

2. *Feedback on processes*. This is analogous to that for deliverables: What works, what doesn't—and here are some specific ways to fix it.

   For example, the instructor says to the team, "Your team has established a regular schedule for meetings, provides a written agenda in advance, and has a perfect attendance record. Really good. But, in your team meetings, one person does about 70% of the talking. I think all of you have important contributions to make, and so I want the less talkative ones to participate more than they do so now. To this end, I want the team to provide me with a memo that records what each of you said in the meeting and a pie chart, one I call an air-time chart, that indicates the proportion of time each of you spoke at the meeting. It's not necessary that everyone speak equally, but I want to see more from those who talk less and less from the one who talks the most. I have no doubt that I'll see statements—substantive statements—from *all* of you."

3. *Feedback for stakeholders.* It may be surprising, but stakeholders often want to know how well they're interacting with project teams and individuals. Judges wonder whether they score higher or lower than other judges, and though they may not comment, they'll pay attention when their scores appear in a comparative scoring chart. Sponsors and clients, too, will respond to feedback from project advisers. One of the most valuable kinds of information relates to the personalities and work styles of individuals on the team. Instructors typically know students better than sponsors and clients do and so can help the latter interpret the kinds of interactions they may see or experience with first-years who have undertaken a project with them.

Furthermore, clients and other sponsors can help team dynamics; for example, where the instructor seeks to encourage more participation from a particular student and so brings the client into the plan to assist the student in talking a little more. Feedback to sponsors takes on its most important role when the outcomes and methods of the project must be negotiated, established, and reviewed. Stakeholders outside the university may have expectations that don't align with the level of skill or amount of time available to first-year students. Stakeholders who are familiar with more advanced teams may fail to communicate as clearly or as timely as needed. They may think a team can work more independently than it can or has access to more resources than it does. For example, many residential universities do not let first-year students keep cars on campus. What may be a 20-minute trip to Home Depot from the client's point of view can be a logistical, and not inexpensive, challenge for first-years grounded on campus. Of course, it is best to leave as much of this clarification and negotiation to the project team, for in their efforts to sort things out they learn, but the adviser must be ready to participate directly and provide the kind of information—the feedback—that makes things work for everyone.

What Are the Challenges and Benefits Educators Encounter?

There are several assessment challenges. They arise in nearly all efforts to promote student work and understanding through assessment, but the nature of PBL leads to different emphases among these perennial concerns.

How Much Feedback?

It is hard to watch a team struggle and not step in to guide the conceptualization, management of resources, dynamics of the team, or implementation of a solution. It may be irresponsible not to do so. In fact, stepping in to help a team may be the very modeling of thought or behavior that makes it possible for learning to take place. But there is no surefire advice as to when and how much feedback there should be.

On one hand, Barrows (1992), a deeply informed and experienced user of projects in professional training, said that the oral statements and challenges the instructor makes should be those he would make to himself when deliberating over such a problem or situation as the one his students are working with. His questions will give them an awareness of what questions they should be asking themselves as they tackle the problem and an appreciation of what they will need to learn. In this way he does not give them information or indicate whether they are right or wrong in their thinking (pp. 4–5).

On the other hand, open-ended, robust, problematic—in other words, authentic—tasks can take a lot of explicit feedback without revealing the answer. For example, professionals use the best work of others to guide their efforts. They look for models. If the audience and topic are similar, then a model of what worked well in the past *should* strongly influence the next round. These models do not "do it for you" when the need or problem is not exactly the same as the one the model addresses.

The difference lies in the extent to which the feedback does all the work or helps the student work smarter. And that difference is a function of the task. That is, supply whatever information helps move the learner toward achievement of the learning outcomes, and if that information easily solves the problem, enlarge the scope of the project.

The Individual and the Team

The fairness issue resides in every team project because teams comprise individuals who work toward a common goal. Not everyone may contribute equally. Assessment should distinguish among efforts and reward equitably.

In the best of all possible worlds, assessment should reward the individual exactly as the team stands, because, as they say in sports, "there is no I in TEAM." But one for all and all for one is rarely fair. Clearly there are cases where individuals contribute unequally, and so various scoring schemes have been developed to partition a team grade (Markham, Larmer, & Ravitz, 2003). The most common use some form of peer review. For example, a three-student team might receive a grade of 85/100 on its project. That score gives the team 255 points to distribute. The teammates can be asked to partition the points, citing reasons for their choices. What usually emerges is a small redistribution of points, a few above and a few below 85. When these apportionments are very similar, it's likely that students' different contributions are well understood and agreed on among themselves. At other times, the team may split the points evenly, each getting 85. This choice can be the result of true equal contributions, or it can be a team that is "looking out for each other." In the latter case, should an outside observer, such as the instructor or a teaching assistant, think that there really isn't an equal partition of the load, it means that one or more students who carried the project have opted to share their points and may, therefore, have given up their A to a C student so that everyone gets a B. To the extent that the instructor is familiar with the team or seeks additional information, there can be intervention and adjustment—or acceptance—of the team's valuation.

Another way to differentiate between the individual and the team is to establish multiple individual tasks throughout the project. In addition to the team project, there are deliverables that come from each student. For example, in the team's search for published sources that relate to the project, each student can be asked to find and evaluate references. These independent assignments generate information about each student's understanding and contribution. Or, at the end of a project, after the team presents its final deliverable(s), each student can be examined to explain, on his or her own, the methods, findings, and impact of the project. Needless to say, some students know what they've been doing better than others do.

Sometimes an individual project log or journal can help. In these, each student records action items, questions, accomplishments, time spent, and other relevant items. A note or two of reflection accompanies the records.

- "Worked two hours today to find relevant sources. Paper by Brown, 2016, is perfect."
- "Tim and I reformatted the website from 3:00 p.m. to 6:00 p.m. Still looks too dense."
- "Finally reached the sponsor, who clarified what to include in tomorrow's meeting agenda. Not what I was expecting."
- "Didn't do a thing for the last three days—sicker than a dog. Team said it'd cover for me."

More elaborate journals ask the student to write about his or her progress in relation to standards or outcomes, such as skill acquisition or the development of habits of mind. First-year students will, if prompted, discuss their ability to entertain alternate solutions disinterestedly, to write logically and fluently, to reflect thoughtfully on comments from teammates before responding, or to use design principles in the construction of a website.

With a good journal that serves as a self-report, an instructor can more fully gauge the level of commitment and progress of any student. First-years usually know what they are supposed to be learning and often have a good, if not always articulate or nuanced, feel for how they're doing. Of course, much depends on the degree to which the instructor reads the journals and responds to their authors.

The Worth of a Project

Some projects are harder to do than others. Some have greater impact. Within a variety of projects, within a given time frame, team size, or team resources, some undertakings are clearly bigger than others. Major factors to consider are the number and depth of relevant disciplines, who is involved, the location, the deliverables, and the technology (Jonassen & Hung, 2008; Larmer, Mergendoller, & Boss, 2015). As a result, teams may be expected to spend 15 hours per week in pursuit of their goal, but one group cannot get the job done with less than 25. Another team writes and presents a good piece of math instruction for a first-grade classroom, while a second team designs a community-relevant health curriculum for an entire fourth grade. Some teams find ways to design, test, and implement a project within a semester, while others end up with a laudable design but no test. In all the foregoing, every project was done well, but each finished with different scales and impacts. What should assessment do?

The answer lies in explicit expectations. The instructor must provide examples at the outset and along the way that clearly state what must be delivered at what level, cost, scope, and so on. At the outset, the expectations will likely be general and will gather specificity only as the project proceeds. For assessment purposes, it helps to put the expectations in writing and periodically discuss these with the team.

Where Do I Get the Time to Do All This?

Educative assessment may need more time than traditional methods. What can be done to address this? There are two major strategies: The first is quality time; the second is assistance. Quality time insists that both instructor and team come to meetings prepared and follow through after the meetings; the attitude is professional, with much required from the team. There's an agenda, notes are taken, and action items are established. An example of such a meeting appears in the opening vignette. See Wolfe (2010) and chapter 10 (this volume) for other examples of effective practices, such as team charters, preparation worksheets, and Gantt charts that contribute to time savings. Similarly, the instructor reads reports and reviews presentations efficiently, with an eye toward key, high-impact concerns. For example, Doug Hesse, director of the University Writing Program at the University of Denver (www.du.edu/writing) recommended editing "only a fraction of a paper: a selected paragraph or page. Make clear up front that you do not aspire to be exhaustive" (Hesse, n.d.). In another example, Purdue OWL, the university's online writing lab, provides specific, concrete, easy-to-apply student check-lists they can use to edit their own work (owl.english.purdue.edu). Overall, the key is to plan and provide explicit expectations about roles, processes, and deliverables so that the students know how to proceed and deliver more effectively and efficiently.

In regard to assistance, several chapters in this book encourage project-based learning faculty to use others in the university and beyond. Significant support can be garnered through undergraduate teaching assistants (see chapter 3). For difficult team dynamics, staff from Student Advising and Counseling often can help a team that needs to reflect on its social psychology (see chapter 12). Instructors can also capitalize on the knowledge and skill of project sponsors and clients (see chapter 8). For example, the head of Food Services can work with a food-waste project team; the Facilities manager can advise a campus energy sustainability project.

To provide a sense of time commitment, in first-year projects undertaken at our university, many faculty meet with a team for one hour each week. The trick is to think differently about the style and content of the time spent with students.

Conclusion

In many ways, the overarching issue for the assessment of PBL, expressed as a question, is "Can I think like a project manager?"; that is, can I plan, organize, supervise, cheerlead, critique, coach, and otherwise make sure that several teams under my direction complete their tasks well? The required skill set for this is not expected of teachers in most universities. Therefore, the instructor must see a PBL program in a larger scale than, say, a course. For example, for each team there is the project launch; then the development of knowledge and skills; followed by the critiquing, refashioning, and retesting of products; and then the presentation of deliverables (Larmer et al., 2015, p. 105). There are the interim deliverables, the due dates, the rubrics and other assessment instruments, and the communication with experts, sponsors, and clients. There are team dynamics, supervision and training of junior staff such as undergraduate or graduate TAs, solicitation and orientation of judges, and perhaps even arrangements for video documentation, press releases, and publication. How well all this proceeds is the bailiwick of assessment—the honest, informed, timely, caring, critical reflection and the report of "how's it all going?"

Try This

1. *It's worth looking at the kind of feedback some faculty give to students.* Here is, what may be, a surprising example of weak feedback. The team has submitted an interim report. The professor reads the report and comments,

   > The paper has some good ideas, and most of the sources are relevant. The team needs, however, to better organize the piece, write sentences that flow more smoothly, and create a more logical sequence among the sources. Also, proofread. On the whole, though, it's an adequate start. C+

   Why is this weak? With this feedback the team knows that something must be done, but it's not clear how to proceed. Which of the ideas are the good ones, and which sources are relevant? How does one better organize a piece, write more smoothly, and create logic among sources? Proofreading they understand, but without specifics, it's hard to know what to look for. In other words, in spite of professorial comments that provide more than the usual amount of feedback, what appears here does not help a great deal. What kind of information will make the professor's response a better guide for students? (This is an exercise in explicitness—after timeliness, it's the single most important criterion for feedback.)

2. *Do you provide educative assessment?* Here are some questions that can be asked to assess your assessment. Take the best learning activity in your curriculum or educational program. (a) Identify the models you use to illustrate what characterizes good work for the activity. Are the models truly illustrative? Are they clear and accessible? Are there enough of them? Even if you are satisfied, can you make the models better—or find better ones? Use student feedback to help you answer the foregoing four questions. (b) Specify the place(s) in the activity where students practice what they need to know or be able to do to deliver good work. Are the opportunities to practice necessary? Do they directly relate to the activity? Are the opportunities to practice sufficient for the average student to develop the skill, attitude, or knowledge to the desired level? Are the

opportunities to practice interesting and worthwhile to students? Again, use students to help you answer these questions. (c) How useful is your feedback? Is it timely and explicit? Do the students say it helps, and, in turn, do the students improve as a result of what you have said or shown to them? And again, ask students to help you examine the value of your feedback.

7

SUPPORTING PROJECT-BASED LEARNING WITH LIBRARIANS AND INFORMATION LITERACY

Marja Bakermans and Rebecca Ziino Plotke

Why Incorporate Information Literacy Into the Curriculum?

Discovering the articles I need from a pile of unneeded ones is like gold washing, tedious at the start but ultimately exciting and rewarding. Sometimes an accidental discovery during research can affect the whole project, and this makes me proud of my work.

What I learned a lot about was how to do research. I feel that my research skills have considerably improved throughout the course and I trust myself finding reliable, scholarly, and reviewed sources that have valuable information. I am glad I was able to take this class because research is not only a skill that will help me throughout college but in life in general. I further learned how to use most of the library resources, which is a skill that few freshmen actually acquire throughout their first months in school.

These student quotes show the joy in having accomplished the major achievement of searching through unfamiliar university resources and differentiating the purpose and use of varied sources to inform and distinguish among fruitful research topics. More important, the students recognize that these skills are critical to their academic and career success. Their success was due to the development of information literacy skills through activities collaboratively designed and implemented by the instructors and a research and instruction librarian.

This chapter explains the need to integrate information literacy skill building into the curriculum and teach it as a foundational learning component, particularly of PBL. Through examples and narratives, this chapter will provide a model for teaching information literacy in tandem with the other course content.

Becoming an Information-Literate Student Is Difficult

First-year students, in particular, are novices in information literacy skills and disposition. These students lack the understanding that research is a process requiring persistence, flexibility, and an ethical approach to using information (Salisbury & Karamanis, 2011). Typically, students are poor at finding information because they don't know of available and appropriate resources (e.g., library search engines, databases, etc.), or they don't know how to use those resources effectively (e.g., search strategies). As one student noted, "Before, I knew how to research, but I did not use databases and library websites. Now I am fully able to use those resources, and I know it will come in handy throughout the rest of my college experience."

Adding to these difficulties, the scope of available information is vast, complex, and filled with confusing language, thus creating a difficult environment to navigate. Students may perceive that there is an expanse of information technology available for searching and a sense that digital content is seemingly unending (Fain, 2011). Students have a difficult time locating appropriate information because, when faced with a multitude of choices, they select a resource that is familiar, easy, and quick to use (Fain, 2011). For example, students rely heavily on Google regardless of the appropriateness or the effectiveness of the content returned (Douglas et al., 2014; Kingsley et al., 2011).

Indeed, faculty often perceive and rank first-year students as having below satisfactory information-seeking abilities (Leckie & Fullerton, 1999; Vander Meer, Perez-Stable, & Sachs, 2012). Students often do not know how to approach an information search. When crafting search strategies, they rely heavily on colloquial or common language terms, lack variety in keyword choices, and add subjective phrases such as "good tool" or "effective solution" to the search strategy (Georgas, 2014).

Students also have trouble evaluating information because they are unfamiliar with differences in and consequences of scholarly work versus non-scholarly work. Thus, it is important for instructors to have activities and discussions around this topic (see the Sample Activity 1, p. 132, this volume). Because of this problem and students' proclivity to search for information on the Internet rather than their library website, they often include inappropriate sources and materials. Novice students initially do not use high-quality sources or information because they have trouble comprehending or accessing information based on the technical, narrow, and expert-level wording, phrasing, and analyses found in scholarly works. Past examples of inappropriate sources and information used in research papers include websites from companies selling a product, landing pages of nonscholarly websites, and blogs. If students find sources through the college library website, their chances of finding information in a text or journal article increases.

Students have trouble applying information gleaned in the search process because their novice knowledge of the topic leads to difficulty in making connections between information (Ambrose, Bridges, DiPietro, Lovett, & Norman, 2010). Thus, they often confuse a synthesis of information with a summary (Megwalu, 2013). For example, students write one paragraph summarizing a paper, another paragraph summarizing the next paper, and so on, instead of integrating like materials together in one paragraph from multiple sources. Critical thinking is a key component of this connection process (Spivey, 1997) where students must carefully pull out related information, whether it is complementary or contrary to their thesis, and weave it together in a narrative. Synthesizing information effectively allows the reader to see where information overlaps but comes from different sources. This is no easy task for students and has been shown to be cognitively demanding (Mateos & Solé, 2009). Indeed, both students and faculty recognize synthesizing as one of the most difficult tasks (Segev-Miller, 2004), and yet a study by Mateos and Solé (2009) found that few instructions are provided to students when they are asked to generate a synthesis.

Students Need These Skills and Abilities

Because information literacy skills are often used in conjunction with a number of additional competencies, including reasoning, critical thinking, collaboration, self-directed learning, and problem-solving, it is thought to be a key component to developing lifelong learners (McGuinness, 2006). During the college experience, students need information literacy competencies because educators expect evidence-based argumentation based on high-quality information, which requires a foundation of information literacy skills (N. Adams, 2014), like the ability to locate, evaluate, and effectively use relevant information (American Library Association [ALA], 1989). Information literacy forms the basis of lifelong learning (ALA, 2000).

Students need to develop these information literacy skills throughout their education—first at introductory levels, including orientation to university resources, and then at more discipline-specific levels and across many years. As students move through their academic careers, faculty place a greater emphasis on requiring library research to complete research papers, projects, and reports (Leckie & Fullerton, 1999). In particular, faculty place high importance on student research skills, evaluation of sources, and reduction of plagiarism (DaCosta, 2010; Hrycaj & Russo, 2007; Vander Meer et al., 2012). In a study by Vander Meer and colleagues (2012), they found that 84% of faculty required searching and using information beyond textbooks in the courses. When requiring library research in a task, faculty overwhelmingly want students to use scholarly sources, like journals, monographs, and review articles (Leckie & Fullerton, 1999).

If these skills are taught early in their academic career (e.g., first-year courses), students will continue to use the skills throughout their college and personal careers (Daugherty & Russo, 2011). Student academic success (e.g., grades or retention) has been linked to repeated information literacy instruction (Bowles-Terry, 2012; Cook, 2014; Moore, Brewster, Dorroh, & Moreau, 2002; Soria, Fransen, & Nackerud, 2013; Vance, Kirk, & Gardner, 2012; Wong & Cmor, 2011). Faculty who integrated library instruction into their courses found that library instruction positively affected the majority (i.e., 77% [Leckie & Fullerton, 1999] and 96% [Cannon, 1994]) of students' abilities. Students also recognize the importance of information literacy skills and place high importance on knowing how to search library databases (Larkin & Pines, 2005). Thus, a trend exists where information literacy is being integrated into more courses, programs, and universities (Singh, 2005).

Faculty Often Do Not Teach Information Literacy

Faculty are not experts on the complexity of resources available through the library and the full scope of the development of information literacy standards and frameworks (Hardesty, 1995). Not surprisingly, then, a large proportion of faculty provide little to no instruction or integration of information literacy in their courses (DaCosta, 2010; Leckie & Fullerton, 1999). In fact, even though most university libraries offer resources to faculty— in-class instruction, workshops, demonstrations, and assistance in designing information-literacy-integrated assignments—the majority of faculty do not use these services (Cannon, 1994; Leckie & Fullerton, 1999; Thomas, 1994; Vander Meer et al., 2012). Thus, there is a disconnect between faculty requiring library research, especially in upper-level courses, to complete assignments and projects and then not providing relevant instruction (Vander Meer et al., 2012). It has been noted that faculty often believe students will pick up information literacy skills along the way, but those same faculty have no clear intention to provide instruction to the students (Hrycaj & Russo, 2007; McGuinness, 2006; Thomas, 1994). Requirements of library research increase in upper-level courses (Leckie & Fullerton, 1999), but often those faculty believe those skills should be developed in lower-level courses. However, instructors who teach lower-level courses often do not incorporate information literacy into their curriculum because they lack resources (e.g., TAs) for large classes, rely heavily on textbooks, and lack the appropriate time to cover information literacy (Leckie & Fullerton, 1999).

Faculty should seek the advice and expertise of instruction librarians to collaborate on information literacy learning outcomes, instruction activities, and assignments. With faculty–library partnerships and in-class instruction, students produce work that reflects more advanced search capabilities. For example, students who receive instruction on information literacy cite more scholarly resources and produce fewer incomplete citations (Wang, 2006). Results from a study by Junisbai, Lowe, and Tagge (2016) confirm the belief that the faculty–librarian collaboration throughout the length of the course in an embedded model produces the strongest results. Their study concluded, "Collaboration both in class and behind the scenes, librarians and faculty jointly provide strategic, systematic instruction to produce information-literate graduates and—in the longer run—engaged, socially responsible citizens" (Junisbai et al., 2016, p. 608).

Why Do Librarians Need to Teach Information Literacy?

Librarians have been teaching information literacy as disciplinary content for many years. In 2000, the Association of College and Research Libraries (ACRL) defined *information literacy* as "a set of abilities requiring individuals to recognize when information is needed and have the ability to locate, evaluate, and use effectively the needed information" (ALA, 2000, p. 2) and produced a set of Standards for Higher Education. In 2015, the ACRL revised the standards to recognize a more complex process and defined *information literacy* as a set of integrated abilities encompassing the reflective discovery of information, the understanding of how information is produced and valued, and the use of information in creating new knowledge and participating ethically in communities of learning (ACRL, 2015).

This definition by ACRL crosses academic disciplines and can be used alongside institutional learning outcomes to create a rich curriculum for teaching information literacy in the classroom and creating information-literate learners. In general, information literacy content taught by librarians ranges from the foundational skills necessary to meet the dispositions of novice learners to the discipline-specific needs for more advanced learners (Bruce, Hughes, & Somerville, 2012). When teaching the content, librarians focus both on the skills necessary for building good information literacy behavior and on how people use the skills and information within any given discipline (Bruce et al., 2012). They understand that the research process is complex and teaching multifaceted elements requires knowing the learners and their background or prior knowledge (Ellis & Salisbury, 2004). Contrary to the misperception that students will acquire information literacy skills throughout their education, these skills need to be explicitly taught and reinforced collaboratively by librarians and faculty.

One-Shot Instruction Is Not Sufficient

Although it is common for academic libraries to deliver information literacy content through initiatives such as workshops and one-shot instruction sessions (Veldof, 2005), when librarians and faculty work together, they can tailor instruction and assignments that increase the relevancy and applicability of the information literacy content. In a study (Bakermans & Ziino Plotke, 2018) that evaluated the effectiveness of information literacy instruction in first-year courses at WPI, we demonstrate that collaborative, integrated, and continuous instruction combined with assignments from research and instruction (R&I) librarians and faculty can improve a student's familiarity with foundational information literacy skills. Analyses indicated there was a significant increase over the semester in the familiarity of library resources, search strategies, and citation formatting and the ability to evaluate source quality. However, improvement of information literacy abilities, like the ability to evaluate the variety of source, source relevance, and ethical use of information, was more difficult for first-year students in these courses. Students from these courses reflected on the improvement of their skills:

> I was able to improve my research skills by taking advantage of the many library resources [this course] had to offer. I found it beneficial that the librarians were so supportive and offered various resources for the students to take advantage of to improve their essays and writing skills.

> In this project I learned how to research a lot better. I did a lot of the research for my group so I was able to get a lot of practice in finding scholarly sources and with using the library page to search for sources. The coursework helped me learn how to take notes on those sources and how to analyze them properly and describe their content so my entire group did not have to read them.

By the end of the semester, most students recognize the importance of using their information literacy skills repeatedly to improve their performance on their final project. One student wrote,

This project included a lot of thorough research. This skill had been practiced in previous assignments in class, and was really put to the test to conduct this project. We needed to use all of the resources we had access to, and learn the most useful search terms and everything to gather the best information. We could not have come up with any solutions if it had not been for a solid background on our topic.

How to Incorporate Information Literacy Into the Classroom

In this section we highlight key steps and examples of how faculty and librarians can integrate concepts of information literacy. First, we explore integration on a larger scale by bringing information literacy into a program or set of courses and partnering with librarians. Second, we provide examples of exercises, activities, and assignments that librarians and faculty use to advance an information literacy curriculum. Third, we describe tools we have used to assess the impact of our teaching of information literacy competencies.

Pair Librarians With Courses

Collaboration between faculty and librarians is integral to a successful integration of information literacy and evidence-based research (Boruff & Thomas, 2011). Keep in mind that integrating information literacy can be at the scale of an individual course or at the programmatic level (Bakermans & Ziino Plotke, 2018; Callison, Budny, & Thomes, 2005), but each scenario represents a partnership where the librarian and the faculty recognize their respective roles as educators working toward shared learning outcomes of the course. When designing a course, collaborate with a librarian at your institution that has a background or specialty in the content matter of your course. However, if your library does not have a subject-specific librarian available, as a faculty member you can work with a generalist instruction librarian. Librarians are aware of their limitations of not being subject experts and welcome learning about the nuances of your discipline and research process. A librarian's familiarity with the content allows for greater effectiveness in designing course assignments and in-class instruction when connecting subject content to information literacy skills.

Faculty depend on and appreciate instruction of information literacy to help students develop research skills, find scholarly articles, reduce the reliance on online search engines, evaluate resources, and foster overall success in college (Hrycaj & Russo, 2007; Manuel, Beck, & Molloy, 2005). To foster respect for the role of the librarian, faculty should introduce the librarian to students as a member of the team at the start of the semester. Remember when designing instruction for the classroom that faculty and students appreciate hands-on active learning strategies and having information literacy instruction tailored to their course content (Manuel et al., 2005; Vander Meer et al., 2012).

Moving Beyond One-Shot Sessions Run by Librarians

Information literacy can be delivered by librarians using a number of different methods. The most commonly used practices include online modules or guides, in-library sessions, in-classroom instruction, or out-of-class consultations. We encourage faculty to employ multiple options to increase student exposure and practice of these skills, as studies have documented that learning gains can occur regardless of the format (Koufogiannakis & Wiebe, 2006). Faculty and librarians should provide multiple occasions (i.e., visits) and opportunities (e.g., activities or assignments) to develop deeper information literacy competencies in students. We recommend that instruction begin with foundational information literacy skills (e.g., identify library resources and how to use them) that all students can use in the research process. As the semester progresses, instruction should provide more catered information (e.g., search strategies, discipline-specific databases) to aid students in their research paper or project.

A detailed list of learning objectives focused on building foundational skills and abilities broken down in the semester is found in Appendix 7.1. Here we provide a quick list of foundational information literacy skills and abilities to target in first-year courses:

1. Identify and locate resources (e.g., electronic, print, tech suite, consultation with librarian)
2. Brainstorm and choose appropriate keywords
3. Navigate searches in online catalogs, databases, and search engines
4. Acquire access to resources through databases or search engines
5. Distinguish between source variety (e.g., journal, magazine, newspaper)
6. Evaluate source relevance based on characteristics such as bias, timeliness, and motivation
7. Interpret source quality by examining connections between source characteristics and the features of a scholarly resource
8. Demonstrate correct formatting of citations (e.g., American Psychological Association [APA], Modern Language Association [MLA], *The Chicago Manual of Style*, etc.)
9. Use information ethically (e.g., citation use in text and in reference list)

Instruction in the Classroom

To assist students in building their information literacy knowledge practices, we bring an R&I librarian into the classroom throughout the semester. The overall goal is to build information literacy skills and abilities that the students will be developing throughout the semester.

Sample first visit. The first in-class visit typically occurs during the second week of the semester. This introductory class lays the foundation by providing an overview of the skills and a path for building those skills throughout the term through different learning activities.

Sample lesson plan. The class begins with an active learning activity and discussion that teaches students how to define different types of authority and bias so that they can develop the ability to appraise varied and credible sources appropriately. The source activity is flexible and can be tailored to the content of the class. The class is asked for four or five volunteers, while being assured that it will be a group activity (i.e., no one is on the spot), and each student is handed a sheet of paper with a source on it. Students present the different sources by reading aloud the key information on their paper, which is also displayed on the screen. Together we break down the various components of each source, such as the title, the author, the DOI (if one exists), the summary, the publisher, the edition, and any other particular elements that tie into explaining the complexity of a source. Through a librarian-led class discussion, we compare and contrast elements and discuss strengths and challenges of each source type. For example, for general background information, we encourage students to avoid an Internet search and look first in a text as their source material.

Crucial to this introduction is learning about the complexity of the research process—where research is a process, an exploration of a conversation, and an inquiry—and that it is okay and necessary to have questions that may have more than one answer. In addition, students learn there are disciplinary experts also excited about their topic, and there are skills and strategies to judge which views to incorporate. Teaching to the complexity of the research process is repeated and refined throughout the rest of the semester.

Sample second visit. For this class visit, which can be incorporated into the first visit (depending on the length of class), librarians teach students to use library research tools and reliable web resources and how to decide where and how their information is published. The goal is to help students begin to develop their ability to discover varied and credible sources and provide appropriate attribution as an ethical user of information. One student reflected on the instruction by writing, "I was also able to refine my researching skills and now I know how to efficiently look for sources instead of just looking up a general term and combing through pages of results and coming up with nothing."

Sample lesson plan. This lesson begins with a brief librarian-led class discussion on access to information. Together the group discusses the cost of information, the price the library pays for access to a database. In this discussion we ask students to think about a topic or health concern that might affect them directly and then imagine if they could not afford the access to information to learn about that issue. This creates a motivation for students to take advantage of the library resources available to them. It makes the process more personal and builds a space for informed learning to occur (Maybee, Bruce, Lupton, & Renmann, 2013). The lesson continues with the librarian demonstrating and modeling for the students how to access and use the library resources to find a variety of sources (e.g., books, journal articles, or newspapers) using effective search strategies and filters. During this exploration of finding sources, the librarian also covers the importance of recognizing the components of each source that are necessary for building a proper citation. Students learn the reasons behind formatting citations properly, specifically that citations give readers the information necessary to find that source again and learn more about the cited topic. Ultimately, citing sources actually helps readers distinguish students' ideas from those of their sources. Students reflect on the information presented and complete a worksheet in class (see Appendix 7.2).

Sample third visit. The third in-class visit usually takes place during the second half of the course. For this class the librarian prepares by reviewing assignments (project report drafts, research notebook entries, or problem statements and solution proposals) submitted by students to gain insight into the various team projects. The goal of this visit is to reinforce the skills learned in the previous classes and to help students recognize that their evidence-based research project is entering them into the ongoing scholarly conversation. This is all part of engaging in lifelong learning. For example, after a semester of information literacy instruction, a student reflected, "I learned that I can research things with efficiency but needed to improve on the reliability of the sources."

Sample third lesson plan. Because this lesson is tailored to the most discipline-specific research needs of projects, it is broken into two parts. The first part is a librarian-led discussion of general trends that the student reports exhibited and require follow-up; for example, integrating new information with current understanding of the project and demonstrating how to integrate citations both in formatting and as evidence for claims. The second part is structured around group consultations tailored to the needs of each project group. The librarian spends about 20 minutes with each group going over its report drafts and discussing strategies for next steps. This may include indicating which specific databases to use, searching for terms and phrases, clarifying citations, and answering any specific questions the group may have. These skills and developing abilities are reinforced through discussions and assignments, as students are repeatedly required to support their claims with information from scholarly sources.

Assignments

We start building information literacy skills as soon as possible in first-year students. In the first week of the semester, we introduce an assignment that combines finding credible and varied sources with assessing their relevance for a larger group topic. Students must work through this process individually by writing an annotated bibliography on at least three sources (see Appendix 7.3 for a sample assignment). Students then come together in groups to share their new knowledge and complete a series of questions that relates to their topic. This particular model is used in a number of first-year courses and is simply tailored to students' particular topic. For example, in a course on environmental impacts, student groups conduct research on a city, the land changes occurring at that location, and how these changes affect the people and environment of that region. Instructors provide the specific location for each group (e.g., Aral Sea, New Orleans, Las Vegas, etc.) and a list of research questions students must answer. In a course focused on energy, students investigate an assortment of energy sources and examine production, extraction, use, and economic, social, and environmental advantages and disadvantages.

We emphasize the importance of information literacy by repeating similar information-seeking skills and evaluation of sources in assignments throughout the semester. In fact, in the first half of the semester, students are given five or six assignments that specifically require them to find, use, and synthesize information from appropriate sources. For example, after team presentations on multiple topics, as with the previous assignment example, students choose one of the presentations (not their own) to summarize its main points and conduct further research. Students need to find three additional scholarly sources that supplement the information presented and explain why these new sources are important and how they contribute to the narrative of that topic. Along the way, it is critical for faculty and librarians to provide verbal and written feedback to students on source relevance, quality, and use.

Librarians engage in the process of providing feedback, formally and informally. Formally, some librarians may grade a homework assignment or review a citation list contributing to the grade. For example, in one class the students were required to provide the librarian with a formatted reference list as part of the homework. The librarian then graded the assignment and provided feedback through a follow-up in-class instruction session. Informally, librarians often attend practice poster sessions at the end of the semester to provide feedback and guidance before the final posters are printed and graded.

Faculty-Led Information Literacy Instruction

Development and instruction of information literacy competencies should not be the sole responsibility of the librarian. Faculty can take on some of this responsibility beyond collaborating and coordinating assignments and visits from the librarian. In this section, we provide sample activities of how to build on the efforts of librarians in the classroom. The first activity focuses on aiding students in evaluating the trustworthiness of a source; the second facilitates students' ability in synthesizing information from multiple sources. See the section "Teaching the Zika Virus and How to Find, Cite, and Evaluate Credible Research Sources" (p. 200, this volume) for an additional example.

Sample Activity 1. Faculty can expand on points that librarians discuss in the classroom, thereby reinforcing concepts for students. A nice example of this would be a class exercise on evaluating the trustworthiness of a source. On the basis of an activity developed by Withgott and Laposta (2015), we guide students in an exercise where they research an online source and assess its trustworthiness by evaluating the authority, motivation, and reliability of the source. The exercise breaks down each component and asks questions that prompt the students to investigate (a) the credentials and knowledge of the author (or organization), (b) what the source is trying to accomplish, and (c) if the information is based on scientifically collected data. Students are then given a scale for each component to assign a numerical score to the source and determine if the source is not trustworthy at all, somewhat trustworthy, or very trustworthy. This type of scoring system provides a tool for students to use in future research. Although this exercise is called "Evaluation of Science in the Media," it can be transferred across disciplines and types of sources (e.g., journal articles, texts, etc.). This activity should occur early in the semester and can supplement the annotated bibliography assignment (see the previous Assignments section). We find that at times students really struggle with interpreting online information and want the tools to help them distinguish whether they should or shouldn't use it as a source of information.

Sample Activity 2. In our programmatic learning outcome around research and information literacy, students learn to find and use sources appropriately. Part of this step in the research process—one that is difficult for first-year students—is synthesis of information from multiple sources. A simple exercise to illustrate synthesizing information with a class is to compare two sets of writing: a summary and a synthesis. Allow students time to read each and then, as a class, work through how the two examples differ in structure, form, and intention. By initially removing the act of synthesis and focusing on the necessary components of a synthesis, you can lessen the cognitive load on handling both tasks at the same time.

Sample Activity 3. Students can have trouble synthesizing information because they come in with novice-level knowledge and organization, with few connections between concepts (Ambrose et al., 2010). To aid students in developing this skill, we employ an exercise in class where students use multiple readings to fill out and cite key concepts of a topic on a concept map. By providing students with the skeleton concept map, we effectively reduce the cognitive load of how to organize the information so that students can focus on performing the task of integrating the information together in a novel way.

This exercise typically takes place midsemester and requires students to read sources before they come to class that day. We start class by taking time (typically 10 minutes) to review and discuss key concepts, terms, research questions, and intended audiences of each article and address any questions or clarifying points with the class. Next, we provide a skeleton concept map for students on the overall topic (in this case, biodiversity; see Figure 7.1) to fill in. We tell students that to understand the big picture of biodiversity, they need to consider some key components: how it is defined, what threatens it, and what strategies can be used to conserve biodiversity. Then we instruct students, who work in small teams, to go directly to the readings and find specific details (i.e., the context in which the information is presented) and write down where they got the information (i.e., article, page, and paragraph).

Next, because students have not completed a similar exercise in class before, we model expectations for them. On a blank concept map and under the document camera, we write an example and explain why we are including that particular information. Students are instructed that upon completion of the maps, they will report to the entire class for a discussion of these topics.

Students work in groups of three to five and are given 20 to 25 minutes if filling out the entire concept map or 10 to 15 minutes if the divisions are split among the groups. During this time, we walk around the classroom and answer questions and further help in clarification of any information in the readings. Once they have completed the diagrams, we open a discussion

Figure 7.1. Skeleton concept map that students fill out to aid in the synthesis of information from multiple sources.

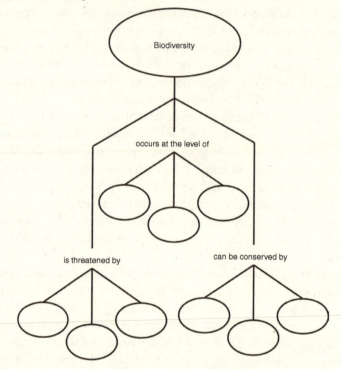

starting with the topic that defines biodiversity and record the information students share on the board. Before switching to the next topic on the concept map, we augment the discussion with lecture information (via PowerPoint slides) on the topic. If time allows at the end of the exercise, we ask students to come up to the board and make explicit connections and cross links by drawing arrows between boxes and describing relationships among information already compiled on the topics (e.g., what strategy to conserve biodiversity relates to a threat). We then add new boxes to the diagram to dig deeper into topics (e.g., consequences of a threat-like climate change).

Throughout, and at the end of class, we ask for reflection on the activity. First, we discuss building in opportunities to practice synthesizing and integrating information in new ways and the implications of the different ways in which novices and experts organize knowledge. Second, we discuss that when we use methods to connect information in meaningful ways, that information becomes more practical and accessible, allowing us to apply it in novel contexts to solve problems (Ambrose et al., 2010).

We find this activity to be effective in engaging students in the material while building the skill of integrating and using information appropriately.

Most recently this activity was used on a day when a colleague was conducting a peer evaluation of teaching. General feedback was that a lot of material was covered while keeping the students engaged and building on their research skills. Interestingly, 18 of 24 students either asked questions or supplied comments during the class period, and this activity reached a number of students who did not regularly participate in class discussions.

Supplemental Instruction

As part of a fully integrated curriculum, students receive instruction beyond the scheduled classroom time. For example, librarians offer office hours, in which students can schedule an appointment and meet as individuals or as a team. In these appointments or consultations, the librarian can cover a variety of skills around information-seeking behavior techniques. Some students meet at the beginning of their project to discuss their topic ideas and learn how to develop keywords and search strategies based on the information they have already found and how to move forward. Other groups meet later in the development of their project and discuss how to cite information correctly or how to understand the difference between citing information and providing evidence for their claims. The librarian and students discuss how different types of sources provide different types of evidence; for example, how a local newspaper may provide insight into the community's concerns on a topic, whereas a scholarly article will provide a more in-depth look at an area of research, providing the students with previous literature, methods, and potential solutions. As one student said, "Meeting with Rebecca Ziino [a librarian] allowed me to utilize the resources that the library provides."

Assessment of Instruction

When implementing information literacy instruction in your courses, do not forget to include assessment components. A wide variety of assessment tools, like surveys, interviews, writing portfolios, concept maps, tests, and rubrics, can be used depending on the situation. See Oakleaf (2009) for a set of guiding questions to help find the best assessment tool for your scenario. Regardless, it may be best to start with an assessment of information literacy skills and abilities of incoming students to develop a baseline of information to inform development of curriculum (Anderson & May, 2010; Oakleaf & Kaske, 2009). Next, include assessments related to instructional practices to gauge student learning gains. Use a mix of formative and summative assessments for continuous feedback and final evaluations. Don't forget that written and oral feedback during the semester can come from both faculty and librarians. Typically, pre- and post-survey methodology is used to measure student learning gains over time (Anderson & May, 2010; Burkhardt, 2007; Greer, Hess, & Kraemer, 2016; Jacobson & Mark, 2000). However, another methodology to employ includes scoring student products with preset rubric categories (Knight, 2002; Oakleaf, 2009). Last, require students to reflect on key learning obtained through information literacy practices to facilitate their ability to identify and adjust their strategies to improve performance (Ambrose et al., 2010). Assessments are a valuable tool for evaluating the effectiveness of instruction and activities so that you can strengthen instruction directed at course, library, or programmatic learning outcomes.

Conclusion

Information literacy competencies are critical to foster throughout a student's college career. First-year students who have exposure to and instruction on using university resources and developing information literacy skills and abilities will be better suited to transfer those skills to other courses. One way to reach students beyond these first-year courses and continue building and strengthening their skills and abilities is to provide resources for R&I librarians and invite them to your classrooms, regardless of the discipline or level. Our R&I librarians provide lecture-based material related to projects or assignments in courses and will create a course guide that focuses on the content outcomes of the course; for example, exploring and understanding primary literature in the sciences. In fact, a student who did not take an information-literacy-imbedded first-year course but had library instruction in a later course wrote,

> I also have never used the WPI research library; I figured one existed but I have never had use for it. It was nice to learn what the true difference is between a reliable and unreliable source; that a landing page is not the page you want to be quoting off of; what the difference between sources is—academic journals, online books, government pages, etc. This is a skill I can truly utilize in my time here at WPI.

Try This

Take some simple steps to promote lifelong learning and academic success of your students and build their information literacy skills. When designing a course, use the checklist provided in Figure 7.2 to integrate information literacy. Read through the checklist and work to include all components in your course design.

Figure 7.2 Checklist to integrate information literacy.

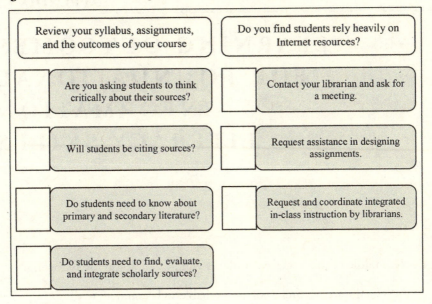

LEARNING OUTCOMES FOR FOUNDATIONAL INFORMATION LITERACY SKILLS

By the middle of the semester, students will be able to do the following:

- Use library research tools and reliable web resources to discover varied and credible sources
- Define different types of authority, such as subject expertise (e.g., scholarship), societal position (e.g., public office or title), and special experience (e.g., participating in a historic event), to appraise varied and credible sources appropriately
- Decide where and how their information is published to provide appropriate attribution as an ethical user of information

Midsemester foundational information literacy skills:

- Define different types of authority
- Use library and web research tools
- Decide where and how their information is published

Midsemester foundational information literacy abilities:

- Appraise varied and credible sources appropriately
- Discover varied and credible sources
- Provide appropriate attribution as an ethical user of information

By the end of the semester, students will be able to do the following:

- Choose appropriate background and specialized sources to provide an in-depth and evidence-based research project

- Use various research methods, based on need, circumstance, and type of inquiry, to access primary and secondary sources of information
- Recognize that information may be perceived differently based on the format in which it is packaged to determine reliability, accuracy, validity, authority, timeliness, bias, and appropriateness of the information found
- Integrate new information with current understanding to be contributors to the information marketplace rather than only consumers of it
- Demonstrate how to use appropriate attribution (in text, references, formatted) to be an ethical user of information
- Recognize they are entering into an ongoing scholarly conversation to engage in lifelong learning, not a finished conversation

End-of-semester foundational information literacy skills:

- Choose appropriate background and specialized sources
- Use various research methods, based on need, circumstance, and type of inquiry
- Recognize that information may be perceived differently based on the format
- Integrate new information with current understanding
- Demonstrate how to use appropriate attribution
- Recognize they are entering into an ongoing scholarly conversation

End-of-semester foundational information literacy abilities:

- Provide an in-depth and evidence-based research project
- Access primary and secondary sources of information
- Determine reliability, accuracy, validity, authority, timeliness, bias, and appropriateness of the information found
- Be contributors to the information marketplace rather than only consumers of it
- Be an ethical user of information
- Engage in lifelong learning

SAMPLE FINDING SOURCES ASSIGNMENT

Getting Started and Understanding Research

Name:

Librarian Contact:

Instructions

Take notes and complete the worksheet as instructed during today's class.

Definitions

- *Varied sources:* Information is created and shared in many different formats. Strong research considers perspectives from many different types of authorities and incorporates different sources when appropriate. Examples of source types include books (e-books), journal articles, newspapers and magazines, government reports, and statistical information.
- *Credible sources:* These are sources the reader can trust. The author's ideas and assertions are backed by evidence and cited properly. The source is written by authors in their field of study.

The Research Process

Define different types of sources and use library research tools to discover those sources.

Searching Summon

Follow along as we navigate to the library website and search for sources using the library research tool Summon.

- *Book*
  - *Search strategy:* Write down what keywords were used.
  - *Citation pieces:* Write down the elements of the source that you will need later to create a proper citation.
  - *Summarize and evaluate:* Take notes about the source: What can I learn from the table of contents, author, introduction, preface, and references? In what way is the information related to the topic? What is the bias and motivation of the source? What did you learn that was new and surprising or contradicted your previous thoughts or knowledge? What new questions were raised?

SAMPLE ANNOTATED BIBLIOGRAPHY ASSIGNMENT

Annotated Bibliography

It is expected that you use scholarly sources of information to research your topic, and you must cite your sources. You will need to find and annotate at least *three legitimate* sources PER PERSON in your group. You must use APA citation format, and you must BE CONSISTENT when citing sources. The research librarian will come to class and provide assistance, but you are STRONGLY ENCOURAGED to meet with or contact him or her for this and future assignments.

Legitimate sources include the following:

- Scholarly journal articles
- Books
- Government, university, and professional association websites
- Popular press such as newspapers and magazines

Guidelines for Annotated Bibliography

- *Proper article citation:* At the top of each entry, you should cite the article according to proper APA style.
- *Annotation:* The annotation should be given in paragraph form and should do three things. First, it should *summarize* the main point or argument that the source offers (and briefly discuss the support offered for it). Second, it should *assess or evaluate* the source: How useful and important do you think the source is? Is it biased? How strong is the evidence presented for the main point? Does it seem objective or biased? Third, you should say something about how this source does or would *fit* into a research project on the topic you have chosen: In what way is it helpful? Does it lend support to your own view of the topic? Does it challenge or change your view? How and why?

Visit http://owl.english.purdue.edu/owl/resource/614/01/ for further instructions and information on writing annotated bibliographies (including examples).

8

SPONSORED PROJECTS

Learning With a Sense of Urgency and Agency

Svetlana Nikitina and Diran Apelian

Why We Do Sponsored Projects

David Siegel's (2012) article "Beyond the Academic-Corporate Divide" starts with a direct invective often hurled at sponsored work within university walls: "Academics often view intercourse with business as a dirty, unchaste affair" (p. 29). He vehemently argued with such a position. And so do we. Our experience in courses that involve work commissioned by real organizations or institutions has shown that direct engagement with the outside organizations could be not only educationally and ethically sound but also exceptionally rich in opportunities to communicate across disciplinary, professional, and cultural divides; to learn with a sense of urgency and agency; and to grow both personally and professionally.

Sponsored research is commonly referred to as work that is externally funded and guided by contract. The contract specifies the time period, the methodology, and other aspects of the work to be accomplished. Such work could legitimately raise questions about commercial control and the university's fundamental mission as an intellectually independent body (Bok, 2003; Krimsky, 2003; Washburn, 2006). This is not the kind of work we do with our first-year students in our "sponsored projects." Our projects are sponsored not in the sense of entering into a contractual relationship with an external agency but in the sense that a viable research topic has been proposed to meet a real need of the proposing (or sponsoring) institution, as well as the educational objective of our course. Our "sponsored projects" differ drastically from what university "sponsored research" departments typically contend with. "Sponsored projects" for us do *not* involve pay for service, contractual relationships, or any legal or financial obligations to sponsors.

They do, however, entail a research assignment that originates from outside but makes topical sense to explore within the frameworks of the course we teach. Our projects are sponsored in the sense that we do have a real customer, or a real end user of our research efforts, and a physical entity that will benefit from our work and will value our contributions. *Sponsorship* in our case implies grounding students' work in the reality of meeting the research or societal needs that palpably exist and demand attention. What we do in our courses is to ensure that the students are exploring a real-world problem in the context of ongoing efforts to resolve it, and their efforts have a tangible impact outside of academia.

While these assignments by nonprofit organizations, college labs, or companies provide an area for investigation by a team of first-year students, these organizations do not control the process. Suggested topics remain fairly open-ended and not subject to strict regulation by such a sponsor in terms of research outcomes or methods. Student teams consult, negotiate, and communicate with the project sponsor and try to address the sponsor's stated need, but the sponsor also allows significant freedom for students to come to their own conclusions in their own way. Our sponsor also operates within the time frame and parameters of the college course and understands the paradigm of PBL endorsed by WPI. The students provide their time and access to institutional research banks, while the sponsors contribute their time, guidance, and access to contacts and data that could help advance the research agenda. We thus define *sponsored projects* as addressing real organizational needs (as opposed to abstract academic assignments) while fully meeting educational research goals and deeply enriching the PBL overall. Performing sponsored research, our students help jump-start a new line of inquiry, contribute to dissertation-related research, perform feasibility studies, or engage in proof-of-concept work. Nonprofits, NGOs, and research labs have been our prime targets for sponsorship of our student projects (see Appendix 8.1). Among the sponsors who have commissioned student projects to our program are Fundación Paraguaya, Seven Hills, Museum of Russian Icons, Metal Processing Institute, the Center for Resource Recovery and Recycling (CR^3), Battery Resourcers, and Tatnuck Brook Watershed Association. Almost all of them had prior contact with WPI faculty and knowledge of our project-based approach.

It is important to stipulate from the outset that the inclusion of sponsors into the teaching process, while significantly enhancing PBL, is an optional step for instructors in our program. Not all faculty choose to include sponsored projects, and those who do are free to scale sponsored work however they like. Some may have just a single team of students pursuing work commissioned by sponsors. Others elect to have all class teams work with sponsors. We have gradually moved to a full-sponsored mode. Initially, none of our projects were sponsored; we allowed students to propose ideas that were significant to them (wind turbines on Cape Cod, road construction in Sierra Leone, etc.). Gradually, we added a few sponsored projects into our roster of projects. Then, a few more. We currently have all teams working on sponsored projects.

There is no question that sponsored projects require extra effort and time to enlist outside sponsors, help them formulate the research question, establish the pattern of student–sponsor interactions, and reach successful outcomes for all involved. Faculty have to offer additional support to sponsors at every turn—from project solicitation to the final handoff of the results. Students need to learn to communicate across corporate, cultural, and disciplinary differences and to bridge academic and industry agendas. The sponsors, likewise, have a lot to juggle. They have to commit extra time and resources to coordinate work with the advisers and students to get valuable results. Here, we present all these challenges and offer some strategies for addressing them.

So, given the extra effort and responsibility involved, why do we do it? We have come to see the rich educational opportunities in working with students on real and authentic problems with real people and organizations. The engagement of a sponsor provides gains in (a) motivating students, (b) offering them a communication-intensive experience, (c) cultivating contextual and cultural sensitivity in solving problems, and (d) fostering personal growth.

Highly Motivated Learning

The overarching mission of any educational initiative is to create a highly motivating learning platform. While working on a palpable societal problem is a huge motivation in itself, sponsored work supercharges it by giving it a human face. World hunger, for example, is a gripping problem, but when you are working on it for a nonprofit that will actually help feed people in a particular community, you will experience the urgency of coming up with a technology, developing a business plan, and collecting data on the legal or economic factors to become an agent of change.

Students in sponsored projects are motivated to jump right into the issue and learn on their feet. Literature suggests that "often, a motivated novice will perform at least as well as a bored expert" (Wolfe, 2010, p. 42), and our experience with sponsored projects supports that. Some of our first-year projects produced patentable work, won poster competitions, got funded for further implementation, and suggested new avenues for fundamental research.

What made these achievements possible was not our students' precocious brilliance but the motivation they got from working with people who look big societal problems in the eye. The opportunity to work on an authentic problem with the realization of the impact they could make as a result of their work is a motivating force that cannot be underestimated. The latter is a source of inspiration and empowerment that goes beyond student engagement.

When working with sponsors, students can get an immediate sense of whether their work is measuring up. Multiple feedback loops (sponsor–adviser–end user) create constructive impetus and opportunities to adjust the intervention to the needs of the community and its circumstances. Learning and tweaking continue all the way through testing and implementation, as students' skills and knowledge get more nuanced and informed by trial and error. Reports on Work Integrated Learning (WIL) experiences by Fleischmann (2015) or Contextual Teaching and Learning (CTL) experiences by Predmore (2005) show a similar surge in motivation and achievement in sponsored situations. Creative arts students placed in projects with industry professionals, for example, "were able to develop problem-solving skills, work with a team, sharpen analytical skills, develop stronger ability to plan and organize, and feel confident about tackling new problems," as reported in a recent study done in Australia (Fleischmann, 2015, p. 28). Overall, students enrolled in sponsored programs are "more motivated, have higher retention of information, and are overall more successful when teachers employ CTL strategies" (Predmore, 2005, p. 22). One reason for higher quality and motivation in learning is that students in sponsored projects receive much more feedback, which gives them a palpable sense of how their work is measuring up. Learning on their feet, the students continue to tweak and improve the results to experience the satisfaction of helping others and doing work that "means something to somebody."

When learning is stimulated by a palpable cause, education becomes a matter of civic responsibility and a deep personal commitment. The urgency of the problem and a tangible need for solutions elevate learning to social service that fosters a kind of motivation that is hard to achieve in a purely academic context.

Communication-Rich Education

Students in sponsored projects interact not only with their team members and advisers but also with the world outside the university walls. They have to learn the language of the corporate or nonprofit cultures and speak it well to be able to gather data, interview stakeholders, and deliver solutions in the format that a company or lab will be able to use. Communication in this context goes beyond the academic requirements of a project proposal, report, and poster. In addition to gleaning information from traditional research sources—books, articles, database searches—students in sponsored projects learn a lot from direct interaction with sponsors and end users. They also need to "pitch" the solution back to them in just the right way. Extra layers of communication are added through Skype sessions, phone interviews, live interactions, and development work in labs and workshops. This communications workout is also a leadership workout in which we see our students evolve into change agents and community organizers at the implementation stages of their projects.

Context-Conscious Education

Helping solve a real problem for a real organization means addressing differences in language, historical context, corporate culture, and the environment. It may also involve understanding legal, economic, and philosophical frameworks to the extent that they are relevant to implementing a solution. Some of our sponsoring organizations have the capacity to connect our students with communities all over the world, as well as those nearby.

Working for a sponsor, students learn to tune in to cultures and places much more than in purely academic contexts. From the start, their engineering skills develop with sensitivity to end-users. They get to see that the best design is not the one that fits all (McDonough & Braungart, 2009) but the one that fits the specific population in a particular circumstance. Sponsored research teaches the art of quick adaptation to changing conditions and resource limitations. Students realize that desk research takes them only so far and that real life holds many unanticipated surprises. Students learn quickly that "problem definition" requires validation and in-depth discussion with those who are the end users, or the project sponsors. This is quite a contrast to the situation when the problem definition is given in isolation, with no connection to the end users, or the "customers." Contextual learning, highly prized in professional work, relies on taking into account all the objective and subjective factors, technical as well as cultural, and trains students to tailor their approach to these critical factors.

Personal Growth

Work on projects sponsored by various organizations allows first-year students to see themselves as more than novice researchers. The self-empowerment and confidence they gain through direct involvement is a strong engine that causes them to reflect on who they are as people and professionals. When students work on issues that have a face they are better able to connect to communities and to themselves.

Through interacting with sponsoring organizations, the students get to reflect almost immediately on what their major in college or their profession in real life might be. Early identification of one's major or passion through dealing with people who have dedicated themselves to others helps our students mature and claim leadership positions in college and beyond. Contextual sensitivity and attention to cultural differences that sponsored work develops in students translate into a respectful regard for differences in ideologies, cultures, and economic standing.

How We Make Sponsored Projects Happen

Our work with sponsors goes through an evolution from engagement and cultivation of contacts to project identification to presentation of the implementation-ready results and recommendations. Each stage of the process presents learning opportunities and challenges. To illustrate them, we use one team's project experience presented through a series of vignettes and student testimonies. The project was sponsored by a Paraguay-based NGO and focused on ways to generate an income stream from the refuse collected by waste pickers on the streets of Asunción (see Appendix 8.2). It was performed by a team of four students enrolled in our course on resource recovery and recycling. The project provided a host of challenges, including long-distance interactions with an international sponsor (based in Paraguay), a different language and culture to contend with, and the changing definition of the problem and of resources available to students that illustrate all stages of the effort involved in working with a project sponsor. Despite all these challenges, the students were able to come up with solutions that gave them a sense of agency and personal accomplishment and gave the sponsor a strategy for going forward in helping the disenfranchised population.

Stage 1: Sponsor Engagement: What to Look for in a Sponsor

Vignette
The student team is agitated during our first advising meeting, bursting with questions:

> How do we set up Skype meetings with the sponsor? Who will contact him? Is he in Paraguay now, not in Africa or Europe?
>
> My Spanish is not that good!
>
> I have worked in a soup kitchen and know something about feeding the poor, but Paraguay . . . that will be interesting. How will we get information from there?

> My father works in recycling in Mexico. Maybe it is similar, maybe different.
>
> Who do we contact? What do we ask?
>
> We need to find out what the local people need, and we have to get in touch with the sponsor.

Cultivating a sponsor network takes time and care. Not every organization or individual will be a good fit for participation in our sponsored projects. Our criteria for selecting sponsors include the following:

- Openness to support academic process: awareness of timelines, familiarity with course content and requirements
- Interest in fostering and building on students' emerging skills and abilities
- Ability to inspire with one's passion for making a social impact
- Balancing inspired leadership of the project with attention to missing data, technical aspects, and desire to guide students through the ups and downs of data collection
- Ability to give the project regular time on a weekly basis to give students feedback on their progress and help them stay focused on the primary targets
- Access and willingness to share critical data and contacts for analysis. The individual sponsor needs to be empowered by his or her organization to share information and to direct the course of investigation
- Humility to give students space to draw their own conclusions and offer recommendations based on their own data analysis

Such collaborations start with an existing personal rapport between the sponsor and instructor(s) and the sponsor's familiarity with academia. The sponsor needs to understand and be able to work with the constraints of time and ability imposed by engagement of college freshmen. The sponsor, Martin Burt in this case, needs to make time to work with students on a regular (weekly) basis. Students rely on him not only for inspiration and basic guidance but also for crucial data and interview contacts. The sponsor should be in a position to exercise authority and initiative to obtain information, provide access, and share important contacts. NGOs and nonprofits typically have contact people or managers who could facilitate students' work because they often rely on outside help and are experienced in coordinating such efforts. Another typical type of sponsor for us has been the Center for

Resource Recovery and Recycling (CR³), a multiuniversity research unit headquartered at WPI and focused on "sustainable stewardship of the earth's resources" by advancing "technologies that recover, recycle, and reuse materials throughout the manufacturing process" (see the CR³ website at http://wp.wpi.edu/cr3/).

Students have worked with CR³ graduate students and faculty members with industry and academic experiences who act as project sponsors and coadvisers. The graduate students get advising experience, and they inspire undergraduate students to pursue the line of research they are passionate about. Seasoned faculty give first-year students opportunities to experience the practice of engineering for the first time and potentially influence the students' search for an academic concentration.

Potential sponsors often appear as guest speakers during the formative lecture period, and such appearances often end with suggestions of topics for future research. Sponsors typically pitch their project ideas after the lecture in private follow-up correspondence or conversations with faculty members who help define and refine project descriptions. Faculty not only explain the parameters of student engagement to sponsors but also offer to stand by and support them in any administrative or work-related matter.

Relationships with sponsors continue to be cultivated after the project has been completed and the semester finished. Maintaining sponsor relationships ensures an ongoing multiyear project and an experienced collaborator. Sponsors often develop a relationship with the campus and feel integrated into its life through attending presentations, poster sessions, and other events; they feel involved enough to come back with project proposals year after year.

Here are our suggestions for cultivating a network of sponsors:

- Develop the network gradually: Start with academic-based projects, then add a few commissioned topics each time to gauge your time investment and student response. This will give you and the sponsor time to adjust expectations and to learn how to support the students better before you scale up.
- Keep an eye on the emerging relationship between the students and the sponsor: Attend Skype meetings, go on field trips, and model to the students the navigation of corporate culture and the proper relationship with the sponsor and sponsoring organization.
- Stay in touch and share your thoughts with the sponsor. Offer guidance in terms of academic requirements and make the sponsor aware that you are involved and ready to support him or her in getting the best results.

- Do not overmanage the relationship between the sponsor and the students—they both need to own it! Give sponsors general guidance, but leave them to inspire and direct the students in data collection on their terms.
- Recognize the sponsor's own pressures (time, resources) and privacy concerns. Make sure students will respect and accommodate them.
- Offer help in brainstorming project ideas and paring them down to a manageable project scope. Set the sponsor up with realistic expectations in terms of both time and student ability.
- Be sure to invite the sponsors to final presentations and poster sessions and acknowledge their support. Student work (presentation slides, poster, report, actual product) should be shared with the sponsor in its entirety. The format and the language of deliverables has to be discussed with the sponsor ahead of time to make sure there is a fit with the sponsor's needs and digital interface.

Challenges at this stage of working with sponsors:

- Securing sponsor's commitment (not just enthusiasm)
- Facilitating student access to sponsor and data
- Developing trust and working relationship
- Cultivating a perception of value to be developed through joint effort
- Maintaining focus on social impact while developing technical solutions

Stage 2: Project Definition and Launch: How to Facilitate Faculty–Sponsor Communications

Vignette

A student team is trying to find a new focus for the project after critical input from the sponsor:

> Did you know that our topic has changed . . . our project has changed? That building, where our waste sorting was going to happen, is no longer available . . .
>
> No, it's available, but it's not as large as we thought.
>
> It's a different building—isn't that what our sponsor said? It's a smaller building, and it means that our waste pickers can no longer collect the large bulky electronics or large bulky anything. Our project is different now. We need to rethink what they will collect.

What is the productive pattern of engagement with sponsors? Here are a few guidelines for faculty:

- Faculty members need to scale up the engagement of the sponsor gradually. Just one or two projects to begin with will give the sponsor a chance to evaluate the time commitment and learn to support the students better.
- Active engagement of the faculty with sponsors is key: Faculty advisers need to attend Skype meetings, go on field trips, and maintain regular contact with the sponsors who need guidance through the academic process.
- Overmanagement of the sponsor during the project could be demotivating and counterproductive. Building a partnership (rather than a supervisory relationship) with sponsors is essential; they need to feel part of the teaching or coaching team entrusted to guide and inspire the students.
- A sponsor's own pressures (time, resources) and privacy concerns need to be recognized and respected.
- Faculty advisers need to stand by when sponsors need help or cannot make the commitment.
- Sponsors typically need faculty assistance in paring the topic down to something manageable in seven weeks by a small team of first-year students.
- Sponsors should be included in campus life to the extent that they are able to participate. Invitations to final presentations, poster sessions, and acknowledgment of their support throughout the project will carry the relationship forward.

After the relationship with sponsors and stakeholders is established and it's time to start the projects, we typically post a roster of projects from which students can choose. In the case of sponsored projects, the list includes names of companies and contacts in addition to project descriptions (see Appendix 8.1). This roster is the result of many conversations between the sponsor and faculty aimed at distilling the general idea to something doable within a seven-week period by a team of four to six first-year students. The topic first suggested by the sponsor is often too broad to manage: "How can recycling benefit the poor in Paraguay?" This question needs to undergo several brainstorming sessions before it boils down to a practical "How can the women involved in waste picking in Paraguay be organized for the sorting and disassembly of small electronics so that they could generate income?" Finding focus within a topic area is not easy, as student Angela MacLeod recalled: "There are so many directions our project could have gone at first, but after some additional research and communication with our sponsor, we were able to set achievable goals for the scope of our project." The emphasis is on focusing on "achievable goals."

The distillation process continues with faculty help after the students select the project to work on and bring their own take and interpretation to bear. Even after some understanding is established, the topic continues to change as new data emerge and context changes. Faculty advisers need to support both the student team and the sponsor at this stage. The manner in which the problem definition process unfolds is a learning experience for the students. The discovery of identifying what the core issues are in an unstructured and fuzzy situation is most rewarding for the whole team.

As the vignette dialogue suggests, interference of real life could be both exciting and frustrating, as it demands cognitive flexibility and thinking on your feet. Neat theories and carefully constructed plans get messy quickly. Both faculty and sponsors try to mediate these frustrations and help students learn to live with uncertainty, divergent viewpoints, and changes of course. Sponsors try to define the problem as tightly as they can, but they also need to report disruptions and introduce corrections as they arise in real time, as was the case in this project. Thus, challenges that faculty advisers face at this stage include the following:

- Negotiating the right scope and problem area for the students to tackle in a limited amount of time and with limited (first-year student) expertise to meet the sponsor's needs
- Negotiating the right balance of social and technical aspects
- Helping students find the right project liaison or contacts in the organization, if the original sponsor is unavailable
- Making time to cultivate crucial relationships with sponsors and to provide just enough support without compromising the sponsor's sense of project ownership

Stage 3: Project Development: How to Facilitate Student–Sponsor Communications

Vignette
The student team is deep into project development with many questions in need of an answer:

We need these numbers, but our sponsor was not able to get them. I guess it is really hard to know how many pickers are there, how much value there is in electronic waste there, and what are the challenges associated with training. We just don't know. Not yet. Maybe never. What do we do? Time is short; we need to prepare the poster, the presentation, the report . . .

But remember what he told us? We have to look at the big picture! It's not so much about electronics and disassembly lines. It's about these women. Nobody cares about them now because . . . many see them as . . . street people. Big picture means we should not get hung up on details but do something that could help these women . . . as much we can with what we come up with.

Once the project is launched and its goals defined (however provisionally), data collection goes into high gear, and the dialogue between the students and the sponsor becomes crucial. The Food Bank team, working on another project sponsored by Martin Burt and Fundación Paraguaya (see Appendix 8.3) took full advantage of sponsor communications:

The experience overall would have been a struggle without our sponsor, Martin Burt. He helped us communicate with the food bank in Paraguay to establish a baseline to start our project. We would Skype with him once a week on our progress, and he would provide feedback and ideas that contributed to our project. One important part of our research came from our sponsor retrieving information from the Paraguay food bank. This information was key to drafting our business model.

Here are some guidelines for facilitating student–sponsor communications:

- Keep an eye on the emerging relationship between the students and the sponsor by attending Skype sessions and virtual meetings and model cross-cultural communications for students.
- Discuss differences in academic and nonacademic business etiquette.
- Foster restraint and humility in students' assessment of their impact on the community; caution against overblown characterization of the solution and a condescending tone toward populations in need.
- Actively discuss sponsor communications with student teams and advise students on how to improve communications toward getting the best results.
- Show respect for the sponsor and appreciation for the sponsor's help and time. Students need to understand fully the sponsor's needs in terms of the form and the content of the final deliverable.
- While the academic and nonacademic goals may be somewhat different, they both could be met with sensitivity to the needs of either party.

- Do not overmanage the relationship between the sponsor and the students—they both need to own it.

Skype meetings, stakeholder interviews, and sponsor calls help generate data, but teams still face challenges as the result of hard-to-control informational flows and gaps, the need to attend to conditions on the ground, cultural differences, and the ever-expanding circles of inquiry that forestall closure and bring in new factors to address.

Data collection inevitably runs into informational gaps and generates uncertainty that students experience despite active sponsor communications. The sponsor's role at this point is not only to stay in touch and help with contacts but also to remind students of the big picture that would help them see all their efforts as worthwhile despite the missing pieces. Olivia Gibbs, a student from a team working to help the Paraguayan food bank turn produce waste into profit, reported how much adjusting and flexibility working with the sponsor demanded:

> From the beginning, we asked our sponsor for a rough idea of profit number but he kept saying, "Don't worry about it." . . . so we didn't. But then, at the tail end of our project, we received a number from the Food Bank folks that represented the amount they would like to see as a profit. It was challenging to have the number at the end, but it taught us to take deep breaths and recalculate.

Needless to say, the students found this change quite unnerving and frustrating. It took faculty and sponsor support for them to adapt and reconfigure their project.

Developing cognitive flexibility in working with sponsors also means learning to attend to the cultural context. There is no point in processing tomatoes into powder, for example, if soup packets hold no appeal to local consumers. It is also pointless to collect electronic waste if there are no local companies that can extract value and pay for it. You must understand what resources local waste pickers actually have at their disposal. This information can come only from communications with people on the ground, either with the waste pickers themselves or with local nonprofits and town authorities who are trying to help them.

Another challenge is that circles of inquiry are continually expanding during such projects and bring in more factors to consider. Working with the Paraguayan food bank led students to contact U.S. food banks to find out how they deal with produce overages. The U.S. experience was both similar and different. One food bank in Texas, for example, quickly developed a for-profit spin-off in a similar situation to handle produce and generate income, which was culturally appropriate. Business expertise and cultural sensitivity were needed at this stage to develop more than just the technology for tomato processing. Help for the development of a business plan came from a local source—the faculty who have experience with developing economies. As more knowledge and data are brought into the net, the project gets more complex and nuanced, demanding both vigilant focusing on the emergent "big picture" and attention to critical detail.

Here are some of the challenges you might encounter at this stage of the process:

- Students could get overly dependent on the sponsor and abuse the sponsor's time.
- Students could oversell their contributions and act superior toward the sponsor and the community they are trying to serve.
- Students could have difficulty navigating corporate or nonacademic cultural differences.
- Students could overfocus on meeting academic requirements at the expense of the sponsor's specific needs, in terms of both content and form of their solutions.
- Students could get overanxious about missing data or gaps in communications and have difficulty dealing with the unknown.

Stage 4: Project Delivery and Assessment: How to Meet Academic and Nonacademic Needs

Vignette

The student team is looking at the project results with a rare sense of accomplishment:

Too bad our sponsor is not here to see our presentation.

Yes, especially that he thinks that our recommendations will actually be used. Like, his nonprofit will use our slides in the workshop for women who are now picking cell phones and radios and other waste on the streets, and they will teach them how to take things apart—electronics, I mean. They will actually do that!

If they do, they may be able to get these women off the street and earning money . . . not much, but real, regular money. The electronics disassembly line might provide the women in this community with a real job and income that they never had before.

First, they will need to find companies in Paraguay or Brazil or somewhere that collects electronic junk and pays for it.

What we did is not just for class. This will actually mean something to somebody.

Deliverables in sponsored research take many forms. The academically required poster, presentation, and report could be secondary instruments for the sponsor who may prefer to see a marketing plan, a prototype, or a proof-of-concept design. To strike a balance between the academic and nonacademic needs, the eWaste team produced a pamphlet and instructional materials in addition to a poster and report, while the Food Bank team added a business plan to the detailed description of dryer technology and recipes for the manufactured tomato product. The challenge is to meet the academic requirements and to deliver it in the format the sponsor will be able to use.

Both the students and the sponsoring company need to wrap up the engagement with a sense that it was all worthwhile. Here are some guidelines to achieve a satisfactory end point and address both academic and nonacademic targets:

- Find a good fit between the sponsor's expectation and your deliverable. The team's findings have to be delivered in a format compatible with the sponsor's interface. This fitting and calibration may take the form of translating the key findings into Spanish or distilling key concepts in a colorful pamphlet. The application of the solution and its format need to be discussed with a sponsor well in advance of completion of the project.
- Make sure that the sponsor sees his or her commitment as worthwhile. This is key. Value added to a sponsoring company may consist of getting important research for the grant application, testing a new technological approach, and critiquing the existing method to justify a switch to a new approach. Clear understanding of where the sponsor sees the most value will help direct the project along constructive lines or reach the best compromise between academic and nonacademic needs.
- Academic evaluation needs to take into account both academic deliverables and sponsor satisfaction by the work the students have accomplished. Students need to be aware that both the quality of their argument and the applicability of their results matter. They need to work toward excellence on both these converging fronts for their work to have the greatest impact.

What are students' efforts worth in the end? It all depends on whom you ask. The feedback students receive from their faculty advisers often differs from what they typically receive from sponsors. Advisers respond to the early drafts, outlines, and conceptualizations presented in writing or in progress report presentations. They pay attention to argument building, research organization, internal logic, and gaps in the report. They care about the quality of writing and presentation skills. Sponsors are much more concerned about the utility of the results and the implementation of the solutions. They also think of how the project report and its recommendations could benefit their grant writing, internal restructuring efforts, or the next phase in business or research development. Those agendas may have a different timeline, evaluation yardsticks, and audience in mind. Faculty advisers need to reconcile students' and sponsors' needs to arrive at a satisfying end point for all.

Overall, sponsored projects require more coordination, collaboration, and mental flexibility to align the efforts of all sides at all stages of project development. Faculty advisers need to cultivate and support their sponsors and help mediate any issues between them and the students. Students are tasked with finding their way into the project and the organizational culture of the sponsoring organization. It is not by chance that many researchers describe sponsored work in academe as "contextual teaching and learning" (Predmore, 2005). The path to personal mastery of the subject is not easy or assured. The mind-set of an independent researcher is not easy to acquire for a first-year student just beginning to develop professional competencies. The agendas of the nonprofit or lab or company need to be carefully synchronized with academic calendars and learning goals. However, those agendas need not be in conflict, and the students need to learn the art of serving "many masters" at once. The many challenges of coordination and alignment are repaid by the rich harvest of insight and mastery of a variety of communication and development tools. The payoff could also be observed in higher motivation, learning quality, and students' ability to transcend cultural and disciplinary boundaries.

Challenges of this stage of project conclusion include the following:

- Aligning academic and nonacademic objectives
- Assessing if the project needs to be extended to the following year and assigned to a new project team if the first phase yielded only preliminary data
- Urging the sponsor to identify the necessary format and content for implementation-ready material and to determine the uses of such materials early on in the process

- Working on additional sets of deliverables on a limited timeline
- Depending on the sponsor for actual implementation

Benefits of Sponsored Projects

Cultivating and engaging sponsors comes at a price, but it also brings its rewards. Faculty take this step when they see a qualitatively different level of engagement and motivation in students who have an end user in view. Another significant benefit is the comprehensive development of communication skills as students are pushed to go beyond library and Internet research and engage with companies outside academia and outside of their familiar cultural context. Communication across academic and cultural lines fosters personal reflection and growth in students who have a chance to clarify their disciplinary commitments and personal passions through active interface with the real world and its needs.

Higher Motivation

In addition to developing communications skills and cultural sensitivity, students in our projects find the pressing urgency and usefulness of the solution to be highly motivating. Sean Kelly, a project sponsor and a former seminar student, reported that students bring "a motivated mind-set to each topic." The urgency of the problem makes the participants transcend the limits of their skills and self-doubt and achieve personal and professional growth. The clear sense of *why* this work is important makes it easier for students to mobilize all their resources to arrive at the *how* of delivering answers. "They learn more about the engineering process, they experience it firsthand, and show true excitement," pointed out seasoned project sponsor Brajendra Mishra, referring to how early engagement helps first-year students "reach a successful outcome" in complex projects. Students themselves report that doing research that "could actually mean something" makes them feel empowered (student comment).

Communications Workout

The most palpable benefit of our sponsored projects is the rich dialogue that takes place between more parties and in more formats than in almost any other learning situation. Team members need to reach out to multiple stakeholders and outside contributors. They are also asked to relate their findings back to sponsors in the form compatible with their needs. The solutions need to be convincing to all parties at the table: the workers who will implement them, the funders that may support the next steps, and the nonprofits that are trying to serve their communities. In addition to writing the required reports, students learn to make elevator pitches, produce succinct posters, raise awareness through pamphlets and workshops, and make presentations at company and lab meetings.

This goes above and beyond the traditional academic templates of written and oral communication and even beyond our communication-rich classrooms that do not engage sponsors. The involvement with sponsoring organizations allows first-year students to grow as presenters, community activists, well-rounded communicators, and teammates. Many of our students go on after this class to present at conferences, poster sessions, and other venues, both academic and nonacademic. They are likely to take leadership roles on future teams, during internships, and in business situations. Through our sponsored projects, they master the art of stepping from behind their research into the limelight of public debate, policy discussion, and community organizing. They also learn to defend their designs and proposals, as well as to solicit input from all the stakeholders and incorporate it into the final recommendations.

Cultural Sensitivity

As students tune in to the sponsor's wavelength, they learn to hear cultural inflections and adjust their recommendation to the particular context in which they are to be used. Solving the problem in many cases involves addressing language differences; attending to the historical context of the company; or understanding the specific environmental, legal, and business frameworks relevant to implementing a solution.

For example, proposing dehydration as a way to handle overripe tomatoes, the students in the project team became aware that they could not talk to their sponsor about dehydrators as commonplace items. Though they are readily available in the United States, they are simply not standard kitchen equipment in Paraguay. While our students easily purchased an inexpensive dehydrator online to experiment with, their Paraguayan sponsor "was amazed we had our own dehydrator," according to student Olivia Gibbs. This made the team aware of the technological gap and pushed it to question the original dehydration solution as befitting the context.

Self-Reflection and Personal Growth

Learning on your feet also promotes search for one's own path in life and supports personal and professional growth. Project sponsor Brajendra Mishra observed in his work with our students that they have demonstrated "a marked improvement in competency toward writing skills, presentation skills, and hands-on researching skills."

Another project sponsor, Martin Burt, sees benefits of sponsored projects for both the clients and the students involved. Students, he described, "have benefited not only the organization I run, Fundación Paraguaya, but also other NGOs in Paraguay, such as the Food Bank and the environmental group Procicla." Our students are "aware of opportunities that are not immediately obvious to people who are running development projects on the ground. For example, the local Food Bank did not know that discharged tomatoes from local food markets could be easily converted into tomato powder and sold as a delicacy."

Another sponsor and project adviser, Sean Kelly, sees the experience in such projects as a thrilling induction of students into the wonders of engineering: "This is probably the first time in their careers where they experience what engineering is, and this excites and propels them into their chosen fields." As a former student, Sean witnessed steady growth in "personal confidence that builds upon the success students see and feel from these projects."

Students themselves report the benefit of these experiences for communication and creative thinking skills. Learning to think big and to be confident through uncertainty is another observed benefit: "We quickly learned to clearly express our ideas and ask questions in a way that he would be able to understand. Martin Burt is an entrepreneur who likes to think big. He put our creative thinking skills to the test and pushed us to think of ideas that could solve the problem. Whenever we had doubts about our project, he encouraged us to keep going to reach our goals" (student comment).

Conclusion

Work on sponsored projects pushes students to draw on deeper resources and demands a higher degree of self-reflection and self-mobilization than traditional learning frameworks require. According to Dehler (2006),

> Action research provides the opportunity to directly relate curricular learning to actual workplace context, and to translate programmatic learning into workplace action. This creates a situation whereby students experience the struggle of coping with turmoil, tension, and the social embeddedness of real organizational problems, enhancing their competencies as a result. (p. 660)

Such a process, Dehler (2006) observed, engages students "in critical reflection to identify, illuminate, and critique your underlying assumptions and how they have, or have not, been affected" (p. 664).

Our own experience with sponsored projects shows that ties with the industry or nonprofits do not compromise student learning. On the contrary, they help students define their professional identities sooner, make them reach deeper into their personal and professional commitments, foster cognitive flexibility, and produce a springboard for highly motivated and focused learning. The immediacy of human interaction, the diversity of cultural perspectives, and the urgency of finding solutions create a highly stimulating learning context. Rather than seeing alliances with outside institutions and with industry as "dirty and unchaste" (Siegel, 2012), we get to experience them as transformational and productive of quality learning. We see firsthand that "corporations are enhancing the learning, not diluting it" (Siegel, 2007, p. 54) in the model of engagement that we practice. The desire to develop solutions that are both "meaningful" and "needed" makes students in sponsored projects grow personally and professionally and bridges many gaps that exist in a freshman's tool kit. Urgency and palpability of the problem lead to a sense of agency and ownership of learning—the ultimate goal of any educational initiative.

SPONSOR AND PROJECT ROSTER

Project Sponsor and Location	Sponsor Type	Project Description
Museum of Russian Icons Clinton, MA	Museum, cultural, nonprofit	Design and enhancement of interactive collection information database that visitors can access via a touch screen system in the galleries to explore the collection. Use of the existing grid system that has been developed to identify each saint and character depicted in many icons for touch screen information access.
Village Light Fund (via Seven Hills Global Outreach) Cameroon, Africa	Seven Hills Global Outreach International Worcester-based NGO	New Energy for a Better Health, Rhumsiki, Cameroon, "Computerized Farming" Project. The goal is to teach local farmers' cooperatives how to use the GPS/GIS technology to increase productivity and yields.
Fundación Paraguaya Asunción, Paraguay	International Paraguay-based NGO	Finding Sustainable Alternatives to Dealing With Waste From Leather Processing in Paraguay: How could the microfinance clients of Fundación Paraguaya who process leather find a low-cost alternative to dumping the waste from leather processing activities into the nearby stream or body of water?
WPI CR³ Worcester, MA	Academic lab with industry sponsorship	The Recovery and Reuse of Aluminum Used in Automotive Applications: What percentage is recycled, and in what ways can the recovery and reuse be increased? A study aimed at quantifying the material flow of aluminum, identifying material losses, and developing recommendations to increase recycling rates.

Project Sponsor and Location	Sponsor Type	Project Description
Fireseed Arts Framingham, MA	A cultural organization serving the local community by transforming trash into works of art	Music With a Re-Purpose: To identify the market for repurposed and recycled musical instruments and to research, contact, and participate in the promotion of the sustainability message—Earth's limited resources are vulnerable and in need of reverence and protection. Students who choose to work on this project will have the additional opportunity to envision unique combinations of materials to be put to use in the construct of playable and original instruments from recycled materials.

INITIAL PROJECT DESCRIPTION AND FINAL PROJECT ABSTRACT

eWaste Project

The original description of the project provided by the sponsor and the abstract of the completed report compiled by the students provide a snapshot of the evolution that an issue undergoes from conceptualization to execution in project work.

Initial Project Description

Develop a plan to help 120 waste recyclers retain and improve their existing microbusinesses. The Paraguayan government is building new homes for 1,000 families living in a slum by the river. However, the new project will not permit waste pickers and recyclers to continue business as usual—that is, to bring the recyclable materials they collect in the streets such as cardboard, cans, and bottles (their "merchandise") to their new homes and do the separation in their front sidewalk. Question: What type of business operation can be created so that recyclers can make a living and generate income?

Completed Project Abstract

The project undertaken by our team focuses on our endeavor to assist in the creation of a recycling program to operate in Asunción, the capital city of Paraguay. Paraguay as a country faces high rates of unemployment and poverty; Asunción is especially plagued by these problems. There is, however, an opportunity in this bleak situation. Solid waste streams have changed constantly through time as humans learn to use different types of materials to their advantage. As computers and consumer electronics have become cheaper and increasingly abundant in everyday life, they have started to form their own waste stream when discarded, called e-waste. These materials can be viewed as a source of profit, as they contain metals that, while minute in volume, are high in value.

Our project aims to use this waste stream in a disassembly and resale recycling program that will aim three things: to build awareness, to build skills, and to build a community. If our project is successfully applied in Asunción, waste pickers can work together to clean up their city, raise awareness about e-waste and their socioeconomic situation, increase their income from an average of $35 per to 10 times that value, and prove to other citizens of Paraguay their value to society. This project will then have an environmental, technical, and social impact.

Fundación Paraguaya is an NGO aimed at eliminating poverty through practical, innovative, and sustainable solutions, as well as a unique self-sufficient agricultural school for the rural poor. Through work with our students, Martin Burt, the founder and executive director of Fundación Paraguaya, has established a long-term relationship with WPI, including advising student projects focused on food and energy sustainability in Paraguay that have evolved into a permanent WPI Global Project Center.

INITIAL PROJECT DESCRIPTION AND FINAL PROJECT ABSTRACT

Food Bank Project

The original description of the project provided by the sponsor and the abstract of the completed report compiled by the students provide a snapshot of the evolution that an issue undergoes from conceptualization to execution in this project.

Initial Project Description

Help the local food bank in Paraguay (http://bancodealimentos.org.py/) transition from being a traditional charity to a social enterprise. Specifically, help develop potential income-generating activities while at the same time reducing food waste and feeding the hungry. For example, overripe tomatoes and other vegetables and perishable foods are picked up by this food bank from farmer markets, taken to a warehouse or cold storage, and then distributed to orphanages and old-age homes. Very little value added. Question: Is there another use for these tomatoes? Can these tomatoes be converted into tomato sauce and sold to low-end or high-end markets? How else can a local food bank, where tax deductions are not allowed, generate income and become sustainable?

Completed Project Abstract

In Asunción, Paraguay, local farmers markets are left with unsold piles of overripe tomatoes every day. Our project focuses on developing a product from this tomato surplus that can generate a supplemental income for the local food bank, Banco de Alimentos. Our proposed solution to this problem involves a dehydration process to dry the tomatoes and turn them into a powder. We conducted a trial to test our methodology and make a prototype of the product, called Mezcla de Tomate, which can be used as a base in a variety of dishes when rehydrated. Using our process, Banco de Alimentos will have the opportunity to sell the product and use the net-positive revenue to help with the expenses that incur from operating the nonprofit organization. We outlined a processing plan and business model for how this product can be used as a profit for the food bank.

The benefits of our proposed solution include reducing tomato waste and creating a product that can give the Banco a form of a supplemental income. The resulting income can be used to pay the salaries of the employees at the Banco so that they can continue to run operations smoothly and feed those who are hungry in Paraguay.

PART THREE

MAKING PROJECT-BASED LEARNING WORK IN THE CLASSROOM

In this section, we offer tools and approaches for putting PBL into practice in the classroom. This section includes strategies that will help you create assignments, in-class activities, and team project management tools geared toward first-year students. The goal of these chapters is to provide you with concrete tools that will enable you to get to work on bringing PBL to your classroom piece by piece or to help broaden and deepen your PBL approaches in your existing courses. The chapters in this section offer sample assignments, modules, activities, and other resources for you to modify for your own courses.

Chapter 9, "Setting First-Year Students Up for Success in a Project," provides approaches and assignments to create a project structure and subtask scaffolding to guide students through PBL work. Stoddard and Spanagel also provide activities and tools to help first-year students identify gaps in research and assess the appropriate scale, size, and scope of a project.

In chapter 10, "Teaching Course Content Through Skill Building," Stoddard and Rulfs provide approaches, as well as examples of specific assignments and activities, to teach course content and transferable skills simultaneously. These skills include oral and visual presenting, teamwork, evidence-based writing, research, values, and cultural awareness.

Chapter 11, "Equitable and Effective Student Teams: Creating and Managing Team Dynamics for Equitable Learning Outcomes," discusses the need to bring greater equity to student teamwork and faculty advising in

PBL. It offers tools, assignments, and modules that set students up for more equitable team dynamics from the start and help them manage teams more equitably and effectively throughout the project. Pfeifer and Stoddard provide stand-alone tools for students and faculty, as well as modules that serve as examples of how you might combine some of the tools in the classroom and through supportive assignments to meet specific needs.

Chapter 12, "Managing Team Dynamics and Conflict on Student Project Teams," provides tools and resources that will enable you to better support team dynamics through specific faculty roles and strategies. Morse offers approaches that you can use to create highly functional teams, manage and facilitate conflict, evaluate team dynamics, and encourage and support project teams.

Each chapter ends with a section called "Try This," which contains suggestions and prompts to help you incorporate PBL into your classroom. Visit our companion website (www.wpi.edu/+fi rstyearprojects) for examples of student project work.

SETTING FIRST-YEAR STUDENTS UP FOR SUCCESS IN A PROJECT

Elisabeth A. Stoddard and David Spanagel

They came into my office, hardly able to contain themselves. "Professor, we finally know what we are going to do for our project. We are going to design, and maybe even build, a desalination plant, using a new, more affordable technology, to increase the amount of drinking water available in desert regions. Now, how the technology works is way above our heads. . . . And we don't know how we'd get the money to build it, or whether we could raise enough with crowd funding to implement it. . . . But, it can make a really big difference in people's lives, and we love it!!! What do you think?"

Working with idealistic first-year college students who are excited and full of hope and passion, without limits of what is realistic, is what makes working with this group so rewarding for many of us. They are often open and willing to try almost anything, and they (usually) lack the jaded, rough edges of experience that can limit possibilities. However, those same qualities also make teaching first-year students challenging. Many of us use pedagogical tools in our history, biology, math, and engineering classes to push our students to ask critical questions and to challenge their assumptions to help them ground their ideas, while fostering their excitement and sense of limitless possibilities.

PBL provides us with additional, and uniquely effective, opportunities to harness the passion and excitement of our first-year students, while also providing our students with new platforms to think critically about the problems they are working on. Students working on projects develop relationships with peers and faculty advisers that enable them to take risks they might not take alone. Having to develop and apply solutions in theoretical or actual cases pushes students to think logistically about the scale, scope, cost, and political–cultural context in which they are working. However, students need structure and support to successfully harness these opportunities and challenges. In this chapter, we discuss a number of strategies we have used to set first-year students up for success in a project, while fostering their passion, creativity, and hope that anything is possible.

Why Do First-Year Students Need Unique Supports in Project Work?

Whenever we teach the first-year project course, the first half of the course tends to revolve around a constellation of course work that combines awareness of current events, societal problems, and human needs, alongside the development of technical skills. One of the goals of this course work and skill development is to prepare students to tackle their own project topic during the second half of the course. Through these preparatory activities, we seek to achieve the following key course objectives: (a) to help students learn how to frame fruitful research questions, and (b) to help them understand that solutions to real-world problems are complex and tend to involve multiple solution strategies.

Helping first-year students acquire basic analytical skills and content knowledge—sometimes in multiple disciplines, techniques of independent inquiry, and a realistic appreciation for the complexity of open-ended problems—can be very interesting and highly rewarding work. However, doing these things simultaneously introduces the students right away to the many serious challenges of doing authentic research and project work. After 10 years of faculty comparing our experiences, sharing strategies, and distilling some helpful approaches, we have identified four key categories of difficulty instructors regularly encounter in teaching and advising first-year students who are engaged in research projects:

1. Helping students choose a problem of appropriate size, scale, and scope
2. Threading the needle: urging students to contribute to existing knowledge without reinventing the wheel
3. Keeping the ball rolling: sustaining student interest and motivation in the research process and project
4. Providing project structure and subtask scaffolding, while meeting individual team needs and promoting student creativity

In the remainder of this chapter, we will discuss specific strategies, supported by examples and sample assignments, that we and our colleagues have developed to manage, or at least mitigate, these challenges.

How to Set Students Up for Success in a Project

Unfortunately, there is no algorithm that can guarantee students will be able to navigate the complex and situational challenges of real world–based project work. We have learned through our own teaching experiences, however, that it often pays to provide students with an appropriate mix of heuristic guidance, on the one hand, and freedom to mess about in the domain of their inquiry, on the other. Rather than leave readers with so imprecise a proclamation as this might seem to be, we offer a few strategies to characterize what we mean here by "heuristic guidance."

Strategies to Help Students Choose a Problem of Appropriate Size, Scale, and Scope

The vast majority of American college students have been too well trained by their previous school experience to know how to assert autonomy when it comes to problem definition. In the standard secondary classroom, the teacher invariably poses questions. The student's job is typically restricted to trying to answer those questions. The entire realm of problem choice is, therefore, an unfamiliar one, and so it comes as little surprise that first-year students may struggle to choose a problem of the right size, scale, and scope to be approachable for a project assignment. To help students grapple with what is for them a novel situation and to help them gain some valuable analytical skills along the way, we emphasize instructional strategies that give students a chance to learn how to choose a right-sized research problem. These include instructional approaches of question reformulation and the use of case studies.

Question Reformulation to Gain Traction on Open-Ended Problems
One key to building student engagement with real-world problems is to assist students in choosing a project topic but allow it to be their own idea. Even within the technical domain, many students find they have come to college ill-prepared for the challenge of real-world, open-ended problems by their secondary school experiences, which most often consist of straightforward homework assignments and textbook-based regurgitation of highly filtered course content. Open-ended problem spaces require a substantial investment of thought and reflection before "the problem" can be isolated and framed

in some manner that will admit of any solution attempt. So many different kinds of questions may arise that it becomes a critical area of student decision-making to discern which problem to try to solve. Fundamentally, though, students must be pressed to ask a question; a topic is not a question, and no amount of "topic hype" can induce fruitful inquiry in the absence of a properly framed motivating question.

Two Canadian scholars of educational psychology, Karyn Cooper and Susan London McNab, examine how a pedagogy of questioning can support both effective instruction and a social justice outcome (equipping students with the capability to frame their own questions). Unsurprising, their study confirms that students who learn how to frame their own questions become more deeply engaged learners. As a result, classroom instruction moves away from traditional models of rote learning but also induces some unpredictability. Autonomous questioners tend to draw more freely on their own values systems, which may or may not be well aligned with those of the instructors (Cooper & McNab, 2009, p. 212). To capture the multiple forms of student and instructor discomfort that can ensue from such situations, these researchers invoked the psychological term *aesthetic dissonance*, which they described as a "disequilibrium in the felt [rather than the rational] realm." Far from being a hindrance to learning, they touted aesthetic dissonance as an "essential discomfort that propels effective questioning" (p. 213). Our experience with WPI first-year students corroborates some of Cooper and McNab's fascinating analysis; students do become more effective and engaged learners when they practice agency through the act of framing questions that are meaningful to them. Though we have not found divergent values systems to be a major problem, we do acknowledge that empowering students to ask their own questions requires more intensive guidance, intellectual flexibility, and coaching. Instructors must be patient listeners to give students room to articulate their own curiosity and at the same time be prepared to offer guidance as students discover that they need it to launch fruitful, appropriately scaled investigations.

Even after choosing some focused portion of the global problem to attack, the student may have to define many other components of the actual task. Typically, for example, students cannot find relevant data gathered in one place or organized in a convenient format. Instead, they have to sift through lots of materials to find a few useful pieces of information, and then they have to exercise some mix of ingenuity and careful judgment in deciding what method(s) to employ in making sense of what they did find. In other words, the whole experience of solving real-world problems bears precious little resemblance to solving homework problems from a disciplinary textbook, which might provide "sample problems" or solution templates and where a selection of answers often appears in the back of the book. There is no "back of the book" for a meaningful real-world-based project problem.

Throughout these experiences, the at-first informal strategy of coaching students to think about framing a fruitful research question proves to be a critically valuable companion to one of our more important learning outcomes: developing an awareness and appreciation for complexity. It turns out that learning how to frame a fruitful question is far more difficult than finding the answer to an already well-defined problem. Students need many opportunities to think "out loud" about their interests and to practice formulating research questions, conferring with each other and with the instructors both before and after testing it "in the field" and then being open to revision and reconsideration. In addition, question complexity and flexibility are important features to examine through discussions with students. For instance, research questions that have a yes/no answer are far less fertile than questions that ask how or why something happens the way that it does.

Nevertheless, to support authentic engagement with problem complexity, we also feel students sometimes need the chance to discover for themselves that their research question is too big (or too small) to match the time and resources available, too vague (or too specific) to support meaningful investigation, trivial and therefore uninteresting, or, at the other extreme, fundamentally insoluble. So, not all obstacles to effective question design need to be anticipated in advance. What does need to be established (usually through conversations that occur during progress meetings with the students) is a clear understanding that research investigation is a living, breathing process of inquiry, which functions best when the researcher gets periodic opportunities to reexamine and refine the quality and/or appropriateness of the question(s) driving the research.

Using Case Studies to Guide Undergraduate Research:
Contextualizing the Size, Scale, and Scope of the Problem

When student research projects begin, we typically find the following issues with students choosing a problem that is of appropriate size, scale, and scope: (a) their interest is too broad and undefined (e.g., "We want to reduce food waste."), or (b) they have identified the solution before they have identified the problem (e.g., "We want to use desalination to create more drinking water."). Case studies are very helpful in both of these cases in guiding students to choose a problem that is of appropriate size, scale, and scope. In case study research, undergraduate (and other) researchers "explore and investigate contemporary real-life phenomenon through detailed contextual analysis of a limited number of events or conditions, and their relationships" (Zainal, 2007, pp. 1–2). Case study research can be a good approach for first-year undergraduate research because it offers a project at a modest scale. It also provides the context to better understand a specific problem, the stakeholders involved and their unique needs, the existing solutions to the problem, and how students might contribute by analyzing one aspect of the problem (Hays, 2004; Rowley, 2002; Zainal, 2007).

In one first-year project course, we have students begin by identifying an area of interest, like reducing food waste or desalination. Then we ask them to identify a specific case in a specific community where this problem (or solution) is taking place. Students present this case in an oral, and then a written, problem proposal, which becomes (over many iterations) the literature review in their research proposal and report.

In the situation where students have an interest that is too broad and undefined, choosing a case helps narrow their scope and contextualize the size and scale of the potential research within the unique needs of community stakeholders. In the scenario where students have chosen a solution before they identified a problem, selecting a case forces them to look at cases where their solution of interest may apply. In both situations, identifying and working on a particular case helps sustain student interest and motivation in the research project and research process (another challenge discussed in this chapter), as the students become invested in a community and the potential for their research to help address a specific problem.

Once the case has been established, we help students continue refining the scope, size, and scale of their project by having them create a Gantt chart to visually map out the different parts of their research plan. "A Gantt chart is a type of horizontal bar chart for visualizing the start and end dates of various tasks on a project" (Wolfe, 2010, p. 47). We provide feedback on their Gantt charts to help them consider the constraints of time, money, and their own levels of expertise.

Strategies to Help First-Year Students Thread the Needle: Identifying a Gap in Research

One classic tactic that all graduate students quickly learn (regardless of discipline) is to present their own work as the answer to a previously unasked (or incompletely addressed) question. Literature reviews for all kinds of published papers thus tend to gravitate rhetorically toward the mode of identifying the "gap" in existing research, which can somehow justify the need for a new intellectual contribution or novel application of existing knowledge. Most first-year undergraduate students, however, have never been exposed to the process of how to identify a gap in existing knowledge. They may also not have been told that the strategy of identifying the gap in research is a key to unlocking how one may pursue a potentially original insight or to develop a valuable extension of existing data into unexamined domains or untried applications.

Analyzing Existing and/or Failed Solutions to Problems to Identify a Gap in Knowledge

Many first-year student research projects take place over a few weeks to a few months. This makes it difficult to identify a gap in research, because first-year students typically lack the time and background knowledge to consider gaps in physical or social science theory. Therefore, we ask our students to look at how others have tried to solve the problem they are analyzing in similar cases (e.g., reducing food waste at a local elementary school). We ask them to investigate how and why those solutions have fallen short or succeeded and/ or how and if those solutions could be applied uniquely to their case. We have found that this allows students to identify gaps through a more narrow scope.

To prepare students as they begin to look for solutions to their problem, we first discuss and provide examples of multiple types of solutions to food, water, energy, and other problems. These include market-based solutions, educational-based solutions, technical solutions, and political- and/or policy-oriented solutions. In this assignment, we ask the students to identify (a) what has already been done to fix the problem; (b) who designed the solution and which stakeholders does it benefit or overlook; and (c) was it successful for particular stakeholders, to what extent, and why.

Students are asked to identify gaps in the development and implementation of solutions to specific cases. For example, in the development and implementation of solutions to reduce hunger, were the needs of vulnerable stakeholders (e.g., immigrant communities) considered? Is something missing from this solution as a result?

Students also use this assignment as an opportunity to analyze how they might fill the gap. We ask them to consider how they might modify or redesign the development and/or implementation of a solution by combining one or more types of solutions (market, education, technical, policy based, or community based) to more effectively and more equitably help solve the problem in an existing or novel case. (You can find the assignment in Appendix 9.1.)

Keeping the Ball Rolling: Helping Students Stay Engaged in the Research Process to Sustain Their Interests and Keep Them Motivated

Our first-year students are always really excited to get started on their projects and research. However, once they delve in, the excitement and motivation often wanes. As students begin to read through peer-reviewed articles on their topics, the project can begin to feel abstract or disconnected to their goal of solving a concrete problem of water or food insecurity. Students often hit roadblocks, for example, when they learn the problem is different from what they anticipated.

At the start of one project, a group of students thought the community they were focused on lacked clean drinking water, so they planned to design affordable water filtration systems for individual homes. However, it turned out that the community had a drinking water filtration system as a result of a recently privatized water system, but the majority of the community could not afford the water. As a result, the problem shifted from a technical problem to which they had a concrete solution in mind to a policy and poverty problem that was considerably more complex and lacking a clear-cut solution. These students (like most who hit roadblocks) felt discouraged, as if their project has fallen off course and they "had to start all over again."

To keep students motivated and the ball rolling, we recommend having regular opportunities for students to report on their progress, challenges, and roadblocks. On the basis of our own experience, and confirmed by relevant literature (Guerin et al., 2013; Hemlin, Allwood, & Martin, 2008), we have found that providing these routine opportunities for students to report on their progress help to (a) build a supportive research community, (b) build student identities as researchers, and (c) increase student ability to effectively write and talk about the process of research. Having a supportive research community, developing an identity as a researcher, and becoming a more confident and effective communicator of research has helped our (and others') students stay better engaged and motivated through the ups and downs of the research process (Guerin et al., 2013; Hurtado, Cabrera, Lin, Arellano, & Espinosa, 2009; Laursen, Hunter, Seymour, Thiry, & Melton, 2010). "Progress reports" can take many forms, including oral presentations, written updates and reflections, and peer-review activities. We discuss these approaches to reporting progress next.

Progress Reports: Research Notebooks and Reflections

In a team-based project, a key component of keeping individual students engaged and motivated in the research process is ensuring that the members of the student research teams feel connected to one another and on the same page in regard to the current pulse and future direction of the project (Wolfe, 2010). We use a type of progress report—we call it a research notebook—to help individual first-year student researchers stay engaged and motivated by keeping them on the same page with one another.

In this assignment, students begin by meeting in teams to discuss where they are in the research process, what objectives they have met, what questions remain, what data still need to be collected, and so on. Then they decide on the next steps in the research process and determine what objective and set of questions and types of data each team member will be working toward. Next, students do research individually by searching for data and answers to their questions in peer-reviewed journal articles and published business, government, or nonprofit organizational reports. The individual students are required to write up information about the databases and keywords used in their search, what they found, what questions were answered or objectives met, and how this shapes the direction of the project. Finally, the students meet again to discuss what each of them has found and to discuss how the collective work shapes the direction of the project.

We have found that this process develops a supportive research community among the team members. Team members are able to stay on the same page regarding the direction of research. Students are held responsible to their teammates, minimizing the occurrence of one or two members doing the bulk of the work while others lose motivation and interest. It also fosters communication about the successes and challenges of the work. Sharing these successes—such as exciting findings or new positive directions—motivates students. Sharing the challenges can build an engaged, empathetic, and supportive team dynamic (Ash & Clayton, 2009).

Progress Reports: Peer Reviews
In a peer-reviewed activity, students provide feedback on another student's assignment, enabling meaningful interaction with peers. Students share ideas and suggestions, which can help create a supportive research community. This process has also shown to improve language and writing ability (Lundstrom & Baker, 2009), and when students write about research, the peer-review process and dialogue can help them build identities as researchers.

One issue with peer review is that first-year students are novices on research and how to give constructive feedback. Therefore, the ability of our first-year students to provide feedback is limited, and the feedback they provide can be inaccurate (Cho & Schunn, 2007). To address this, we use the expertise of the director of our writing center to both review our peer-review assignments and activities and provide our students with a workshop on how to give constructive feedback in writing as editors and through dialogue as reviewers.

Research also shows that greater learning opportunities arise when feedback (e.g., on a research proposal) is put into a dialogue. Nicol, Thomson, and Breslin (2014) explained, "If students are to learn from feedback, they must have opportunities to construct their own meaning from the received message: they must do something with it, analyse it, ask questions about it, discuss it with others and connect it with prior knowledge" (p. 103). These multiple opportunities for written and oral dialogue also help increase students' ability to effectively write and talk about research, which, in turn, can sustain their interest and motivation in the project and research process.

Therefore, in our peer-reviewed assignments, we often give our students multiple opportunities for such dialogue. For example, after our student teams have completed their problem proposal (proposing what problem they will be analyzing and why), we assign an activity in which individual students are tasked with reading and providing written feedback on another team's research proposal outside of class. Back in class, the students who reviewed each other's team proposal discuss the feedback. Then the student research teams reconvene and discuss the feedback they got from their individual peer-review partners. (You can find the assignment in Appendix 9.2.)

When we do this activity, the room is always abuzz. You can see excitement around new ideas, and the furrowed brows debating how to overcome a particular challenge that the reviewers brought to the team's attention. Student confidence builds during this dialogue and interaction, as they engage in their identities and abilities as researchers and reviewers. This can help sustain their interest and motivation in the project and research process.

Providing Project Structure and Subtask Scaffolding, While Meeting Individual Team Needs and Promoting Student Creativity

One of the challenges of teaching a course in which you are advising multiple projects is finding a balance between providing a course and assignment structure that guides students and the advisers who are coaching and creating a flexible enough course structure to accommodate teams who are farther along or farther behind in the research process. We often hear from students that the structure is incredibly helpful, especially in the beginning and middles stages of the research process. As we get toward the end of the research process, some teams find the structure inhibiting, as they may be at different stages of the research process. We have worked to create a structure that allows us to support all our student teams by providing a unifying frame that enables faculty to advise multiple teams at once in the classroom and via assignments.

One way we can create structure and subtask scaffolding is by having the student teams' project goal, objectives, and research questions serve as a grounding mechanism or home base for student teams and faculty advisers.

Using project goals, objectives, and research questions to guide research and research advising is not novel; it is an established practice (Hennick,

Hutter, & Bailey, 2010). Our goal here is to provide some tips regarding specific approaches and assignments to create a structure that benefits both students and faculty while meeting individual team needs and enhancing student creativity. The goal, objective, and research questions are used to guide student research-related assignments and to guide faculty coaching and assessment of student teams and their progress. We also discuss strategies we use to meet individual team needs and enhance creativity, specifically using concept mapping and the research notebook assignment described earlier.

Once students have done the initial work to identify the problem in their specific case study, we then help them draw on this knowledge of the case to develop a project goal and project objectives. Each student on the team submits a set of project goals and objectives and receives detailed feedback from the faculty. Students submit individually at first to ensure that all voices can be heard in the process of developing project goals and objectives. The team then meets to discuss all the feedback and, using this feedback, drafts the group's goal and objectives. The team submits this to the faculty, who give feedback and a grade. The students revise it a final time. The multiple drafts, though they create extra work for both faculty and students, are important because the goal and objectives frame the rest of the project. We have found that the additional time spent developing solid goals and objectives saves us and the students from the work of salvaging projects that lack focus and direction later on.

Next, students use their goal and objectives to structure, develop, and write up the methodology for their research. They develop mini research plans to meet each objective (e.g., interviews, types of secondary data they will collect, etc.). The research notebook assignments (discussed in detail earlier in this chapter) are used to document and facilitate individual research and group strategies to meet particular objectives. Within this structure, students are able to act individually and creatively, as the individual researchers and the team drive the actual research—whom they interview, what sources they investigate, and the use of their own passions, interests, and skills to creatively meet the objectives they set for themselves.

The project objectives also structure the team's write-up of their results or findings. The teams are required to create a "living results" document, which they work on when they meet to discuss what they accomplished with their most recent research notebook assignment. In it they record findings, data, quotes from interviews, and potential conclusions under each objective. This develops into their results section over multiple drafts.

When the students are about three weeks from submitting a report and presenting a poster on their project, we do a concept mapping activity in class on large sheets of paper or on the blackboards, structured by the project goal and objectives. They show how they have met each objective methodologically with interviews and secondary data collection. They map out their findings under each objective—what parts of the objectives have not yet been met—and sketch out a plan as to how they will fill these gaps in the limited time remaining.

Often these maps are turned into informative visuals for students to include in their reports for a quick summative visual that illustrates how the project was organized and carried out methodologically and its key findings. Students report finding this activity productive in identifying their remaining gaps and developing a relative plan. They love the creativity involved in a visually effective map—the activity helps them see all they've accomplished and provides motivation to finish at a key time. (You can find a map template in Appendix 9.3.)

Challenges of Incorporating These Strategies Into Course Instruction

One prominent challenge of trying to teach students to engage with these problems is the reality check provided by the real world. None of the problems actually get solved within the space of several weeks or months. Students who signed up to take on the exciting prospect of working on a global problem like hunger, energy, or health can sometimes feel disappointed at the end of a semester of extremely hard work. Their efforts, no matter how high the quality or how well intentioned, may not make an appreciable dent in the very large scope and complexity of the global problem. When David Spanagel taught Power the World, some fraction of his student evaluations always reported some dismay along these lines:

> Why work so much harder in a [PBL] course as compared with other freshmen we know who are taking standard science, math, and humanities and arts courses? At least on their final exams they can end up feeling like they have mastered some content, whereas we only come to realize after all this work that we have barely begun to scratch the surface of the problem we had set out to solve.

They wanted to build a desalination plant. They wanted to create controlled nuclear fusion. They wanted to end the ravages of hunger and disease. The very reason a great problem appeals to our most adventurous students in the first place can come back to haunt us at the end of the course.

Instructors are well advised to encourage students to reflect along the way about how their research question formulation or project definition efforts, for example, are nourishing an important process of maturing and sophistication. Realistic acknowledgment of the difficulties of global problems need not be discouraging, especially if they are reframed as strong motivations for students to develop expertise within their chosen discipline (major) and as a reminder for all students to appreciate the value of bringing a diverse set of skills and methods to bear on the messiness of real-world challenges.

Students who complete a meaningful first-year project experience can emerge with a highly favorable combination of attitudes and commitments. They can cultivate their own areas of expertise to the best of their ability but not to the disparagement of other kinds of expertise. Rather, they can aim to excel in their majors in hopes of being able eventually to work alongside community members, collaborators, and the best practitioners of every other field of study. All kinds of expertise, channeled and tested through the widest variety of solution approaches, may ultimately be needed to help crack the puzzle of a really complicated global challenge. This is a sobering reality but potentially a deep source of inspiration. This inspiration may help students persist through whatever challenges, unpleasant tasks, and intervals of tedium they may encounter throughout their subsequent undergraduate, graduate, and professional careers.

Conclusion

The array of strategies we outlined in this chapter may seem overwhelming, especially if one is trying to integrate PBL into a standard content course within one discipline or another. The key is not to treat the project as an add-on to an already full content agenda. To manage a project-based course experience successfully, one needs to adopt a different model of learning and teaching.

What the students are learning is not just a textbook-provided list of terms to be defined, concepts to be comprehended, and algorithms to be practiced. Projects intervene between the learners and the traditional sources of authority, so that the problem itself becomes the demanding teacher and the guide to what most needs to be learned. If you can perform just such a gestalt switch, the task of teaching a project-centered course becomes neither easier nor harder but just as fully engaging of the instructor's talents and knowledge as any other course might be and potentially a far more interesting teaching experience. For more on the shifting role of instructors in project-based courses, see chapter 4. For more on teaching course content through skill building, see chapter 10.

Try This

1. *Framing and refining research questions.* Provide your students a relevant topic description for a research assignment. Ask them to pose three to five possible research questions they would like to investigate, all of which fall within that domain. Then ask them to analyze both the scope and the potential complexity of each question they proposed: (a) Can it be answered with yes or no? (b) What kinds of research methods might be required to obtain relevant data or evidence needed to address that question? Finally, ask them to rank their questions in order of the anticipated value and significance of the findings that each research investigation could yield (which ones matter more) and to be prepared to explain why they ranked them in that order. Then, collect the results of this work and lead a group discussion in which you assess (by commending and critiquing) the questions the students generated and how well they characterized and prioritized those questions. Help them, in this manner, gain a better sense of just what your discipline does, what problem aspects it is best (or poorly) designed to illuminate, and what kinds of question features can lead to more (or less) "promising" avenues of investigation.

2. *Peer review.* Think of one assignment (writing, presentation, etc.) where you feel your students would benefit from some early feedback. Reach out to your writing center to develop a guided peer-review activity that will help your students get, give, and discuss the feedback in pairs or groups.

3. *Concept maps.* If you have a project in your course or plan to incorporate one, think of a moment in the project process when it would be helpful for your students to step back and assess their progress and what remains to be completed. Consider including a concept mapping exercise at this point for students to physically and creatively document their progress and the gaps that remain.

GREAT PROBLEMS SEMINAR: WORLD'S WATER

Professor Elisabeth Stoddard and Professor Derren Rosbach

Worcester Polytechnic Institute

Project Solutions Presentation

Goals of This Assignment

- To build research, teamwork, cultural awareness, problem-solving, and presentation skills
- To become knowledgeable about and analyze some of the most effective solutions surrounding your particular problem

Instructions

In an exciting and captivating seven-minute presentation:

1. State the specific problem your team is working to address.
2. Describe the first potential solution in detail.
3. Analyze the pros and cons of this solution in terms of the economic-, environmental-, social-, ethical-, and/or social-justice-related costs and benefits of this potential solution to your problem.
   a. What aspect of the problem does this solution address?
   b. Does this solution specifically address the main cause of the specific problem? If so, how? If not, why not?
   c. Is the solution aimed at . . . individuals? . . . families? . . . communities? . . . corporations? . . . government? . . . business? . . . institutions? Are they responsible for the problem or just suffering from the effects?
4. Describe the second potential solution in detail.
5. Analyze the pros and cons of this solution in terms of the economic-, environmental-, social-, ethical-, and/or social-justice-related costs and benefits of this potential solution to your problem.
   a. What aspect of the problem does this solution address?

    b. Does this solution specifically address the main cause of the specific problem? If so, how? If not, why not?

    c. Is the solution aimed at . . . individuals? . . . families? . . . communities? . . . corporations? . . . government? . . . business? . . . institutions? Are they responsible for the problem or just suffering from the effects?

6. Discuss the following relevant questions regarding your two potential solutions:

    a. What are other people doing to solve this problem in your particular case or in a similar case elsewhere?

    b. How can you build on their proposed solutions?

    c. How might you improve on their proposed solutions?

    d. How might you take the solution in a different direction?

    e. How can you apply others' solutions uniquely and/or appropriately to your case?

Presentation Requirements

1. *Content and Length of Presentation*

    a. The presentation should start with an introduction, telling us the name of your presentation, the name of the team members, and what you are going to discuss today. This should be very brief (about one minute).

    b. The presentation should be seven minutes long. Presentations that are significantly shorter will have points deducted. Presentations that are longer will be stopped, and points will be deducted. *Practice, practice, practice.* Presentations that have not been practiced at least once are *always* disjointed and poorly timed and clearly have not been practiced. Don't make this mistake.

    c. You must have at least 6 slides and no more than 11 slides in your presentation. The general rule in good presentations is about 1 slide per minute.

    d. Your slides should be primarily images and graphics. They should not be all words (makes presentations boring).

    e. The questions we posed regarding your problem topic should guide and provide a framework for your presentation—do not just walk through the questions and answers with us.

    f. The last slide should list your image and reference citations.

2. *Presentation Style*

a. Be persuasive! Use clear reason and evidence to explain the problem and make your case. These are problems that currently affect people's and animals' lives! Help us see what life is like from their point of view.

b. Try to discuss the issue with us instead of reading from cards. However, if you feel most comfortable reading from cards, be sure to read with a lively voice and make occasional eye contact.

c. You must practice your presentation as a group at least once before your presentation. We are here to learn from you. Give yourselves and us the respect of doing a great job presenting your problem and pleading your case on issues that affect people's lives from around the world.

3. *Sources*

a. You must have at least three sources per team member that pass the CRAP test.

b. These sources must be listed on the last page of your presentation. They must be cited properly. Please use the APA style. For image sources, please provide links only.

4. *Work Shared Equally by Group Members*

a. Divide tasks equally.

b. Make time to work together as a group.

c. Make time to practice at least once together.

Questions

a. Contact your professors anytime via e-mail with questions or concerns.

b. Come during office hours or make an appointment to meet with your professors.

Presentation Rubric: Possible Grades for Each Dimension

Dimension	Excellent A	Good B	Fair C	Needs Substantial Improvement
Completeness (20 points)	• Questions 1 through 6 are covered	• Most questions answered	• Some questions answered	• Most questions not answered
Sources (10 points)	• At least three per team member • Sources cited properly	• Missing one source • Some citation errors; moderate need for editing	• Missing two sources • Citation errors distract readers; significant need for editing	• Missing three or more sources • Citation errors interfere with readability
Group Presentation Style (10 points)	• 6 to 11 slides • Slides are primarily images and graphics, not words • Group presents information with smooth transitions from one team member to the next • Presentation well practiced	• 5 to 12 slides • Slides have equal amounts of graphics and words • Group transitions generally well, a few stumbles; still able to follow case study • Presentation seems moderately practiced but still a little bit rough	• 4 to 13 slides • Slides have more words than graphics • Group transitions are distracting; hard to follow case study • Presentation seems barely practiced and quite rough	• 3 to 14 slides • Slides are primarily words • Group presentation and transitions are disjointed; difficult to impossible to follow case study • Presentation seems unpracticed and is disjointed
Ideas and Content (60 points) State problem Describe solution 1 Analyze solution 1 Describe solution 2 Analyze solution 2 Discuss solutions	• Solutions and analysis are clear and straightforward • Ideas are well elaborated • Details are effective, specific, and relevant	• Solutions and analysis are generally clear and straightforward • Ideas and details are usually effective, specific, and relevant but may be limited in depth	• Solutions and analysis are vague • Ideas are thinly developed; details, when provided, may be irrelevant, unfocused, or too general	• Solutions and analysis are not clear or straightforward • Ideas or details are very limited, unclear, or difficult to follow • Discussion seems off topic, disconnected, or random

GREAT PROBLEMS SEMINAR: FOOD SUSTAINABILITY

Professor Elisabeth Stoddard and Professor Kris Wobbe
Worcester Polytechnic Institute

Problem Proposal Peer Review

Goal

The goal of this assignment is to help you (a) practice evaluating the quality of evidence-based writing, (b) continue developing your skills as editors, and (c) identify what was done well and what needs work in other teams' writing in order to identify similar issues in your own report.

Instructions

Download your assigned partner's problem proposal. Review the proposal based on the following criteria. Bring a digital or paper copy of your comments and feedback to class on [DATE], where you will go over your feedback in class with your partner.

Review Criteria

Use these criteria to comment on the proposal. Make note of what aspects of the assignment are done well and what aspects could be done more effectively. The following are different types of comments one can give as an editor:

1. Give EVALUATIVE comments (e.g., "I like this first paragraph"; "You did a really good job describing the problem"; "The writing is really good"; "I didn't like the part where you talk about stakeholders.").
2. Give DESCRIPTIVE comments (e.g., "I was confused in the first paragraph"; "After reading your account of the problem, I don't feel convinced it's that big a problem"; "One suggestion would be to discuss how the problem specifically affects people's lives."). Descriptive comments

are more effective in pointing out parts that need revision. Evaluative comments—both positive and negative—tend not to contribute much to a writer's specific sense of what to do. So, do your best to give your partner as many descriptive comments as possible.

Questions to Address in Your Peer Review

1. The introduction should summarize the problem by clearly identifying what the problem is, where and when it is taking place, and why it is important. How did they do this well, and where could they do this better?
2. The introduction should indicate what we can expect to read in the rest of the paper, similar to the way you introduce your presentations. How did they do this well, and where could they do this better?
3. Is it clear exactly what the problem is and where it exists?
4. Does the proposal discuss a particular case the team will be focusing on? Where is this done well, and where could it be done better?
5. It should be clear who is affected by this problem and how. Where is this done well, and where could it be done better?
6. Does the team discuss at least three different dimensions of the impacts of the problem (e.g., environmental, economic, political, technical, or other)? Where is this done well, and where could it be done better?
7. The proposal should discuss how various communities are affected by this problem differently than others. Where is this done well, and where could it be done better?
8. Does the team discuss at least three different dimensions of the causes of the problem (e.g., environmental, economic, political, technical, or other)? Which causes are clearly laid out, and which could use some further clarity and explanation?
9. Does the team state the goal of its project? Is the goal clearly linked to the problem laid out in the proposal? If not, how might it be improved?
10. Are you convinced this is indeed a serious problem that needs to be addressed?
11. Are the facts and claims about the problem and stakeholders backed up with properly cited evidence?

CONCEPT MAPPING TO EVALUATE PROGRESS ON MEETING PROJECT OBJECTIVES

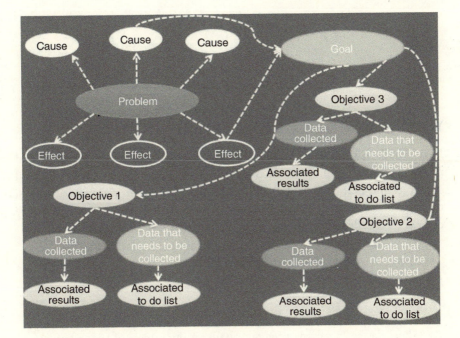

TEACHING COURSE CONTENT THROUGH SKILL BUILDING

Elisabeth A. Stoddard and Jill Rulfs

Why Teach Content Through Skill Building?

First, we discuss the value of integrating the teaching of course content and transferable skills in project-based and other courses. Second, we offer several strategies and examples of skill and content integration in the areas of values, teamwork, research, writing, presenting, and cultural awareness. Third, we discuss the challenges of integrating content and skill in courses.

Teaching Health Distribution Management and How to Analyze One's Own Values: A Story

> Everything I've been taught since kindergarten is a lie! Throughout grade school classes, I've always been told about the importance of fair and equal treatment of others, such as giving everyone a box to stand on. But while the treatment may be equal, the result is not. That is the main difference here between equality and equity—treatment vs. the result of treatment. When everybody is different, fairness and success also differ. Giving out the same portion, when people start on different levels of privilege, simply keeps the gap open.

As Jill was working her way through 60 student writing assignments, the opening sentence of this student reflection certainly caught her attention. This student was reacting to the image shown in Figure 10.1.

Figure 10.1 Equality versus equity.

Note. Interaction Institute for Social Change. Artist: Angus Maguire.

The assignment was to "study the image, share it with another student not in the class, and talk about your thoughts and his or hers after seeing the image. Then think about that interaction, revisit your reaction to the piece, and finally write a thoughtful reflection." In this class focused on issues in global health, Jill aimed to reinforce two of the course's specific learning outcomes: (a) articulate problems from the perspectives of diverse stakeholders and (b) explain some of the complexities of solving problems on a global scale. Because the course content focused on issues of both biology and management, it was important for students to think about the concept of equity in designing concrete aspects of their projects, such as health distribution criteria and delivery management of health-related services and supplies.

This assignment is an example of an opportunity to have students learn course content, while simultaneously developing skills that they will need to be successful in their college and professional careers. Our first-year project-based courses have several skill-based learning outcomes. These include teamwork, research, evidence-based writing, presenting, approach to problems, cultural awareness, and values. This assignment enabled students to engage in the "values" learning outcome—asking students to evaluate, articulate, and critically analyze their own values as they relate to the great problem the course is focused on. While the assignment fostered the development of this skill, it also laid the groundwork for using more specific disciplinary content around health distribution and health management to reinforce the product of that reflection.

This student's response made it clear that he had, indeed, taken stock of his values and reflected on and even rethought his ingrained understanding of fairness and equality. Not all students reach this level of personal insight or reflective thinking. As first-year students, many of them wrote formulaic essays, likely meant to showcase their fund of knowledge, focusing on communism or socialism or the tax code. But often they can be redirected to focus on the concepts of equity and equality when applied to a concrete, discipline-based example. In this case, the student's reaction to the picture became important again when he was working on some very practical aspects of his project, which required the management of supply chains and inventories, as well as a determination of how to best distribute the resources at hand. The very practical aspects of developing a resource management scheme (how many, how often, how much) became much more nuanced in light of the concept of equity and attaining the desired outcomes of the plan. Thus, understanding and articulating one's values (or perhaps those of a company or corporation) gained importance beyond the realm of personal philosophy. It became something that could have an impact on business decisions.

The Importance of Integrating Content With Skill Building

Accreditation and quality assurance agencies in the United States, in the United Kingdom, and elsewhere have identified a number of transferable skills that they see as essential to develop in higher education. These include oral and written communication, teamwork, research skills, ethics and values, critical thinking, recognition and valuing of diversity, global and multicultural competency, and the ability to apply knowledge in real-world settings in order to assess and solve problems (Fallows & Steven, 2000; Hart Research Associates, 2015). The development of these skills is seen as critical for today's college graduates in a world where long-term careers and lifetime job positions are no longer the norm.

Graduates today will likely have multiple jobs in different sectors and positions throughout their lifetime and therefore need skills that are directly transferable to a wide range of employment opportunities (Fallows & Steven, 2000; Hart Research Associates, 2015). As a result, universities need to provide their students with transferable skills and applied learning experiences that will enable them to be flexible, to be prepared to work on a global stage, and to solve problems with colleagues and clients who have views and backgrounds different from their own (Hart Research Associates, 2015).

There are generally the following approaches to teaching skills to undergraduate students: (a) embedding and integrating skill development within course content and throughout the university curriculum and (b) providing a skills course apart from specific course content, where students focus entirely on learning and practicing a broad list of skills in one or more classes (Durkin & Main, 2002; Fallows & Steven, 2000). While both approaches have benefits, research has shown that teaching skills divorced from content is not as effective as integrating the two.

Teaching skills apart from content is problematic, as it does not enable students to deeply engage with the process of learning, where they create, analyze, critique, develop, and share knowledge with others (Wingate, 2006). Students who understand the process of learning, creating, and sharing knowledge have developed a lifelong transferable skill, which will allow them to be flexible in the workplace and valuable in multiple fields (Fallows & Steven, 2000; Wingate, 2006). Research has also shown that students benefit from the *experience* of using skills (writing, presenting, teamwork) in the context of a course, where they are engaged with complex and challenging content in a high-stakes scenario (Wingate, 2006; Wingate, Andon, & Cogo, 2011). When skills are taught in multiple courses across the curriculum, students benefit from regular and repeated experiences using and developing a wide range of skills (Fallows & Steven, 2000).

We have found that our students recognize the benefits of these skills and value the opportunity to improve on them, while learning content at the same time. The following are some student responses to the midterm course evaluation question ("Identify one or two specific things you like about this course.") in a course that integrates skill building with content:

> I really enjoy working on group projects. I've learned a lot about researching and presenting in addition to the material.

> I like how it's teaching me how to effectively work in teams, teaching me to be a better presenter, and learning about interesting topics.

How to Integrate the Teaching of Content With the Teaching of Skill

In this section, we provide strategies and examples of how to integrate the teaching of content with the following skills: teamwork, research, writing, presenting, and cultural awareness. Teaching first-year students skill and content through projects with open-ended problems can create some anxiety for our students who are often used to multiple-choice tests or problem sets with predetermined answers. Therefore, as you will see, we provide a fair amount of support and structure to facilitate and document student learning of skill and content. We find that structure and support can also be helpful for faculty who are just getting into PBL and skill-content integration. For those of you who are trying this for the first time, we were once in your position. All of the strategies and examples shared here began through trial and error, and they were implemented piece by piece, year by year, each time we taught the course. This gradual approach can help faculty work on PBL and skill-content integration one assignment and content area at a time, without having to begin with a complete course overhaul.

Integrating Teamwork With Course Content

Teamwork is one of the transferable skills considered essential to develop in higher education (Hart Research Associates, 2015). The ability to effectively work on a team is considered a critical skill by all employers, and research has shown that student learning can increase significantly when students work effectively on a team. However, we also know from experience and research that student experiences on teams are often negative, and their learning can suffer as a result (Meadows, Sekaquaptewa, & Paretti, 2015; Wolfe, Powell, Schlisserman, & Kirshon, 2016). Therefore, it is critical for students to know how to work effectively in a team and what effective teamwork looks like.

Because our students are often dubious about time spent in and out of class on teamwork and prefer to just start their project, we assign brief readings documenting the value of learning to work effectively on a team in terms of learning outcomes, product outcomes, and employability. We have found that providing these data gives credibility and weight to the time and energy spent on developing good teamwork skills.

At the start of a team-based assignment, we provide our students with some team management tools. We ask each team member to create an asset map, which details the strengths, skills, and experiences that might be relevant to the project. Asset maps allow students to think through what they have to offer the team and the project, help members get to know each other, and allow the team to assign work based on areas of members' skills, interests, or areas they want to develop (see chapter 11 for details on asset mapping and equitable team dynamics). Students bring this map to class for their first meeting with their team members.

At this first in-class team meeting, we discuss two other team management tools: a team charter and a task schedule. A team charter is a brief contract that states the team's goals and individual members' goals and describes how the team will handle conflict, missed deadlines, or poor-quality work

(Wolfe, 2010). A task schedule helps a team delegate project tasks and stay on schedule by detailing who is in charge of which tasks, when each task is due, and the contribution value of the task (Wolfe, 2010). We give teams 15 to 30 minutes in class to introduce themselves, discuss their assets, and begin drafting their team charter. Their charters and task schedules are later submitted for a grade and faculty feedback. Following Wolfe (2010), we also ask teams to identify a team manager, a student who will remind the team members about deadlines and keep meeting minutes, prepare meeting agendas, and facilitate team meetings.

Wolfe (2010) created team charter and task schedule templates for students to use. (See Appendix 10.1 for a sample team charter and task schedule created by WPI students.) In chapter 11, Pfeifer and Stoddard provide additional recommendations for team management tools and roles to increase equity and reduce issues associated with bias and stereotyping on student teams.

We also discuss styles of team collaboration: "face-to-face" (students work together in person), "divided" (students work separately), and "layered" (students take turns working on the document, adding their expertise in "layers") (Wolfe, 2010). Drawing on Wolfe (2010), we detail which approach is most effective at each stage of the project. For example, face-to-face meetings are ideal for brainstorming and drafting plans. A divided approach can be useful for drafting sections after students have brainstormed together to generate a plan. A layered approach can be helpful when editing and revising each other's sections and the entire document.

After the completion of the project, we assign a critical reflection, where we ask students to think through their teamwork experience. The goal here is for students to document their learning on (a) their own role on the team, (b) how and when the team was effective and ineffective and why, (c) what the individual student could've done better as a team member, and (d) what the team could've done better as a collective. Research has shown that this kind of processing helps solidify and deepen learning (Ash & Clayton, 2009).

In student reflections, as well as in course and assignment evaluations, we found that even the most dubious and resistant students found these teamwork strategies and tools useful:

> I was annoyed that we had to create a task schedule because it felt like busy work. But having to stick to the schedule we created meant I couldn't procrastinate until the last minute, which was actually nice.

> I like to be in control on group projects. Because of the designated roles, I couldn't be in control as much as I would like to. I had to actually trust

that others would get their work done and do a good job. This made me anxious, but my team all did their parts on time and did a good job. Once I could let go of wanting to do it all myself, it was actually fun and interesting to work with others on this.

Integrating Research With Course Content

One of the learning outcomes for all of our project-based first-year courses is for students to be able to find a diversity of credible sources, assess their claims and relevance, and use them appropriately. We have found this to be more challenging for our first-year students than we had anticipated. Therefore, we have developed a number of assignments that teach both content and research skills. In student assessments, students report making the greatest gains in this learning outcome and often note that learning how to conduct research was the most valuable skill attained in this course. We provide two examples of integrating research skills with course content.

Teaching the Zika Virus and How to Find, Cite, and Evaluate Credible Research Sources

As we teach research skills, we have a wonderful opportunity to help students discover, evaluate, and reinforce content knowledge. Perhaps because they can type with their thumbs on tiny phone keyboards better and faster than we can with 10 fingers on our full-size computer keyboards, we often make the erroneous assumption that they are equally good at using technology-based resources for finding credible information. We have discovered that although nearly all of our first-year students reported having done research assignments in high school, many of them have no idea what a database is and how it differs from a publisher or a journal. We often get citations for articles identified as having been published by JSTOR or PubMed.

To address this issue, the librarian who was part of our instructional team came to class with hard copies of bound journals, textbooks, trade journals, newspapers, and magazines. She had identified articles in each for teams of students to read and worksheets for them to complete (see chapter 7). To follow that up and tie it directly to course content, Jill assigns students individually to use different databases to complete the following assignment:

Each of you has been assigned a database or search engine with which you should work. Use the simple search term "Zika virus." Copy and paste the first five returns from your search. From these, select one, retrieve it, and read it. Answer the following questions:

1. Which of the five did you choose and why?

2. What is the source? Indicate the name of the source and what type of publication it is; for example, the *Wall Street Journal* (a business-focused daily newspaper) or *The Journal of Infectious Diseases* (a peer-reviewed journal that publishes reports of original research on infectious diseases, the official publication of the Infectious Diseases Society of America).

3. Briefly, what is the subject of the article? Please be more specific than "the Zika virus." Is it a policy recommendation about how to combat a global Zika epidemic? Is it a research report regarding the link between the virus and microcephaly? Is it a World Health Organization directive for physicians? If it is a very long or very technical article, you may be able to get this information by reading the abstract or executive summary.

The databases the students were assigned (e.g., JSTOR, ERIC, PubMed, the *Wall Street Journal, The Economist*) would return a variety of types of information. After completing the assignment individually, students convened in groups of increasing size (two, then four, then eight) and ascertained how many different, and different types of, sources they had identified and what kinds of information each had. After several rounds of this, using the whiteboard in the classroom, we constructed a table of the databases, the types of articles they returned (peer review, op-ed, research reports, academic theses, etc.), and the kinds of information (educational research, policy assessment, event analysis) one might look for using this particular database or search engine.

Because Jill controls the precise search term that all students used, each student added to his or her content knowledge about the Zika virus and its impact from at least one source. Because these students eventually worked in teams on other assignments related to the same topic, they also had the opportunity to share their knowledge and gain knowledge from other students related to the impact of Zika on global health from biologic- and management-related perspectives.

Teaching Water Pollution and How to Conduct and Analyze Research as a Team

In a seven-week project on water pollution and other water problems, one way we teach students about the research process is by having them keep a research or source analysis notebook. For each notebook entry, students are required to find two peer-reviewed journal articles and respond to questions on their research strategy, the key arguments and evidence in the articles, and the articles' significance for the project.

Prior to assigning each notebook entry, the teams meet in class to coordinate their research efforts. They decide who will research what and what research objectives will be met as a result. (See Appendix 10.2 for the guide sheet we provide our students with to facilitate this process.) We have found that if we don't provide time in the classroom to do this, students (a) don't realize they should be coordinating their research activities and (b) don't know what others are researching and so may be duplicating efforts or taking the research in different directions.

After the teams have submitted their notebook entry, they meet in class to discuss the outcome of their research efforts. Each student briefly summarizes the articles and supporting evidence, discusses what objectives were met (or not met), and tells how he or she sees this research shaping the direction of the project. They collectively discuss any problems with research and the direction of the project (and any relevant problems); create, revise, and/or update any task schedules; and discuss how the team is functioning. This is supported by a guide sheet (found in Appendix 10.3).

After the group discussion, we ask the students to add two more pieces of information to their notebook: what they see as next steps in meeting each of the project objectives, and what they see as major gaps in their understanding. We ask for thoughts on how to start to fill these gaps, to list particular struggles with the research or the project, and to provide a plan for how to tackle these. When this second piece is submitted, the assignment is graded, and the students are given feedback. (The research notebook assignment is found in Appendix 10.4.)

Having students plan, document, and reflect on the research process teaches them, through practice, that their research objective is the organizing force that drives their research. It requires them to think through their research strategy—what search engines and keywords were used and why—instead of just Googling or choosing databases at random. It helps them concisely summarize articles in their own words, supporting claims with evidence in their own and in others' work. It also pushes them to think about the role of one study or piece of research in the broader context of the project.

Integrating Writing With Course Content

Among the many aspects of writing students need to learn and practice is evidence-based writing. As the scientist in her instructional team, Jill is constantly asking students to "show me the data." It becomes a bit of a standing joke among the members of the class, but it feeds right into teaching evidence-based writing and the need to identify and critically evaluate evidence before reaching conclusions. Jill's instructional team partner is a professor of management—in particular, organizational behavior—and introduces students to evaluating the value proposition of an idea or innovation using the NABC approach (Carlson & Wilmot, 2006), where N stands for *need*, A for *approach*, B for *benefit*, and C for *competition*. While this is a business model, we have easily adapted it for use in helping students assess their proposed project.

In an early writing assignment, we ask each student to identify a problem in global health that she or he would like to use as a basis for the project. While their original inclination often is to focus on an approach—what they'd like to *do* rather than the problem they are trying to address—this assignment makes them focus squarely on the *need*, as the model intends. Having identified a need, they must write a one-page persuasive piece, identifying the problem they have articulated and providing evidence that it is indeed a problem in need of a solution rather than the other way around. This requires that they do research to find the evidence and, as they are problems in global health, often requires students to begin to master vocabulary related to problems in health, such as *morbidity*, *mortality*, *incidence rate*, and *prevalence*. The assignment also requires that they use and properly identify credible sources for their evidence. But the emphasis of what follows is on writing. Students are asked to bring two copies of their assignment to class: one to turn in and one for peer review. Then, in class, each student is given the paper of another student and a set of colored highlighters. After reading the paper they have been assigned, students are asked to highlight the problem statement in green. Using different colors, they highlight each piece of evidence that supports the claim, each in-text citation, and the overall conclusion the author reached. The effect is very visual and very immediate.

Reader response or peer review has been shown to be beneficial to both the original author and the reviewer (Van den Berg, Admiraal, & Pilot, 2006), and the exercise has been described and can be designed in a number of ways: identify accurate and questionable interpretations of data, make assumptions with no supporting evidence, and so on (Brookfield, 2012). What we like about this writing skills approach is its visual impact.

Thus, this assignment integrates multiple skills with content. In terms of content, it reinforces the hypothesis generation and testing paradigm in a slightly different format, and it exposes the peer reviewer to a second problem in global health. A management tool is used as the foundation for the assignment. In terms of skill development, research is embedded in the preparation. And, finally, the practice of identifying the components of a good, evidence-based piece of writing has been reinforced through the physical act of highlighting.

Integrating Presentation Skills With Course Content

In this section we discuss two dimensions of presenting: oral and visual. Being prepared to deliver engaging oral materials effectively requires different skill sets than being prepared to deliver engaging visual materials. But to be effective, either or both must begin with a clear understanding of the message to be delivered.

Teaching the Zika Virus and Effective Visual Presentations

Our students, who are digital natives, often arrive on campus with experience using a variety of presentation software packages (e.g., Prezi, Keynote, SlideShark) that include lots of bells-and-whistles. While these can be used to create effective visual presentations, too much emphasis on the technology affordances can obscure the clarity of the message.

One of the tenets of Edward Tufte's work is that content counts most of all (Tufte, 2006). Translated, it means that a presentation stands or falls based on the quality and relevance of the content. Thus, any information that does not directly contribute to the message should be omitted. This "less is more" message is one of the most difficult to convey to many students who may have been rewarded for the volume of information they include in assignments and feel as though quantity is a measure of value.

That said, presentation is perhaps one of the easier skills to integrate with disciplinary content, because the content of the presentation can be based in any discipline, and the skills needed to make an effective presentation—oral or visual—apply broadly across disciplines. We are lucky to have a teaching and learning team in our academic technology center who will come into the classroom and conduct workshops focused on making effective presentations. The team will also review and critique student presentations. Introducing students to the resource early in their college careers makes it more likely they will continue to hone their presentation skills across other courses and projects. However, absent this resource, a variety of resources are available online that can provide guidelines and even presentations that can be used in the classroom (e.g., Bourne, 2007; Erren & Bourne, 2007).

Jill uses an infographic assignment to focus specifically on the visual presentation of information. Every year Jill has taught this course, we have (unfortunately) faced some global health issue that provides fodder for this exercise. Most recently, it was the Zika outbreak (think about it—Ebola, SARS, avian flu, AIDS; the list is seemingly endless). Each student team (three to five students) was given an article to read. The workshop on designing and making their infographic began with simply deciding what story their infographic was to convey. Putting the focus on the information first (decide on the data) gave them a framework for reading the article and actually learning about some aspect of Zika (symptoms, viral infection, sequelae, etc.). Thus, content was put ahead of design.

Again, students often begin with what they know and what they are comfortable with—the technology. Here, working with the Academic Technology Center (ATC) member of the instructional team, we reinforced the concept that content or information must come first. Only after this was completed were students allowed to move on to design. For both aspects of the project, message and design, the overriding theme was "Simplify!" Once the message was defined, design work focused on layout, creating graphs and charts, and eventually on specifics of color, font selection and size, and visual balance. Students were provided with lots of resources, such as the color-emotion guide (yellow conveys optimism, clarity, and warmth; blue conveys trust, dependability, and strength) but are given creative latitude (The Logo Company, 2017). They were also provided with a simple-to-use software program called Piktochart. The final test was to answer the question "Was it effective?" To do that we used peer review. Students were given infographics from another team, with all identifying information redacted, and were asked to score the product on a scale of 1 to 5, using the following questions:

- Is the story clear and easy to understand?
- Are there data to support the message?
- Is the visual balance consistent with the emphasis of the message?
- Is it visually attractive (color and design)?
- Is it easy to read (size and distribution of text and graphics)?
- Is it effective?

Students were also encouraged to provide open-ended comments for improvement. The scores and the comments for each infographic were combined and returned anonymously to the team that produced it. Because each team had a different article, this again gave students an opportunity to gain information about the Zika outbreak that was not the subject of their assigned article.

In final course evaluations, a number of students commented on this particular assignment as one they both enjoyed and learned a lot from. One student said, "When I went to do my final poster, I felt confident that I knew where to begin."

Teaching Water Technology and Effective Oral–Visual Presentations

In "The World's Water," students learn about various water technologies and about how to give an engaging and effective oral–visual presentation by researching, preparing, and presenting material on water technologies. In oral–visual presentations (e.g., PowerPoint, Prezi, or PechaKucha), students have to work to develop a presentation where the visual presentation supports the oral presentation and vice versa. The images or words on the screen cannot distract the audience from the verbal narrative. For example, many students (and professors) will put bulleted lists, quotes, or even paragraphs on slides. While these words are in view, the presenter will often continue with a verbal narrative that does not match the words on the slide, forcing viewers to read *or* listen or be too distracted to do either. Students (and professors) sometimes put unlabeled images or figures on a screen (e.g., a graph without a title or legend, or an image of a person or scene without a caption). Again, while these images are in view, the presenter will often continue with a verbal narrative without explaining what these images are or how they are connected to the verbal narrative. As a result, viewers can be distracted by trying to understand how the image is connected to what they are hearing.

On the day we assign the water technologies presentation assignment, we invite a staff member from the ATC to explain how to give an effective oral–visual presentation. He or she provides students with guidance as follows: (a) the importance of creating a written outline of the narrative for the presentation *before* drafting the slides, (b) the importance of identifying the clear takeaway message of the presentation (what should the audience walk out of the room remembering?), (c) how to *emotionally* engage your audience (research has shown that an effective presentation engages the audience emotionally every three to five minutes), (d) how to tailor the presentation to specific audiences (i.e., what can you assume they know or don't know?), (e) the ideal image-to-word ratio on slides, and (f) examples of effective and ineffective graphs and other visual aids.

We have half of the teams present on one day and half present on another day. This allows for peer-to-peer feedback and mentoring. After the first round of presentations, the teams who presented get peer feedback from the teams who did not present, using a peer feedback guide sheet. Next, the teams who presented mentor the teams who have not yet presented, using a mentoring guide and by drawing on their experiences of what worked and what did not in preparing for and giving their presentation. On the second day, students receive peer feedback in the same format. However, because the second group does not have the opportunity to mentor another set of teams who will be presenting after them, we ask them to collectively write up a page of advice for next year's students.

Providing peer evaluation has the following major benefits: (a) Research has shown that students are often more motivated to impress their peers than their faculty, creating pressure for students to perform at a higher level (Hanrahan & Isaacs, 2001), and (b) research has shown that peer evaluators learn to better assess and critically analyze their own work by evaluating the work of their peers and others (Lundstrom & Baker, 2009). The opportunity for students to mentor one another as peers allows students to develop trust and deepen relationships as students, friends, and colleagues, which leads to the creation of a supportive community of learning in and outside of the classroom (Colvin & Ashman, 2010).

Integrating Cultural Awareness With Course Content

Our learning outcome focused on cultural awareness aims for students to be able to articulate the differences in experiences of a "great problem" for various stakeholders, across nationality, gender, race, ethnicity, class, and other identities. In this section, we discuss a course activity we have used to help students develop the skill of thinking through and articulating the different ways people experience great problems, like unequal access to environmental goods (e.g., clean water or clean air).

Teaching Wetland Conservation, Environmental Justice, and Cultural Awareness

The National Center for Case Study Teaching in Science at the University at Buffalo has an amazing reservoir of case studies and supporting materials available to teachers at all levels (sciencecases.lib.buffalo.edu/cs/). Elizabeth A. Stoddard used one of the case studies, "First in Flight, Last in Wetlands Preservation?" to teach her students content on wetland conservation and environmental justice, as well as the importance of thinking through a case from the perspective of multiple stakeholders.

Before engaging with the case study in class, we introduce our students to information and concepts around wetland ecology and conservation; we also introduce them to the issue of environmental injustice and relevant concepts. *Environmental injustice* and *environmental racism* are terms used to describe the fact that low-income communities and communities of color are disproportionately affected by environmental harms and pollutants as compared to wealthier, Whiter communities. This is a result of a lack of socioeconomic and political power in these communities, as well as classist and racist siting practices, environmental policies, regulations, and enforcement (or lack thereof) (Westra & Lawson, 2001). These concepts, and the discussion of them, provide our students with the knowledge and conceptual tools to think about how problems like pollution are experienced differently by different groups of people.

The students come to class equipped with the concepts and background to engage with the case study. This case looks at issues associated with land development and wetland loss from the perspectives of multiple stakeholders, including an EPA officer concerned with adhering to EPA procedures, a businessperson concerned with economic development, an ecologist concerned with wetland preservation, and a person concerned with preventing urban sprawl (Petersen & London, 2003). We add a fifth stakeholder, an environmental justice organization concerned with the environmental harms and associated health impacts of building and operating an airport next to the low-income minority neighborhood it represents.

Students are divided into stakeholder groups to talk about the issues they face as stakeholders and their goals (e.g., stop the development of the airport or modify the proposed plans). The students are then reassembled into groups of five, with one representative from each stakeholder group. These multistakeholder groups write a position paper on whether the airport should be built and, if so, under what conditions. Then, as a class, we do some processing around the various stakeholder perspectives, the impact the decisions will have on various stakeholder groups, how stakeholders experience the same environment differently, and the impact of this, as well the challenges and benefits associated with taking everyone's issues into account.

As students use the concepts around wetland ecology and environmental injustice in context, student learning of the content deepens (Ambrose et al., 2010). By having the students engage in an activity that forces them to analyze the issue from the perspective of multiple stakeholders, we give them the opportunity to practice thinking through the differences in experiences of this "great problem" for various stakeholders across race, class, and other identities and interests and the impacts of these differing experiences.

Challenges to Integrating Skills and Content

Incorporating the teaching, development, and building of skills into our classes takes a fair amount of time and thought—time and thought we have traditionally put into the teaching of content. However, experts on the teaching and learning of high-impact practices tell us that to be good practitioners of the art, we must do this.

In a post titled "Stop Assigning Team Projects . . . Unless . . ." on the Lilly Conference blog The Scholarly Teacher, Erik Eddy and Caroline D'Abate (2016) wrote,

Teamwork is here to stay. It is important for faculty to realize, though, that it isn't enough to simply place individuals together and call them a team. We must provide our students with education and ongoing support as they build the skills necessary to be successful in a team context.

Likely you could substitute any of the other specific skills we have identified—communication, evidence-based decision-making, cultural awareness—into that text and have it be just as valid. The skills required of the twenty-first-century college graduate go far beyond disciplinary content. One might argue that with the speed at which information is being amassed and evaluated in many fields, the value in disciplinary knowledge is in the application of skills—such as teamwork, critical thinking, decision-making, and communication—rather than in some of the more traditional definitions that compose learning in a discipline.

What is clear from our experience is that this approach requires us as teachers to redefine some of our long-held approaches to teaching and shift the emphasis in the classroom to accommodate the time and effort needed to provide the education and support referred to by Eddy and D'Abate (2016). Even students, often coming from a more content-focused system, driven by content-rich, high-stakes testing, may have significant adjustments to make. Students in Jill's class occasionally say, "I wish I had learned more biology." Her response is to ask what had prevented them from doing so. It is her way of reminding them that in a problem-based approach to learning, the questions to be asked and answered are not only "What do I know?" but also "What do I need to know?" and "How can I best do that?"

Biology content learned in a meaningful context will be more valuable, and likely more retained, than that learned in a content for content's sake context. The faculty as well as the students must be willing to shift the emphasis, particularly in the classroom. The flipped classroom approach can be particularly helpful here. Given we have only so much time to teach both skill and content, moving some aspects outside the classroom makes room for other things that may need more careful guidance.

From an institutional point of view, this can lead to some concern about disciplinary credit. In institutions with general education requirements, perhaps this is more easily accommodated than it is at our institution. Especially, more traditional faculty have voiced concerns about whether the students in these courses are learning what they need to know to go on to the next course in the disciplinary curriculum. These concerns are not easily addressed, but our assessment of the success of students who have taken these courses suggests it is not a significant concern. However, each institution may have to address this for itself, A careful analysis of the critical content knowledge required for success is a good place to start in developing learning outcomes for each course. In the early days of offering these courses at our institution, our dean made a list of the learning outcomes we had agreed on for all of the GPS courses and asked individual department heads which of these they wanted their students to gain mastery in. Of course, almost everyone agreed they were all valuable skills across all majors. While that does not, and did not, stop the skeptics from being critical, it no doubt won some people over to our side.

Conclusion

Clearly, the people contributing to this book are advocates of the cause, and the teaching of skills and content is integral to its success. So, it is not surprising that at the conclusion of this chapter, our message is not only that it can be done but also that it can be remarkably effective. In a course evaluation, one student explained,

> The whole experience was invaluable to me. My presentation, research, and teamwork skills improved immensely. More important, I learned how to think in different ways. I had to think of a system even when focusing on a certain aspect in that system. . . . That one class was invaluable to opening my eyes to the possibilities of new knowledge just from the way in which research is conducted or seeing things in a different perspective.

We recommend that faculty begin with clearly defining the learning outcomes, both general and disciplinary specific, and then find, discover, or invent ways to combine them. Don't be afraid to give up "content" time in the classroom. With the easy availability of online content delivery (YouTube, Khan Academy, eBooks), not to mention such traditional tools as textbooks, moving some of the foundational content acquisition outside the classroom can free up time to focus on applications and skills during face-to-face meeting time. And more than being effective—and sometimes challenging—it can be fun and invigorating to find new ways to support student learning. Last, incorporating PBL and content–skill integration does not have to be done through a course overhaul. Start with one assignment, one lecture, or one activity. Use the suggestions in the following section to consider how you might get started.

Try This

1. Choose one particular course to think about. What transferable skills do you want your students to develop in this course?
2. How might you modify one of your existing assignments or activities to give your students an opportunity to explicitly and intentionally develop one or more of these transferable skills?
3. What new assignment might you develop in this course to give your students an opportunity to explicitly and intentionally develop one or more of these transferable skills?

EXAMPLE TEAM EQUITY CHARTER

Note. Student names have been changed to protect identity.

Team Member Roles

Team Manager: Eliza
Team Facilitator: Jose
Production Manager: Suvi
Facilitator: Malik

Team Goals

Broad

- Maintain an environment in which everyone can contribute
- Understand, keep in mind each other's assets
- General support in all areas

Time-Specific Goals

- Have all work done at least 12 hours in advance of deadline
- Meet all project requirements
- Have practiced the whole presentation before the due date

Team Member Assets and Personal Goals

- *Eliza:* Some of my assets include creativity and my presentation skills. My main personal goal is to become more punctual.
- *Jose:* My assets include presentation skills, leadership skills, and good research skills. My personal goal is to become a better writer.
- *Suvi:* I think that some of my assets are my creativity and my organizational skills. I hope that through this project I can become a better researcher.

- *Malik:* I believe I provide valuable leadership that isn't too overpowering and well-developed writing skills. I am a confident presenter when I know what I am talking about. I hope to become more receptive to others' ideas and be considerate of different project approaches.

Communication and Stability Rules

- Reply to the GroupMe (in a timely manner)
- Let others talk, don't interrupt, make sure everyone is heard
- Be engaged, minimal phone time
- Make meeting times a priority, don't bail last minute
- Stay on task, be productive in time allotted

Conflict Resolution

- No texting, no phone, no e-mail when resolving situations
- See it as a way to step back and reevaluate the process
- Follow rules for communication and stability (and there shouldn't be a conflict)
- No one comes out on top, make it an equal playing field

Missed Deadlines

- A member who misses a deadline is responsible for contacting the professor and reaching a solution that won't negatively affect the other members.
- Ask for help if a deadline is creeping up too fast.

Unacceptable Work

- Peer review should help prevent this.
- If you realize you need to take a shortcut, ask for help instead.
- Communicate if a standard is not met where a member does not see using specific feedback.

Team Member Contributions

- Eliza: 26
- Malik: 25
- Jose: 25
- Suvi: 26

Sample Task Schedule

Deadline	Task	Assigned to	Contribution Value (Lowest 1–5 Highest)	Type of Task	Status
9/18	Finish equity charter	Collective	3	Organizational, writing	Complete
9/18	Finish equitable task schedule	Collective	3	Organizational	Complete
9/18	Annotated bibliography, two sources	Each member	5	Research, writing	
9/19	Open Piktochart account and e-mail everyone with access information	Malik	2	Supporting, organizational	
9/19	Review infographic tools and techniques and sketch draft of sections	Jose and Eliza	5	Lead, technical	
9/20	Write up background section content and sketch this section on infographic	Jose	4	Lead, writing, production, technical	
9/20	Write up Egypt case study content	Eliza	4	Lead, writing, production, technical	
9/20	Write up Singapore case study content	Suvi	4	Lead, writing, production, technical	
9/20	Write up filtration process and technology content	Malik	4	Lead, writing, production, technical	
9/21	Meet to get feedback on draft	Collective	3	Supporting	
9/21	Incorporate feedback into draft	Malik and Suvi	5	Lead, production, technical	
9/22	Final aesthetic touches	Eliza and Suvi	3	Supporting, production, technical	
9/23	Upload assignment to ePortfolio site and to Canvas; make sure can open in correct formats for presentation	Jose	2	Supporting, organizational	

*Eliza and Suvi have an extra point because of the final aesthetic touches. Malik and Jose have an exam on 9/23 and Eliza and Suvi do not. So, they volunteered to take on this work.

STUDENT GUIDE FOR ALLOCATING GROUP RESEARCH TASKS

FY1100 Great Problems Seminar: The World's Water

Professor Elisabeth Stoddard and Professor Derren Rosbach

Worcester Polytechnic Institute

Student Guide Sheet: Team Meeting to Plan for Team and Individual Research for the Research Notebook Assignment

Use the following questions to guide your discussion and planning around who will be researching what for their research notebook assignment to help you meet which research objectives:

1. What research objectives have not yet been met?
2. What questions or topics within these objectives need attention first, and why?
3. Come up with a strategy that will allow you to begin to meet one or more of these objectives and answer some of these questions. Decide who among your team will work on which objectives, questions, and topics for this research notebook assignment.

STUDENT GUIDE FOR MID-PROJECT GROUP DISCUSSION ON RESEARCH PROGRESS

FY1100 Great Problems Seminar: The World's Water

Professor Elisabeth Stoddard and Professor Derren Rosbach

Worcester Polytechnic Institute

Student Guide Sheet: Team Meeting to Discuss Research Found for Research Notebook Assignment

Use the following questions to guide your discussion of what each of you found for Part A of your research notebook and how this shapes the next steps of your team's research. Each team member should take turns answering and discussing the following questions and topics with each other.

1. Summarize the articles you read, only the main points that are relevant to your research.
2. Did what you learned help you toward meeting any of the project objectives? Explain. Did it answer any specific questions the group had? Explain.
3. How might what you found shape the direction of your team's research and project? What new questions do you have? What are the relevant next steps?

SAMPLE RESEARCH NOTEBOOK ASSIGNMENT

FY1100 Great Problems Seminar: The World's Water

Professor Elisabeth Stoddard and Professor Derren Rosbach

Worcester Polytechnic Institute

Research Notebook Assignment

As research is a key activity of much of college work, it is helpful to develop a methodology around doing it that will be adaptable to other situations. To help develop that methodology, we are asking you to follow this guide as you find two articles that will be useful for your project.

There are two parts to this assignment. You will complete Part A before class by [DUE DATE HERE]. You will complete Part B after you meet with your team in class on [DATE HERE]. You will submit Parts A and B together by [DUE DATE HERE].

Part A

Each research notebook entry will consist of three sections.

1. *Research log (20 points):* Record your research activities.
   a. What were the specific project objective(s) that guided your research?
   b. What database or search engine did you use?
   c. What search terms did you use?
2. *Reading notes (40 points):*
   a. Provide a citation in APA format for at least two sources you found useful. One must be from a peer-reviewed scholarly journal; the other could be from a technical or professional report, newspaper, magazine, or website that passes the CRAP test. If in doubt, ask your PLAs, professors, or class librarian.

    b. Beneath each citation, provide two to five sentences describing the useful information found in these sources.

3. *Research reflection (40 points):* Briefly answer the following questions:

    a. In what ways is the information you read related to your topic, project goal, and/or particular objective?

    b. What did you learn that was new or surprising or that contradicted or confirmed your previous thoughts or knowledge?

    c. What new questions were raised while reading these sources and thinking about your project?

    d. How will the information you learned shape your next steps in the project?

Part B

Answer the following questions after meeting with your team on [DATE HERE]:

1. After learning about the collective research of the group, what do you see as the next steps in meeting each of the project objectives?
2. What do you see as the major gaps in your team's understanding?
3. What are your thoughts on how to begin filling these gaps?
4. Are there particular struggles with the research or the project?
5. Do you have a plan for tackling these struggles? Would you like our help or input?

EQUITABLE AND EFFECTIVE STUDENT TEAMS

Creating and Managing Team Dynamics for Equitable Learning Outcomes

Geoff Pfeifer and Elisabeth A. Stoddard

We, and many of you reading this book, are bringing PBL into our classrooms and even integrating it across our university curriculum. As a result of this exciting shift in higher education, we are requiring our students to work in teams on a more regular basis. Many universities are also working to increase access to higher education to typically underserved populations, such as low-income communities, first-generation college students, and students of color (Wolniak, Flores, & Kemple, 2016). As such, student teams are becoming increasingly diverse.

Why Do We Need to Teach Equity in Teamwork?

Learning and working on diverse teams has multiple benefits for students and (future) employees, including the ability to take more risks, enhanced creativity and innovation, work that is more fun and purposeful, and projects that are more successful (Rock & Grant, 2016). However, simply placing students on teams does not inherently result in these benefits; students need to be provided with the knowledge and resources to work effectively and equitably. Women and students of color are often marginalized in team settings as a result of unconscious bias (Meadows et al., 2015; Wolfe et al., 2016). This results in reduced learning opportunities for all students, with compounded harms to the self-efficacy and retention rates of female students, students of color, and other underserved populations—particularly in the STEM fields (Meadows et al., 2015; Wolfe et al., 2016).

Following is an excerpt from a first-generation student of color at WPI who was reflecting on her experience working on a project team. (All names in student quotes in this chapter have been changed to protect student identities.)

> Our group is very diverse but the some of the stereotypes we discussed in class were true. . . . Our group just had minor problems with two [White male students] talking too much, and two [female students of color] barely talking. . . . During one of the meetings with our PLA, only Karl and I were able to attend and we were telling our PLA about the progress of the project. I was very disappointed when our PLA would direct a question to me and Karl would answer every time. I was getting frustrated that I was not given the chance to answer the questions, which made me feel a little stupid because I was thinking if Karl thinks I don't know the answers to the questions or if there was something else. I learned from that meeting and I will make sure it never repeats, but that feeling of being looked down on did not feel great.

Research tells us that this student's experience is common. For example, Wolfe and colleagues (2016) found that most students have some negative experiences on teams, including having their ideas ignored or stolen, having their voices silenced, and/or being given project tasks seen as less intellectually challenging or valuable. However, female students and students of color experience these problems at disproportionate rates, with 23% of White male students, 37% of White female students, 41% male students of color, and 58% female students of color having the experience of being ignored, silenced, and/or presumed less capable (Wolfe et al., 2016).

In this chapter, we discuss some of the research that analyzes the issues and impacts of unconscious bias on student project teams. We offer several strategies and tools to (a) bring equity into the process of forming teams, (b) enable students to work with each other and manage their teams more equitably and effectively, and (c) bring what Bensimon (2007) terms *equity-mindedness* to faculty project advising. Equity-mindedness refers to understanding that part of the role of a faculty member is to be aware of and work to rectify patterns of inequality in student experience and learning outcomes as well as being race-conscious and aware of the ways that practices in higher education (including high-impact practices like PBL) have historically failed minoritized students (Felix, Bensimon, Hansen, Gray, & Klingsmith, 2015; Bensimon 2016). Finally, we discuss the challenges of bringing the conversation and practice of equity into teaching and advising project teams.

Why Do We Need Equity-Mindedness in Team-Based Learning and Teaching?

By 2020, more than half the children younger than the age of 18 are expected to be youth of color from multiple racial and ethnic backgrounds (Wazwaz, 2015). As a result, the combined population of Black, American Indian, Asian, Pacific Islander, and multi-racial, multi-ethnic groups in the United States is expected to rise from 33% to 56% of the total American population by 2060 (Wazwaz, 2015). Higher education institutions must prepare now for the shifting demographics that will shape student populations and their attendant needs in the coming decades. As our students enter a diverse work-force, they need to be prepared to work equitably and effectively with people who are different from them.

Recent studies have shown that diverse teams are better at solving problems and innovating, precisely because there is a diversity of perspectives and backgrounds that can be brought to bear on problems (Phillips, Liljenquist, & Neale, 2010; Rock & Grant, 2016). Team-based project work among diverse peers has been shown to have multiple benefits for problem-solving, for students in general, and for women, underrepresented, and underserved students in particular (Kuh, 2008). This includes an increase in learning opportunities, improved performance, and improved confidence (Wolfe et al., 2016). However, this assumes that the people working on those teams can take advantage of that diversity and are not hampered by bias and problems related to biases.

Collaborative learning on teams is challenging for students as they work to manage grade-dependent interpersonal relationships. This approach can also be challenging for faculty as they work to advise students not only on content but also on how to delegate roles and responsibilities, communicate and organize, and handle conflict. These problems are confounded by the fact that most students and faculty have never been given any formal training on how to work in or coach academic teams (Wolfe et al., 2016). Collaborative learning and teamwork can be particularly challenging for women and students of color, as research has shown that these students are often stereotyped as poor performers or underperformers, particularly in STEM fields. For example, Meadows and colleagues (2015) explained that these students can experience additional challenges in team-based learning, including task assignment biases, intellectual marginalization, and a lack of work recognition.

Task assignment biases occur when students assign themselves or others tasks based on unconscious biases regarding who is more or less capable of or suited for particular tasks. For example, Meadows and colleagues

(2015) found that female undergraduate students are more often assigned social and organizational tasks, stereotyped as "women's work," while male students take on more technical roles. This results in reduced learning opportunities for both male and female students, as women lose opportunities to learn and present technical content, and male students lack the opportunity to gain key communication and organizational skills necessary for effective teamwork critical in today's workplace (Meadows et al., 2015).

Intellectual marginalization refers to when students' ideas are ignored or not taken seriously (Meadows et al., 2015). Research has told us that women and students of color experience intellectual marginalization on project teams more frequently than their White male counterparts (Wolfe et al., 2016). A female student of color on a project team at WPI relayed her own experience having her ideas ignored or shut down:

> Even though I normally lead in group settings, in this group I often do not speak. I feel like every time I say something everyone, except Theresa, shuts my ideas down. Mike and John always take charge. They always call the shots. Through this group project I found out that I hate confrontation and I don't like disagreeing with others. I also hate not being heard. In order to fix this I will try to not be as intimated by Mike and John. I believe they do not ignore me intentionally so I should not be scared to speak up for what I believe even though I might be shut down.

Students who experience intellectual marginalization may experience a loss of confidence in their chosen field and, as a result, leave the program (Meadows et al., 2015).

A *lack of work recognition* refers to when students' contributions are not acknowledged, when credit for the work is stolen, or when individual credit is subsumed under the work accredited to the whole group (Meadows et al., 2015). A female student of color on a project team at WPI explained, "There were several incidences when either Grace or I would mention something during our meetings but we'd be ignored and one of the guys would say the same thing as we said and he gets the credit for it." Another female student on a project team reported that her voice is "swallowed" by those of her male teammates. Students who fail to get recognized for their hard-earned work often seek to avoid projects and other beneficial high-impact practices that their institutions have to offer as a result of their negative experiences on teams (McNair, 2017).

Research has shown that female students and students of color often put in more effort and volunteer for the harder tasks to prove themselves and overcome stereotypes (Meadows et al., 2015). A White female student on a project team at WPI explained,

I am also the only girl in the group, so I naturally feel like I have to pull my full weight on the project to prove that I am a very important group member. Because I am different from the rest of my group members gender-wise, this naturally motivates me to do more.

This pressure and need to work harder can lead students to self-select away from White- and male-dominated fields, like STEM fields (Meadows et al., 2015; Williams, Philips, & Hall, 2014). While White- and male-dominated STEM fields may experience issues of race and gender bias more acutely, problems of racism and sexism on student teams exist across all disciplines (Birmingham & McCord, 2002; Williams et al., 2014).

Most students who are marginalizing others in group settings are unaware of their actions or their impacts, as it is often the case that the biases that underlie this operate below the level of conscious actions and choices (Meadows et al., 2015). One White male student on a project team at WPI explained his surprise when he discovered that he might have unintentionally been acting in ways that caused others on his team to feel marginalized:

> Prior to our discussion about communication, I had assumed that Oona and Maria wouldn't participate in conversations because they had nothing to say. I was surprised when they told Oliver and me that they feel excluded from our conversations and often have things to say but don't say them. I felt awful about this because I never meant to exclude anyone. . . . Oliver and I would just get caught up in our debate over ideas.

As universities embrace high-impact practices, like PBL, and require students to work in teams, we must enable our students to work effectively and equitably in teams. In doing this, we as faculty must, as Bensimon (2007) argues, take an active role in understanding the ways that institutional racism, bias, and other forms of marginalization impact our students of color. Working toward equitable teamwork in project based learning is essential to ensuring that we are putting equity-mindedness into practice and working toward breaking down barriers to learning as well as helping to graduate students who will go into the workforce with the tools to continue to work equitably with others in industry.

How Do We Bring Equity to Team-Based Project Learning?

In this section, we discuss how to bring equity into the formation of student teams, describe a set of tools that faculty can provide their students to enable them to work more equitably and effectively, provide a description of a class module that faculty can use to discuss team conflict and the role of unconscious bias, and provide faculty with some tips on how to advise student teams more equitably.

Bringing Equity to Team Formation

Chapter 12 describes some of the pitfalls with letting students choose their own teams and recommends providing students with the real-world work experience of being assigned to a team based on strengths, experiences, and other assets. Asset mapping is an approach often used in community development, in which a community identifies its assets and then builds on and leverages these assets to solve community problems, like hunger, instead of focusing on community deficits (Lightfoot, McCleary, & Lum, 2014). Scholars and educators have recommended using an asset- or strengths-based approach in education (Maton & Hrabowski, 2004), and we have found that it can help bring equity to team formation. Because female students and students of color are often stereotyped as underperformers, forming teams based on assets or strengths—and then having student teams share and discuss these "asset maps"—can help overcome some of these biases (Meadows et al., 2015; D. Whitehead, personal communication, June 2017).

Students can create asset maps in the style of a concept or mind map. See the example in Figure 11.1 of a student's asset map for a project course on water problems. As this concept and practice has evolved, we have asked our students to include in their maps the areas in which they want to grow and develop.

Faculty can use asset maps to form teams based on a diversity of strengths (e.g., writing, proficiency in Excel, etc.) and experience (e.g., international, jobs, etc.), as well as in areas in which students want to grow. To avoid isolating women or students of color on project teams, faculty should consider demographics, in addition to assets, when forming teams (Meadows et al., 2015). Research has shown that having women on teams with other women and students of color on teams with other students of color can increase the confidence of these students when working on teams (Dasgupta, Scircle, & Hunsinger, 2015). A female student of color on a WPI project team explained,

> We're from different parts of the United States and are different races and cultures. But we have much in common as women pursuing STEM pathways. We were in a unique position in which we experienced working with a

Figure 11.1. Sample student asset map for equitable team formation.

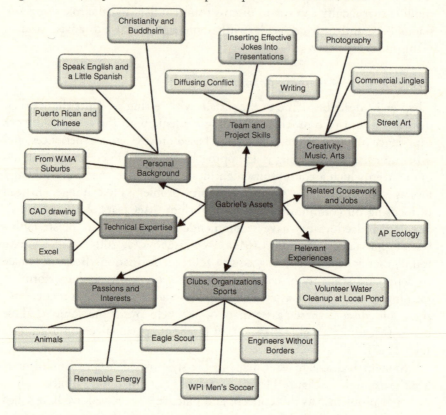

male and then working with only the three of us. We agreed that we felt more comfortable in challenging each other's ideas and voicing opinions with only the three of us. This was a positive consequence as we could be more adventurous in our ideas and were not limited by a subconscious bias from males.

Ensuring that women and students of color are not isolated on teams is particularly important in first-year projects, where students are transitioning from high school, are still building their confidence, and may not yet have strong social and academic support networks. It is also particularly important in shorter term projects where students do not have the opportunity to get to know each other in depth to get beyond initial stereotypes and biases (Meadows et al., 2015; B. Walker, personal interview, May 16, 2017).

Once faculty have created teams based on assets and demographics, student teams should have their first meeting during which they share and discuss their asset maps, the diversity of strengths, where and how each member wants to grow, and the potential benefits and challenges of the diversity on their team. We discuss this in more detail in the sections that follow. The downside of the asset-mapping exercise is that it requires more time on both faculty's and students' end. But it has a number of benefits—it allows students to think through and map out the strengths, skills, backgrounds, and experiences they bring to the table. It also allows them to discuss with their peers and faculty where they want to grow. It allows faculty to talk about why having a diversity of these assets on a team is a benefit to the team and the students' ability to assess and solve problems and how to support one another strategically through assignments in areas in which each student wants to grow.

The maps also allow students to learn about each other and get to know each other better, which can help in overcoming stereotypes and biases (Meadows et al., 2015). Comprehensive Assessment of Team Member Effectiveness (CATME) Team-Maker is another tool faculty can use to aid in the creation of more equitable teams (https://info.catme.org/). The benefit is in its ability to save time. Students fill out an online survey, answering questions about demographics, skills, and assets. An algorithm is then used to form teams based on a set of criteria chosen by the faculty member (Simmons, 2015).

Equitable Team Management

The following section is an equitable team management toolbox. Faculty and students can use these tools in isolation or in combination, as many build on and incorporate the others. After the toolbox, we discuss a set of modules that faculty can use to facilitate the use of these different tools.

Equitable Team Management Toolbox

> *Tool:* Student Asset Mapping and Team Asset Charting
> *Description:* Students create a concept or mind map of their assets and the areas in which they want to grow to aid in equitable team formation, development, and management. Maps can be used to help teams get to know each other early on, moving past stereotypes. They can help facilitate early team discussions around similarities and differences and how these might benefit and challenge the team and the students' work. The team asset chart can be used by the team to assign project- and assignment-related tasks based on students' strengths and the areas in which they want to grow (Stoddard and Pfeifer, 2018). Find a team asset chart template in Appendix 11.1.

When to use: Faculty can use these tools when forming student teams. Students can use them to facilitate introductions during initial team meetings and to aid in the division of labor.

Tool: Student Self-Assessments: Personality, Communication, and Conflict Styles

Description: Self-assessments include personality tests, such as modified Myers–Briggs introvert–extrovert and perceiving–judging tests (see Appendix 11.2). Others assess students' conflict resolution style (see Appendix 11.3). Wolfe (2010) developed self-assessments for students to assess their discussion style (competitive or considerate), presentation style (self-promoting or deprecating), and problem-solving style (holistic or action oriented) when working on teams. A student with a competitive discussion style might be more likely to interrupt his or her peers and not listen to or acknowledge others' ideas. A student with a considerate discussion style may be more likely to give up trying to talk when interrupted. Self-assessments help students identify and name these traits in themselves and their teammates and develop strategies and agreements to ensure all students are heard equally.

When to use: Students can take these assessments prior to their first meeting and use them to facilitate introductions and discuss how similarities and differences might affect the team and the students' work. Students can take or retake these assessments midway or two thirds of the way through longer projects to help them (re)evaluate how they interact on *this particular* team, as communication and conflict styles will shift based on the project, who is on it, and issues of bias. Our peer learning assistants suggest that assessments like introvert and extrovert be shared among peers. However, other assessments that are more revealing about students' vulnerabilities, such as the Wolfe (2010) assessments, should be used for individual (not group) reflection.

Tool: Team Building Exercises

Description: Team building exercises can help students learn how to communicate and collaborate effectively with the diverse members of their team and begin to forge relationships and develop trust, which can help overcome stereotypes (Al-Atabi, Shamel, Younis, & Chung, 2010; see Appendix 12.2). Some exercises can be tailored to incorporate course content.

When to use: Team building exercises can be used as early as the first team meeting to help students open up and discuss their self-assessments and asset maps or to see those traits and styles in action. In projects that take place over several weeks or months, team building exercises can be used at times of low energy to motivate teams or in times of heightened stress to reduce conflict.

Tool: Discussion of Team Members' Similarities and Differences: Benefits and Challenges

Description: As students meet for the first time, have them use their asset maps and self-assessments to discuss their similarities and differences. Teams are unable to gain the benefits of diversity unless these differences are discussed explicitly (Rock & Grant, 2016). Discussing similarities can help students overcome stereotypes (Meadows et al., 2015).

When to use: Use this exercise when team members are first meeting. This exercise can also be used midway or two thirds of the way through longer projects to help students reconnect and reevaluate their assets and how they interact on this particular team.

Tool: Team Equity Charter

Description: Wolfe (2010) created a template for teams to write up a team charter, a short contract that states the team's goals and the personal goals and commitments of individual members. It also defines how the team will handle conflict, missed deadlines, and poor-quality work. We recommend adding a section on rules for civility and communication to this contract to enable more equitable team interactions. We also recommend adding a section on team member assets, as seeing each other's strengths can help students overcome stereotypes and inform personal goals for growth. Find the assignment for developing a team equity charter and an example of a team equity charter in Appendix 11.4 and Appendix 10.1, respectively.

When to use: A charter should be written up by the team at the start of a project, ideally after asset mapping, self-assessments, and team building exercises. We recommend that students revise team charters halfway or two thirds of the way through the projects to address conflict and issues of inequity on the team. We discuss this further in the module after this section.

Tool: Equitable Task Schedule

Description: Wolfe (2010) created a template for a task schedule, which helps teams stay on track by noting who is in charge of which tasks, when each task is due, and the contribution value of the task based on difficulty and time required. To reduce task assignment biases and increase equitable access to a range of project tasks, we recommend adding a column to Wolfe's (2010) template that notes the type of task, such as technical, organizational, lead, or supporting. Explain to students that they should use this column to keep track of who is being assigned or taking on which roles and to make sure to rotate roles among members to ensure everyone has a chance to develop skills in all areas. Find the assignment for developing an equitable task schedule and an example of an equitable task schedule in Appendix 11.5.

When to use: Task schedules should be made at key points or as new assignments arise in project work, such as when drafts or presentations are due, when interviews or data collection is planned, and so on.

Tool: Team Member Roles and Role Rotation

Description: Wolfe (2010) discussed the need for and role of a team manager or supervisor who keeps the project on schedule. The manager reminds the team members about deadlines and responsibilities on the task schedule, keeps meeting minutes, prepares meeting agendas, and facilitates disagreements using the task schedule, meeting minutes, and team contract. We have found that this role is too large for first-year students and even upper-class students. It is also very time-consuming and, as such, the manager has less time to work on more content-driven tasks, which can lead to inequity in student learning and experience. Therefore, we recommend dividing this role into two: manager and facilitator. The manager takes meeting notes, updates the task schedule, and sends out deadline reminders. The facilitator writes up the meeting agenda, uses the agenda and a facilitation guide to facilitate the meeting, and helps manage conflict. We also recommend two additional roles—lead producer and lead researcher—to increase opportunities for equitable learning experiences. The lead producer helps organize and facilitate project products, such as a written draft or presentation. The lead researcher helps facilitate the research plan at various project stages. To ensure equity in learning and experience, we recommend rotating these roles so that each team member takes on each role during the course of the project or class. In Appendix 11.6, find a description of the team member roles, a sample meeting agenda structure, a sample meeting note structure, and a sample meeting facilitation guide. Ultimately, the goal is to have lead roles for each member, to tailor the roles to your specific project or assignment, and to create roles that your specific student population will benefit from.

When to use: Roles should rotate among students throughout the project.

Tool: Peer and Team Evaluations

Description: Chapter 12 details the value of periodic peer and team evaluations. They provide students with the opportunity to reflect on their teammates and their own contributions to the project, develop their ability to provide positive feedback and constructive criticism, and identify and discuss conflict before it blows up. We see peer and team evaluations as an opportunity for students to identify and discuss equity in terms of task assignments, project roles, and equitable communication. Find sample team evaluations in Appendix 12.4. CATME Peer Evaluation is another tool that faculty can use to aid in peer assessments (https://info.catme.org).

When to use: Periodically use evaluations throughout the course of the project.

Tool: Student Reflections on Team Dynamics

Description: Providing students with the opportunity to reflect on team dynamics helps them articulate their learning about how to act effectively and equitably on a team. It can also help them prepare for and facilitate conversations with team members about team dynamics and keep faculty aware of potential equity and other issues on teams. We provide more details on using reflection, as well as a sample reflection assignment, in the second module later in this chapter.

When to use: Periodically use reflection throughout the course of the project.

Modules for Equitable and Effective Teamwork

These modules aim to help students learn about the benefits and challenges of diverse teams; issues of racial, gender, and other biases on teams; and how these biases affect team dynamics. They also provide students with the tools to work together equitably and effectively, take advantage of the diversity on their team, and manage issues of conflict and bias. Our goal here is to show you one possible way of using some of the tools we described in the context of a longer term project. It is not meant to be an exhaustive or prescriptive model but rather meant to be an offer of some sense as to how some of this can work.

Module: Establishing an Equitable Team Culture

The goal of this module is to help students learn about and use tools that will create the context and ground rules for an equitable team culture. In this module, students come to class with their completed asset maps and self-assessments and having read some literature on the benefits and challenges of diverse teams, such as Rock and Grant's (2016) *Harvard Business Review* article "Why Diverse Teams Are Smarter." Teams can participate in a team building exercise at the start of class or at any point during this module, if faculty choose to include this component. Faculty should discuss the assigned literature with students to help them think through the benefits and challenges of diverse teams as it relates to their upcoming project work in the class, in their undergraduate careers, and in their future professions.

Students then work on creating a team asset chart, where they list the team's relevant skills, experiences, interests, and background. This asset chart will help members learn about each other's strengths, background, and interests, which can help them overcome stereotypes (Stoddard and Pfeifer, 2018). Faculty should briefly discuss the value of learning about one another's assets and experiences in terms of taking advantage of members' strengths and diverse backgrounds and experiences.

Faculty should then introduce the concept of the team equity charter and its purpose, and students can begin to write up their team equity charter in class, using the asset chart to inform their team equity charter. The charter can be completed by the team in or out of class. The team should submit it for a grade and faculty feedback, and students should be given the opportunity to revise if necessary. The creation and use of the chart, assessments, and charter should help new teams members get to know each other and establish a culture of equitable and effective teamwork.

Module: Team Dynamics, Conflict, and Issues of Unconscious Bias

The goal of this module is to give students the tools to recognize when unconscious biases are at play, how these biases can negatively impact student learning and team productivity, and how to take advantage of that recognition to confront these biases and create more equitable team dynamics. We teach this module about halfway to two thirds of the way through the project, when most project teams have experienced some conflict (see chapter 12 for more on stages of team development). Students come to class having reviewed the asset maps and self-assessments they completed at the start of the project. We ask them to submit a short reflection on the following questions before class: (a) Because your self-assessments were based, in part, on previous team experiences, have your communication, conflict, and personality styles remained the same on this team, changed some, or changed a lot? Explain. (b) Have you used your assets on this team? Have your team members used your assets? Have you used theirs? Explain. The goal of having students reflect on these assessments and assets is to prepare them to think through their team dynamics as we discuss issues of conflict and bias in class.

This module begins with a review of the literature on the benefits and challenges of diverse teams. To get students engaged and talking, we use Poll Everywhere software (www.polleverywhere.com) to pose questions about diversity on teams. We project the questions and have students use their electronic devices to answer live. We discuss that one of the challenges of differences on teams is that it can lead to conflict over ideas and approaches, but if managed effectively and equitably, that conflict can be productive and beneficial to the team. However, we explain that there are better and worse ways to deal with conflict to produce effective and equitable teamwork and, as a result, high-level project and learning outcomes.

It is at this point we show the students a video in which a project team is engaged in conflict. The video, produced by Joanna Wolfe at Carnegie Mellon University, depicts a team of three engineering students in conflict over which materials are most suitable for their project design. During the conflict, a male student tells a female student that "anyone with half a brain" would know that his ideas on materials are better. The female student responds by asking the third team member (student of color, gender ambiguous), who has been silent, "What do you think?" The male student immediately interrupts this third member, who then returns to being silent.

We ask our student teams to take five minutes or so to discuss the following: (a) What did they see in this interaction? (b) How might this affect the learning and experience of the individual students? (c) How might this affect the learning and the efficacy of the team? Then we ask students to share what their teams came up with in a larger class discussion. We use this broader discussion to bring up "the slacker": a student who is not doing their share of the work, not showing up to meetings, and/or not participating in group discussions. This is one of the most commonly reported issue on teams (Wolfe et al, 2016). We ask the students how the student who is told she has "half a brain" or how the student who is shut down and silenced might feel about coming to the next meeting. Most say they would dread coming to the next meeting and may not come as a result. Most also say they would do the minimum required to just get through the project. The "loss" of this student, perceived as slacking can result in a loss of learning opportunities and the loss of that student's contributions to the project (Meadows et al, 2015; Finnegan, 2017). We talk about what students might do to recognize, support, and reengage their peers who are experiencing marginalization on the team, and how they might seek support if they themselves are experiencing these issues.

We then explain that being on a team is a process of socialization and that as students divide up roles and responsibilities, unconscious biases and stereotypes can come into play. These biases and stereotypes can contribute to some of the problematic dynamics they saw in the video. We explain that an unconscious bias is a bias often below our conscious level. For example, women who self-promote are perceived more negatively than men who self-promote (Wolfe, 2010). We then begin a discussion about unconscious bias by looking at biases around introverts and extroverts. We use this approach as a way to provide safe entry into a difficult discussion and to help students in privileged categories (who do not regularly experience bias associated with gender, race, class, sexual orientation, ability, etc.) identify with bias in a context that might be more familiar to them. However, while discussing biases against particular personality types can help lay a foundation for more privileged students to engage in these difficult conversations, it is important to not conflate biases against particular personality types with biases against people of color or other historically marginalized communities.

The instructor asks the students for a show of hands based on who is an introvert and who is an extrovert. We then asked the students to imagine that it is the end of a busy week, and we ask them what they will do to unwind and relax. The introverts typically want to watch YouTube or movies, read books, or play video games either by themselves or with a close friend. Extroverts, on the other hand, want to be social, go to parties, and so forth.

We then ask each group what it thinks of the other group's chosen activities. The result is often that each group views the other group's choices negatively. For example, the extroverts claim the introverts' activities are "boring" or "lame," and the introverts see the extroverts' choices as "obnoxious" or "attention seeking." This is done in a friendly, poke-fun-of, joking fashion, which can help get students talking and more comfortable to discuss more difficult topics, like bias and team conflict.

We point out here that these are examples of biases and then also point out that when students get to know each other, these biases tend to go away. For example, an introverted student who is friends with an extroverted one may not see her as obnoxious—she is just into different things. We explain that these biases can lead to misinterpretations of team member behavior. For example, an extrovert might think an introvert isn't engaged and doesn't want to participate, when really the introvert is still thinking. As a result, the introvert could be left out of the brainstorming process of providing input on project design, for example.

We use this discussion of unconscious bias on teams and impacts on introverts to segue into a discussion of unconscious biases around race, gender, or national origin. We explain that research tells us such unconscious biases can also lead to students being left out of project work. This includes having their ideas ignored or shut down, having someone else take credit for their ideas, being talked over or interrupted, being assigned tasks deemed less difficult or valuable, or not having their work recognized or valued. We use Poll Everywhere—again, to show students these data and to ask them questions (see Figure 11.2).

We have found that sharing these data with the class "publicly" helps students who are experiencing these issues make sense of their experiences, validate their experiences, and give the whole class a common language and set of facts to discuss these issues on their teams.

We then invite our PLAs to talk with the class about their own experiences on teams, including as female students and students of color. Sharing experiential knowledge can provide critical peer-peer support and mentoring (Patton et al, 2015). Our PLAs are an integral part of course and assignment design, and we depend on their input for this and other modules. We ask them if they have experienced issues on teams and if they would be willing or interested to share them with the class. The goal here is to have first-year students hear from upper-class students who have firsthand experience navigating these situations. We ask that, if possible, they share stories of when they (or their peers) were marginalized on teams and instances where the dynamic was more equitable. We ask them to share what strategies helped them deal with being, for example, talked over or given lesser tasks. We also ask them

Figure 11.2. Using polling tools to discuss data with students on unconscious bias.

A 2016 study of 4 STEM universities did research on bias on student project teams, what do you think they found?

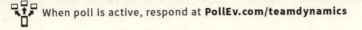 When poll is active, respond at **PollEv.com/teamdynamics**

14% of white women, 23% of women of color, 19% of men of color, and 10% of white male students reported having their ideas ignored/shut down; someone else take credit for their ideas; assigned tasks deemed 'less important', or have their work not valued.

23% of white women, 35% of women of color, 39% of men of color, and 20% of white male students reported having their ideas ignored/shut down; someone else take credit for their ideas; assigned tasks deemed 'less important', or have their work not valued.

40% of white women, 58% of women of color, 41% of men of color, and 23% of white male students reported having their ideas ignored/shut down; someone else take credit for their ideas; assigned tasks deemed 'less important', or have their work not valued.

to share what they or others on their team did to create a more equitable and inclusive team dynamic and to discuss the impact of these approaches for their team and their project. Our PLAs have found this experience to be productive for themselves in reflecting on these situations and to be empowering as they serve as a role model for others.

Finally, we ask our students to use a guide sheet to work through some questions about their team dynamics. We reiterate that the differences on their team—from personality to gender to national origin to race to communication or learning styles—can only be a benefit to their team and bring their project to the next level if these differences are discussed and used intentionally as an asset. We ask them to discuss their current team dynamics, issues, and conflicts to address problems and better use the differences on their teams.

The guide sheet includes questions such as the following: Who talks the most in your group? Who talks the least in your group? Why might that be a problem? How might that affect the productivity of the group? How might you change this dynamic moving forward? (See Appendix 11.7 for the full guide sheet.) This activity helps the team begin to see patterns around their team dynamics; for example, the exclusion of the voices of some members of the team or the unequal delegation of tasks. We ask the students to review and revise their team charters in light of this discussion. The module concludes with having them individually reflect on their experience with this project team to date, including issues of inequity and conflict, as well as strategies that have led to equitable and effective teamwork. (See Appendix 11.8 for this reflection assignment.)

While this module is a continual work in progress, we have seen benefits for our students. For example, we have had project teams recognize, as a result of this workshop, that some members of the team are unintentionally dominating the discussion, leaving others to feel that their voices were not valued or welcomed, and as a result, they worked to change this dynamic. For example, on one team two White male students regularly dominated the conversation and decision-making, and two female students of color struggled to be heard or acknowledged. During the guided discussion at the end of the module, the team discussed these issues openly and came up with strategies to ensure that everyone's voice would be heard and that everyone would have the opportunity to lead. A White male student on this project team explained,

> The importance of group diversity is something that I was skeptical about coming into [this course]. To me, all that mattered was how much effort someone was prepared to put into the project. . . Becuase Demetri and I were the more assertive group members, I assumed that we cared the most about the project, and that Sonia and Kira weren't as committed. This prompted me (as group manager) to give them fewer tasks and smaller roles. I only realized how wrong I was when we had an activity in class where we discussed identities and group dynamics. I discovered that Sonia and Kira were not indifferent toward the project, but that they were being shut out by Demetri and myself. In group meetings, Demetri and I would go back and forth debating ideas, all the while Sonia and Kira didn't want to interrupt with their own ideas. In future projects, I am going to be sure to avoid this issue by paying more attention to other group members and inviting them to share their ideas. If Sonia and Kira had felt comfortable sharing their ideas from the beginning, I am sure our team would have been more productive in less time.

Faculty Project Advising for Equity

In our role as project advisers, faculty can further support equitable team development. The following is a toolbox for equitable project advising that can be used as needed by faculty and students but can also be part of modules taught in the context of PBL.

Project Advising Equity Toolbox for Faculty
(Drawn From Meadows et al., 2015)

> *Tool:* Develop and regularly affirm an equitable classroom environment.
> *Description:* This tool can be employed in a variety of ways. It can be as simple as having a statement on the syllabus making students aware that the classroom is an equitable one and that any form of racism or sexism (implicit or explicit) is not, as Meadows and colleagues (2015) put it, "expected nor tolerated" (p. 12) and then making time to discuss what this means (thinking with the students through the ways such biases manifest, reading articles, and/or employing a module like the one described previously). You can also make it clear that students who experience any sexism or racism or other forms of discrimination can discuss this with you and their peers and that steps will be taken to ensure that this does not happen again. This latter part usually requires more than a simple syllabus statement—in our experience, it requires that faculty themselves feel comfortable discussing racism and sexism with the class, in a public way, and do so with some regularity, thereby demonstrating their own willingness to work through these difficult topics.
> *When to use:* Use this tool at the beginning of the course or project and regularly through the duration.
> *Tool:* Carefully explain all components of assignments and/or expectations for student work. (Don't assume knowledge of any of these.)
> *Description:* Some students, especially first-year and first-generation students, have no history with professional academic norms (norms of citation, norms of professional interaction, norms of reading and note taking, etc.). Therefore, being explicit about all of these norms reduces class-based implicit bias and creates a more egalitarian learning environment. It is also good to be aware of, and discuss with your students, the ways that some of these norms are themselves biased in favor of certain groups because of the history of the academy (Meadows et al., 2015). Doing this can also help with the first tool discussed earlier.
> *When to use:* Use this tool whenever giving assignments.
> *Tool:* Be a role model of equitable peer interaction yourself.
> *Description:* As a member of the project team (in an advisory capacity), faculty should also practice equitable interactions with student teams

(and other faculty), exemplifying what good egalitarian collaborative behavior looks like.

When to use: Use this tool throughout the duration of the class or project.

Tool: Any peer learning assistants or other class support staff should also work to model equitable collaborative methods.

Description: Support staff, such as peer learning assistants, graduate assistants, and so on, should also work to not mirror stereotypes in their roles in the classroom, such as female students in organizational roles and male students in technical roles (Meadows et al., 2015). You can share literature with your PLAs about the powerful role they play as role models, particularly for underserved students, empowering them to better support their students (Riegle-Crumb & Morton, 2017).

When to use: Use this tool as needed.

Tool: Encourage teams to use multiple collaborative methods and not just in-person work on the project.

Description: Giving students the tools to work in ways other than solely in person can help students who may have substantial nonschool responsibilities (e.g., jobs, child care) be effective members on teams with more traditional students. Wolfe (2010) offered a guide to different collaborative methods.

When to use: Use this tool at the beginning of the project.

Tool: When interacting with student teams, be sure to give equal time and speaking opportunity to all team members.

Description: Be sure to address all students in your interactions with student teams and pay special attention to any members of the team that may be quieter.

When to use: Use this tool as necessary.

Tool: Get regular feedback from individual team members on the team dynamics throughout the duration of the project.

Description: Have individual team members write regularly about how the team's work is going. Ask them to address questions about the team's decision-making process and division of labor and about any conflicts they might be experiencing. Then address any issues that arise.

When to use: Use this tool regularly.

Challenges

One of the main challenges of addressing inequity on student teams is faculty discomfort. Most faculty, naturally, feel most confident in teaching students about topics for which they have received master's and doctoral degrees, like chemistry or Greek history. Teaching students how to work on teams and how to manage racism and sexism on teams is something most faculty have not been taught, and many struggle to manage dynamics and bias on their own faculty teams. Many faculty feel that they shouldn't bring up issues of racial, gender, or other biases if students have not brought them up. However, Meadows and colleagues (2015) argue, "The absence of discussion more often effectively treats everyone as a white male, erasing differences rather than achieving intentional equality" (p. 5). If not discussed, issues of bias will only persist in our classrooms and on our student teams.

This work did, and still can, make us (the chapter authors) uncomfortable. As White faculty with privilege (who have done critical work but do not have degrees related to team dynamics), we did not want to make mistakes in how we approach or discuss these issues with students or faculty. However, we also know that work around equity and inclusion is not just the work of experts or of those who have experienced marginalization. It is the responsibility of everyone, particularly those of us in privileged positions.

Faculty can work to become more confident discussing these issues by reading research and literature on the topic of bias on student teams and in higher education, some of which is cited in this chapter. Faculty can also become more comfortable discussing these topics through practice, just as faculty have become more comfortable and skilled in teaching through projects or using other high-impact practices, something most of us were not trained to do. We can tell our students that while this is not our field of expertise, it is our responsibility as their faculty and advisers to prepare them to succeed outside of these walls and in their careers in a global and diverse world. We can explain that we know, from research and experience, that it is critical for them to learn how to work effectively and equitably on teams—both in their academic experience and in their future careers working with diverse colleagues and global customers. Finally, we hope this module and these tools will provide faculty with some concrete ways to introduce, guide, facilitate, discuss, and manage issues of bias on your student teams and to help our students take advantage of the differences among themselves.

Another challenge with this work is student pushback. Students (and faculty) don't want to have their behaviors attributed to racism, sexism, or other biases. In addition, many of us in privileged positions find it difficult to see these biases in our own actions. One White male student on a project team explained why he believed it was something other than race or gender that resulted in two White male students dominating the team and two female students of color finding it difficult to talk or contribute:

> I had never thought that our different identities would negatively impact our group. While the most obvious division in our group is between Sam and me (two White males) and Kate and Naomi (two female minori-

ties), I don't think this is caused by gender and ethnicity, but by something more simple. Kate and Naomi are roommates and have known each other longer than anyone else in the group, making them naturally stick together.

This student made a good point that race and gender are only two of our complex identities, and two of many components (e.g., friendship) to consider when thinking through issues of team dynamics. However, as faculty, it is our responsibility to push our students to think critically. For example, we might ask this student to think about the fact that our classrooms exist and operate within a society in which gender, racial, and other biases exist. Therefore, why should he consider only the role of a friendship within the context of team dynamics? Might he consider all potential contexts at play, like gender and/or racial stereotypes of bias, when thinking about why two team members rarely talked and found it difficult to get a word in? It is important to explain to students that this bias is most often unconscious, after years of being exposed to bias in our education, families, culture, politics, and media. We *all* have biases, and we *all* are responsible for identifying, acknowledging, and working to overcome them. When we do, we will function more effectively and more productively and create the potential to know each other and learn from each other in ways we have not before.

After the module, this student and his team discussed issues of equity on their team. The team, and this student in particular, worked extremely hard to ensure that particular members (himself included) did not dominate the conversation moving forward. They came up with strategies to make decision-making more equitable and to more equitably divide tasks and roles. While he wasn't ready to consider whether racial or gender bias was at play, he recognized that there was an equity issue on his team and that he played a role in limiting the voices and equal participation of others. The change in the team's dynamics, as well as the behavior of this student, was drastic. The team went from tense and quiet to laughing and active in the classroom. While no one course module will change how students or faculty see the world or how we act in it, this student and this team show us that we can make a lot of progress just by broaching the subject, reflecting on our own actions, and using team management strategies to interact more equitably.

Conclusion

The benefits of PBL are made clear throughout this book. As we discussed at the outset of this chapter, the context in which PBL takes place is one in which student populations are increasingly diverse in race, gender, class, sexual orientation, national origin, religion, immigration status, and more.

Such increasing diversity is good for the PBL environment, as we know from recent studies that diverse teams are better at solving problems, coming up with more innovative solutions, and learning more from working with individuals who are different from them (Rock & Grant, 2016). But these benefits accrue only if students have been explicitly told to try to take the perspectives of their teammates and given the tools to help them do so.

Only when people feel welcome and respected will the team be able to benefit from diversity of perspective and experience. Data also tell us that gender- and race-based biases (both explicit and implicit) exist in university environments at the same levels they do in the rest of society. Our students are experiencing these biases, and this has the potential to hamper the effectiveness of teamwork in PBL and student learning as a result. We hope these tools and examples offer some guidance for faculty and students to better understand and overcome these issues and to support students and faculty in the creation of more equitable team and classroom environments so that all students are able to benefit from the kinds of positive outcomes PBL has to offer.

Try This

1. In reflecting on your own courses, have you seen issues of task assignment bias, intellectual marginalization, and/or lack of work recognition? Which equitable team management or equity-minded project advising tools might help address some of the specific problems you are seeing in your own classroom?
2. How might you add one or more of these tools (e.g., asset mapping, team equity charters and equitable task schedules, role rotation) into the schedule of one of your existing project assignments?
3. Team building exercises help teams develop trust and overcome stereotypes, but team building exercises also compete with our time to teach content. How might you modify a team building exercise to incorporate content from your course?

TEAM ASSET CHART TEMPLATE

Asset Types	Member Names and Bulleted Description
Team and Project Skills	• A • B • C • D
Creativity—Music, Arts	• A • B • C • D
Related Course Work and Jobs	• A • B • C • D
Relevant Experiences	• A • B • C • D
Passions and Interests	• A • B • C • D
Technical Expertise	• A • B • C • D
Clubs, Organizations, and Sports	• A • B • C • D
Personal Background	• A • B • C • D

MODIFIED MYERS–BRIGGS TYPE INDICATOR (MBTI) TEST: INTROVERT, EXTROVERT, JUDGING, PERCEIVING

Modified by Charlie Morse
Worcester Polytechnic Institute Counseling Center

Quick Test for MBTI Introvert–Extrovert Type

1. When you are with a group of people, would you usually rather:
   - join in the talk of the group (E)
   - talk individually with people you know well (I)
2. In a large group do you more often:
   - introduce others (E)
   - get introduced (I)
3. Would you say it generally takes others:
   - a lot of time to get to know you (I)
   - a little time to get to know you (E)
4. Do you spend a lot of time:
   - by yourself (I)
   - with others (E)
5. Can you:
   - talk easily to almost anyone for as long as you have to (E)
   - find a lot to say only to certain people or under certain conditions (I)
6. Can the new people you meet tell what you are interested in:
   - right away (E)
   - only after they really get to know you (I)
7. Would most people say you are:
   - a private person (I)

- a very open person (E)
8. Do you find being around a lot of people:
   - gives you more energy (E)
   - is often "draining" (I)
9. Do you usually:
   - mingle well with others (E)
   - tend to keep more to yourself (I)
10. At parties do you:
    - do much of the talking (E)
    - let others do most of the talking (I)

Quick Test for MBTI Perceiving–Judging Type

1. Would you say you are more:
   - easy going (P)
   - serious and determined (J)
2. In most situations you are more:
   - deliberate than spontaneous (J)
   - spontaneous than deliberate (P)
3. Are you more frequently:
   - a fanciful sort of person (P)
   - a practical sort of person (J)
4. Do you tend to notice:
   - disorderliness (J)
   - opportunities for change (P)
5. On the job do you want your activities:
   - unscheduled (P)
   - scheduled (J)
6. Is clutter in the workplace something you:
   - tolerate pretty well (P)
   - take time to straighten up (J)
7. Is it preferable mostly to:
   - just let things happen naturally (P)
   - make sure things are arranged (J)
8. Do you prefer to work:
   - just whenever (P)
   - to deadlines (J)
9. Are you more:
   - whimsical than routinized (P)
   - routinized than whimsical (J)

10. Do you usually want things:
   - settled and decided (J)
   - just penciled in (P)

CONFLICT RESOLUTION STYLE ASSESSMENT

Which of the following best describes how you handle conflicts?

1. I don't like conflicts, and I try to avoid them. I would rather not be forced into a situation where I feel uncomfortable or under stress. When I do find myself in that kind of situation, I say very little, and I leave as soon as possible.

2. To me, conflicts are challenging. They're like contests or competitions— opportunities for me to come with solutions. I can usually figure out what needs to be done, and I'm usually right.

3. I try to see conflicts from both sides. What do I need? What does the other person need? What are the issues involved? I gather as much information as I can, and I keep the lines of communication open. I look for a solution that meets everyone's needs.

4. When faced with a conflict or even a potential conflict, I tend to back down or give in rather than cause problems. I may not get what I want, but that's a price I'm willing to pay for keeping the peace.

5. I want to resolve the conflict as quickly as possible. I give up something I want or need, and I expect the other person to do the same. Then we can both move forward.

Interpretation

If you chose #1, your conflict resolution style is *evader*. This is a lose–lose strategy. When one partner avoids a conflict, neither partner has an opportunity to resolve it. Both partners lose.

If you chose #2, your conflict resolution style is *fighter*. This is a win–lose/lose–win strategy. Either you win and your partner loses, or you lose and

---

Note. Used with permission of Stephen Dent. Dent, S. 2002. "What is your Conflict Resolution Style?" The CEO Refresher . . . brain food for business! Refresher Publications Inc. www.refresher.com/asdconflict.html

your partner wins. It's survival of the fittest. But conflicts are not contests, and this style precludes the possibility of finding a fair solution.

If you chose #3, your conflict resolution style is *negotiator*. This is a win–win strategy. Both you and your partner have the chance to express your needs and resolve the conflict in a mutually acceptable way. While this strategy may sound simple, it's actually the most difficult to use. It requires each of you to articulate, prioritize, and satisfy your own needs while also addressing the other person's needs.

If you chose #4, your conflict resolution style is *harmonizer*. This is a lose–win strategy. You lose because your needs aren't met. Your partner's needs are met, but the partnership suffers because you eventually become resentful and unsatisfied.

If you chose #5, your conflict resolution style is *compromiser*. This is a lose–lose strategy. Both you and your partner give up something you need just to make the conflict "go away." Invariably, you end up addressing the same issues later.

ASSIGNMENT FOR DEVELOPING TEAM EQUITY CHARTER AND ROLES

Team Equity Charter and Team Member Roles

Instructions for the Team Equity Charter

1. Read Wolfe (2010), chapter 3, "Getting Started With the Team Charter," in *Team Writing: A Guide to Working in Groups*.
2. Wolfe provided a sample team charter on page 38. We would like you to add three sections to Wolfe's sample team charter to increase equitable team dynamics:
   a. A section on rules for civility and communication to enable more equitable team interactions (see example in the following Sample Team Equity Charter section)
   b. A section on team member assets, which should inform your "personal goals" section (see example in the Sample Team Equity Charter section)
   c. A section on team member roles (roles defined later; see example in the Sample Team Equity Charter section)
3. Use chapter 3 in Wolfe, the Sample Team Equity Charter section, and the Team Member Roles section to help draft your team equity charter.

Sample Team Equity Charter

Note. Sections added to Wolfe's template are marked with an asterisk.

Broad Team Goals

1. Find a problem that is realistic and that we have the ability to help address.
2. Create a group atmosphere that people want to work in so that we are excited and prepared to work together effectively and equitably.
3. Be organized in our work and help each other out throughout the project.

Measurable Team Goals

1. Meet or beat all deadlines.
2. Have all the required components in both the presentation and the essay.
3. All team members must find at least four valid sources, including at least one peer-reviewed journal article.

Team Member Assets*

Member A's name and assets:
Member B's name and assets:
Member C's name and assets:
Member D's name and assets:

Personal Goals

1. Member A's name: Keep the team on schedule, help facilitate communication among team members during conflict, and improve my presentation skills.
2. Member B's name: Stay well ahead of deadlines, avoid procrastination, and improve research skills.
3. Member C's name: Improve my writing skills so that I get my points across in a clear and concise manner and make sure to answer e-mails and texts from team members within the hour.
4. Member D's name: Improve teamwork skills so that the project is more cohesive, make sure I don't interrupt, and make sure I ask those who have not spoken what they are thinking.

Individual Commitments

- We are all willing and committed to putting in 100% effort into this project so that our grade reflects the amount of work put in.

Other Concerns

- Because we are all athletes on different sports teams, we are concerned that we may be busy with practice and competitions and that our schedules may conflict, but we will work together to be able to meet when needed.
- Finals week is coming up, so we are concerned about being busy with other school work, but if we manage our time well, we will be able to meet all the deadlines of our project.

Team Member Roles*

We are committed to changing the roles during the project so that every member has the opportunity to act in each role during the course of the project.

1. Member A's name: team manager
2. Member B's name: team facilitator
3. Member C's name: product manager
4. Member D's name: research facilitator

Rules for Civility and Communication*

1. No interrupting.
2. All ideas will be written down during brainstorming sessions.
3. If someone is dominating the conversation, the team facilitator will use a two-minute timer to ensure everyone has a chance to be heard.
4. If disagreements get heated, we will take a break.
5. The expectation is no name calling; if that happens, we will take a break, and all parties will apologize upon return.
6. Members will stay present during meetings; no doing other work or chatting online or on phones and so on.

Conflict Resolution

- If two team members experience a conflict, the other team members will be asked to add in their opinions. If the conflict is not resolved within two days, then we will ask an instructor to weigh in on the conflict.
- If someone is not paying attention during meetings and is on a device doing other work or socializing and so on, he or she has to buy everyone a cookie from the café.

Missed Deadlines

- If a team member misses a deadline, the team manager will send out a reminder e-mail or text message. If that member does not respond within the day, then we will have a team meeting on how to proceed.

Unacceptable Work

- If a team member turns in unacceptable work, other team members should contact the team facilitator with their concerns. The facilitator will then communicate the concerns with the individual, and if the individual has questions, the group will meet to resolve the issues.

Team Member Roles

Team Manager

The team manager takes meeting notes and sends them to the group after the meeting. He or she updates the equitable task schedule based on the meeting and sends it to the group. He or she also sends out deadline reminders, based on the meeting notes and equitable task schedule.

Team Facilitator

The team facilitator writes up the meeting agenda for the upcoming team meeting. To construct the agenda, he or she draws on the previous meeting notes, equitable task schedule, and communication (e-mail, in-class discussion) since the last meeting. He or she sends the agenda out before the meeting, asks the team members if anyone has anything to add, and uses the agenda and a facilitation guide to facilitate the meeting. The team facilitator helps manage conflict by ensuring that everyone's voice is heard (potentially using the facilitation guide) and by drawing on the team contract to remind everyone about agreed-on rules of conduct.

Production Manager

The production manager helps organize and facilitate project products, such as a written draft or presentation. For example, on a written draft or presentation, he or she would help organize the document or presentation by working with the team to outline the narrative of the piece. Once the big picture narrative is created, he or she might help facilitate the division of labor to determine who will take on which section. The goal is to help manage the production of the project but not to be in charge of or dominate the vision of the production or the division of labor.

Research Facilitator

The research facilitator helps facilitate the research plan at various project stages. The facilitator should use the team's research objectives or questions as facilitation guide. As the team members are assessing where they are with the project and what the next steps are, the research facilitator should use the team's research objectives or questions to facilitate the discussion and next steps. For example, "Which objective will research X help us achieve?"

Keeping these big picture objectives or research questions in mind, he or she might help facilitate the division of labor to determine what research objectives or questions still need to be worked on and who will work on researching what is next to help meet those objectives or answer those questions.

ASSIGNMENT FOR DEVELOPING AN EQUITABLE TASK SCHEDULE

Equitable Task Schedule

Instructions for the Equitable Task Schedule

1. Read Wolfe (2010), chapter 4, "Getting Started With the Task Schedule," in *Team Writing: A Guide to Working in Groups*.
2. Wolfe provided a sample task schedule on page 46. We would like you to add a column to Wolfe's (2010) template that notes the type of task, such as technical, organizational, writing, research, production, lead, and/or supporting. This is to increase equity in the types of tasks you are assigned and/or volunteer to take on. This can also help you document the areas in which you are gaining experience and/or need more experience in. Use this column to keep track of who is being assigned or taking on which roles and to make sure to rotate roles among members to ensure everyone has a chance to develop skills in all areas.
3. See the following sample task schedule with the modified template that includes "type of task." This is for a group assignment where students did research on a sustainable water technology and created an infographic about the technology.

Sample Equitable Task Schedule

Note. Student names have been changed to protect identity.

Team Member Contributions

- Eliza: 26
- Malik: 25
- Jose: 25
- Suvi: 26

Deadline	Task	Assigned to	Contribution Value (Lowest 1–5 Highest)	Type of Task	Status
9/18	Finish equity charter	Collective	3	Organizational, writing	Complete
9/18	Finish equitable task schedule	Collective	3	Organizational	Complete
9/18	Annotated bibliography, two sources	Each member	5	Research, writing	
9/19	Open Piktochart account and e-mail everyone with access information	Malik	2	Supporting, organizational	
9/19	Review infographic tools and techniques and sketch draft of sections	Jose and Eliza	5	Lead, technical	
9/20	Write up background section content and sketch this section on infographic	Jose	4	Lead, Writing, Production, Technical	
9/20	Write up Egypt case study content	Eliza	4	Lead, writing, production, technical	
9/20	Write up Singapore case study content	Suvi	4	Lead, writing, production, technical	
9/20	Write up filtration process and technology content	Malik	4	Lead, writing, production, technical	
9/21	Meet to get feedback on draft	Collective	3	Supporting	
9/21	Incorporate feedback into draft	Malik and Suvi	5	Lead, production, technical	
9/22	Final aesthetic touches	Eliza and Suvi	3	Supporting, production, technical	
9/23	Upload assignment to Eportfolio site and to Canvas; make sure can open in correct formats for presentation	Jose	2	Supporting, organizational	

*Eliza and Suvi have an extra point because of the final aesthetic touches. Malik and Jose have an exam on 9/23 and Eliza and Suvi do not. So, they volunteered to take on this work.

STUDENT RESOURCES: TEAM ROLES, SAMPLE MEETING NOTES, AND TEAM FACILITATION GUIDE

Team Member Roles

Team Manager

The team manager takes meeting notes and sends them to the group after the meeting. He or she updates the equitable task schedule based on the meeting and sends it to the group. He or she also sends out deadline reminders, based on the meeting notes and equitable task schedule.

Team Facilitator

The team facilitator writes up the meeting agenda for the upcoming team meeting. To construct the agenda, he or she draws on the previous meeting notes, equitable task schedule, and communication (e-mail, in-class discussion) since the last meeting. He or she sends the agenda out before the meeting, asks the team members if anyone has anything to add, and uses the agenda and a facilitation guide to facilitate the meeting. The team facilitator helps manage conflict by ensuring that everyone's voice is heard (potentially using the facilitation guide) and by drawing on the team contract to remind everyone about agreed-on rules of conduct.

Production Manager

The production manager helps organize and facilitate project products, such as a written draft or presentation. For example, on a written draft or presentation, he or she would help organize the document or presentation by working with the team to outline the narrative of the piece. Once the big picture narrative is created, he or she might help facilitate the division of labor to determine who will take on which section. The goal is to help manage the production of the project but not to be in charge of or dominate the vision of the production or the division of labor.

Research Facilitator

The research facilitator helps facilitate the research plan at various project stages. The facilitator should use the team's research objectives or questions as facilitation guide. As the team members are assessing where they are with the project and what the next steps are, the research facilitator should use the team's research objectives or questions to facilitate the discussion and next steps. For example, "Which objective will research X help us achieve?" Keeping these big picture objectives or research questions in mind, he or she might help facilitate the division of labor to determine what research objectives or questions still need to be worked on and who will work on researching what next to help meet those objectives or answer those questions.

Sample Meeting Agenda

GPS Project Agenda
Date:

1. Last week's accomplishments:
   - Eliza: Revised methodology
   - Malik: Revised literature review
   - Jose: E-mailed and filled out the IRB, assisted in revised methodology
   - Suvi: Drafted outline of results
2. Documents to review:
   - Introduction
   - Revised literature review
   - Revised methodology
   - Interview and focus group questions
   - Drafted outline of results
3. Discussion items for meeting:
   - Interview and focus group meeting set up
   - Attaining more contacts for interviews and focus groups
   - Other sources of data collection
   - Team communication
   - Plan for next week

Sample Meeting Notes Structure

GPS Project Meeting Minutes
Date:

Attendance: [Names]

Discussion: This section summarizes what was discussed at the meeting. It can be written in clear, short, summary bullet points. For example:

- Decided to change mode of communication from e-mail to text.
  - No texts later than midnight.
- Divided up next steps for research. They are . . .
- Chose TA office hours to practice presentation (date and time here).
  - Ask for feedback on our introduction.
  - Ask for feedback on including short video.
- Decided to meet with class librarian if can't find credible and relevant sources.
- Chose time and place to meet to discuss research found and questions that still need to be answered, which is . . .
- Chose time and date to revise PowerPoint and do first practice round, which is . . .

Next Steps and Action Items

Here include a description of agreed-on next steps, with student names listed next to each item.

Sample Team Meeting Facilitation Guide

1. Team members provide updates on their progress and any problems they are having, for two minutes each. Other team members should jot down questions or comments during this time. No interruptions or questions during this time.
2. Provide eight minutes of open time for questions or comments on progress and problems reported out by the team. Stop at four minutes and ask those who have not participated in this discussion to add their thoughts.
3. Each member provides his or her thoughts on the next steps for two minutes. Other team members should jot down questions or comments during this time. No interruptions or questions during this time.
4. Provide eight minutes of open time for questions or comments on thoughts for next steps reported out by the team. Stop at four minutes and ask those who have not participated in this discussion to add their thoughts.
5. Research facilitator and project managers should help the team organize, facilitate, and move forward on the next steps at this point.

EQUITABLE TEAM DYNAMICS DISCUSSION GUIDE

Equitable Team Dynamics Discussion Guide

Instructions

1. Write out each of your identities, based on the (a) MBTI personality assessments and (b) discussion, presentation, and problem-solving style assessments from Wolfe (2010), chapter 7, "Communication Styles and Team Diversity," in *Team Writing: A Guide to Working in Groups* and from the Conflict Resolution Style Assessment.
2. Discuss the following questions.

Team Communication
- Who talks most in your group?
- Who talks the least in your group?
- Why might that be a problem?
- How might that affect the productivity of the group?
- How might that affect equity on the team?
- How might you change this dynamic?
- How are you handling electronic communication?
- What is considered a timely response?
- Have you set boundaries for what can be conveyed and when electronic communication happens?

Team Leadership
- Who takes the lead in your group most often?
- Who takes the lead in your group least often?
- Why might that be a problem?
- How might that affect the productivity of the group?
- How might that affect equity on the team?
- How might you change this dynamic?

Team Decisions and Equity
- Who makes decisions in your group most often?
- Who makes decisions least often in your group?
- Why might that be a problem?
- How might that affect the productivity of the group?
- How might that affect equity on the team?
- How might you change this dynamic?

Team Member Assets
- Are all team member assets being used, meaning are you using and building on the skills of each member? List at least one way that you are using the assets of each team member. List at least one way that you are not using the assets of each team member and/or how you might use at least one of their assets more effectively.
- What problems have been caused from not effectively using all assets?
- How might that affect the productivity and equity of the group?
- How might you change this dynamic?

Team Problem-Solving
- What are the problems that your team seems to have repeatedly (e.g., work is turned in late, people don't show up for meetings, one person dominates the conversation, one person doesn't participate in conversations, etc.)?
- How might you change this dynamic?

Team Value Rubric
Take a look at the AAC&U Team VALUE Rubric (www.aacu.org/value/rubrics). Assess where your team is, and discuss where you think you can get to.

CRITICAL REFLECTION: TEAM DYNAMICS, CONFLICT, AND BIAS

Targeted learning outcomes: Teamwork

Goal of this assignment: To reflect on the ways that stereotyping, bias, and difference in personality, communication, and conflict styles shape your team dynamics, your role and experiences on teams, and the roles and experiences of others on teams

Instructions: Write a 2- to 3-page reflection. The reflection is a formal piece of writing and should be well written, thorough, and concise. Any sources used should be cited in the text and should be listed in a bibliography in APA format. Sources are not required for this assignment. The reflection should be written using Times New Roman font, 1.5 spacing, 12-point type, and 1-inch margins.

The essay should be informed by your asset map, self-assessments, and following articles you read for class:

- Read: Meadows, Sekaquaptewa, and Paretti (2015) *Interactive Panel: Improving the Experiences of Marginalized Students on Engineering Design Teams.* The ASEE (American Society for Engineering Education) publication can be downloaded here: https://peer.asee.org/interactive-panel-improving-the-experiences-of-marginalized-students-on-engineering-design-teams.
- Read: Finnegan (2017) "It's Good Till It's Not: Does Group Work Really Help All Students?" *Inside Higher Ed* article found here: https://www.insidehighered.com/advice/2017/08/01/helping-diverse-learners-navigate-group-work-essay?utm_source=Inside+Higher+Ed&utm_campaign=1b0d729230-DNU20170801&utm_medium=email&utm_term=0_1fcbc04421-1b0d729230-198477221&mc_cid=1b0d729230&mc_eid=47613e59d6.
- Read: Williams (2015) "The Five Biases Pushing Women Out of STEM," *Harvard Business Review* article found here: https://hbr.org/2015/03/the-5-biases-pushing-women-out-of-stem.

Questions

1. Review your self-assessments and asset map you wrote up in A term. Your self-assessments were based, in part, on previous team experiences. Has your communication, conflict, and personality styles remained the same on this team or changed some or a lot? Explain.

2. Have you used your assets on this team? Explain.

3. What kind of communicator or personality type are you? What kind of conflict or problem-solving style do you have?

4. How do these styles affect your ability to communicate effectively with others on your team?

5. How do your styles and the styles of the others in your team affect your team's ability to communicate?

6. You have seen some data on how diversity on teams can have positive effects and can create conflict. You have also seen both in our class today, the ways in which stereotyping, biases, and other factors can affect whose ideas are listened to and taken seriously; whose voices are heard and who is talked over or shut down; who is assigned what task; and so on. In your group, whose ideas are listened to and taken seriously, whose voices are heard and who is talked over or shut down, who is assigned which tasks, and so on?

7. Reflect on how stereotyping, bias, and/or other factors may be shaping your team dynamics.

8. You have finished or in the process of revising your team charter with your team. Where is your team on the AAC&U Teamwork VALUE Rubric? What is a realistic goal of where you could get to on that rubric? What would you need to do to get there?

9. What are the strategies that you and your team came up with to make your team dynamics more effective and equitable?

Assignment Rubric: Possible Grades for Each Dimension

Dimension	Excellent: A	Good: B	Fair: C	Needs Substantial Improvement
Format	All formatting requirements are met.	Most formatting requirements are met.	Some formatting requirements are met.	Most formatting requirements are not met.
Content	Answers are specific and detailed.	Answers are generally specific and detailed.	Answers are vague and not detailed.	Answers are not specific and detailed.
	Clear examples are provided.	Examples provided are generally clear.	Examples provided are vague.	Clear examples are not provided.
	Ideas are well elaborated, and details are effective, specific, and relevant.	Ideas and details are usually effective, specific, and relevant but may be limited in depth.	Ideas are thinly developed; details, when provided, may be irrelevant, unfocused, or too general.	Ideas or details are very limited, unclear, or difficult to follow. Writing seems off topic and disconnected.
Writing conventions	There are few or no grammatical, mechanical, or usage errors; there is little or no need for editing.	There are some errors, but they do not interfere with meaning; there is moderate need for editing.	Errors do not block meaning but do distract the reader; there is significant need for editing.	Errors interfere with readability and meaning.

MANAGING TEAM DYNAMICS AND CONFLICT ON STUDENT PROJECT TEAMS

Charlie Morse

A s a guest presenter on "Effective Project Team Dynamics" within classrooms, I often start the discussion by asking students, "By a show of hands, how many of you have been involved in highly functional project teams?" Inevitably, and thankfully, almost every hand in the room will go up. Then I ask, "How many of you have been a part of teams that were highly dysfunctional?" and again practically every hand will go up. It seems that almost everyone can relate to the highly energized feeling of functioning "in the zone" on a team, as well as to the tension and stagnation inherent in trying to push through dysfunctional team dynamics.

Students can also readily identify the characteristics of highly functional teams: equitable commitment and participation, trust and respect among team members, mutual understanding of roles as it relates to work and team functioning, effective team organization and structure, and open communication involving both positive feedback and constructive criticism. But understanding these variables does little to ensure a successful teamwork experience; faculty can and should assume an active role in educating students about team dynamics. This chapter provides some guidelines and resources to support faculty in just such an endeavor.

Proactive Team Management

After I completed dozens of student project team consultations of faculty-referred "underperforming teams," a general pattern of problematic team functioning becomes apparent. The story typically goes like this: As student teams begin working together, predictable tensions emerge that may or may not lead to overt conflict within the group. These tensions are ignored, bypassed, and avoided for the sake of preserving harmony within the group. The source of these tensions goes unaddressed, tensions persist, and mounting frustration and resentment among team members interferes with effective communication and teamwork. Declining team outcomes become apparent to faculty, and when these are reflected back to the team, pressure mounts. The team is heading toward total breakdown.

Most often at the core of problematic student team functioning is the avoidance of tension and conflict. For multiple reasons I'll highlight later in this chapter, students tend to avoid tension and conflict, which ultimately leads to the project team under functioning. This is reflected most obviously with teams where there are problems due to overt tension and conflict and less obviously in teams that appear functional but aren't reaching their full potential because of conflict avoidance. Also within this chapter we'll highlight how faculty can significantly influence, for better or for worse, student perceptions of and ability to manage conflict within their projects teams.

High Team Functioning Matters

The importance of faculty injecting team dynamic skills into their classes is underscored by the fact that businesses are relying increasingly on team-based models and name "the ability to function on a team" as their number-one skill in hiring new professionals (S. Adams, 2014). Universities do well to prepare students for the job market by providing them with multiple opportunities to function within teams. Simple exposure to team-based learning opportunities has been shown to improve student learning outcomes (Davidson, Major, & Michaelsen, 2014), and faculty have the opportunity to enhance student teamwork skills and satisfaction immensely by designing course work with team development in mind and including teaming skills in course content (Eddy & D'Abate, 2016).

Useful Models to Support Team Dynamics

Tuckman and Jensen's (1977) model of team development provides an excellent framework from which to understand student experiences within teams and opportunities to actively enhance the development of teamwork skills within the design and content of a course. Tuckman and Jensen's model reinforces the importance of the development of interpersonal knowledge, trust, and respect as an essential factor at every stage in a team's development.

Perhaps one of the most important lessons to be learned within project teams is this: Only in the context of valuing and embracing personal, cultural, racial, and gender differences will teams achieve their highest potential.

Tuckman and Jensen's model breaks team development down into a series of stages that place differing tasks and demands on the teams and also call for different types of instruction and support from faculty. These stages are labeled *forming, storming, norming, performing,* and *adjourning.* During the *forming* stage, group members begin to develop understanding, respect, and trust—the glue that will hold the group together throughout the project. *Storming* occurs as unavoidable differences and disagreements emerge within the group and the team tries to "work out the bugs." *Norming* involves establishing a set of expectations and rules, written and unwritten, providing a structure within which the group will operate. *Performing* occurs as group members fully engage each other while constructively challenging and bringing out the best in one another. *Adjourning,* most often brought about by the end of a semester, provides an opportunity for students to disconnect from the team, celebrating their achievements and consolidating what they've learned from the course.

While this model appears linear, realistically, student project teams will move back and forth between these stages. All teams begin with forming and end with adjourning—the bulk of the life cycle of most teams is spent back and forth between storming and norming. Only the healthiest teams will be able to enter into the most highly functional stage of performing. I'll highlight later how successfully engaging the tasks and demands of each of the first three stages provides the necessary fuel to propel groups into their most functional performance. I'll also highlight how the concept of team synergy—at the core of highly performing teams—provides students an experience that helps them appreciate the importance of recognizing and embracing differences of all kinds as the fuel that propels groups and communities toward being the best version of themselves.

Project Teams in the Forming Stage

On the basis of their strong interest in the topic, four students are assigned to work together on a semester-long project to design rainwater collection systems in rural Namibia. The group members, Priya, Vanessa, Laurie, and Javier, are all known as very strong students. Each of them is engaged fully in classroom discussions, with insightful comments and observations. They sit together in class and appear to be getting along well as they research existing rainwater collection systems, as well as local infrastructure, resources, and cultural elements that may affect the project. Their first assignment, a research report, though very well written, omitted information about resources and cultural elements. As their faculty adviser, you are surprised that this group of talented students would make this mistake, and you provide clear written feedback encouraging them to work harder to finalize their research and begin the design phase.

Student Experience

Students coming together to work within project teams are, quite often, working with project partners they've never met and who are quite different from them. As such, during the team formation stage, it is expected that there will be a combination of excitement and anxiety. Team members are typically excited about the possibilities that lie ahead, somewhat optimistic and hopeful about team performance, and eager to dig into the work. At the same time, many questions and uncertainties are a source of anxiety, especially if students have been a part of dysfunctional teams in the past. Fears occupy the minds of students at these early stages of team formation: whether they will like and be liked by their projects partners, whether they will fit into the group if possible disagreements or tensions emerge, whether they will be able to contribute meaningfully to the project.

Generally, student project teams will "keep things safe" as they come together with their uncertainty and excitement. Group members will avoid controversial topics and seek out safety in areas of commonality and agreement. Strong feelings and disagreements will be pushed aside while students get a feel for similarities and differences that may exist within the group.

In addition, the students are tasked with getting their bearings in the work that lies ahead. Uncertainty about project definition, scope, approach, and structure weighs on the emerging team, and students are eager for direction and input from faculty and project sponsors so they might find some safety in "having a plan." All too often student project teams will bypass the task of forming secure working relationships—built on understanding, trust, and respect—in their eagerness to engage in the task-oriented work of moving ahead on the project. You will soon see how this strategy potentially undercuts the group's ability to sustain and maximize functioning as the project progresses.

Faculty Roles and Strategies

The strategies employed to form student project teams and the roles and involvement of these strategies in the early stage of team formation can greatly affect how these teams come together and perform overall throughout the life of the project. Initial structural factors in the design of the class have the potential to greatly influence team dynamics. Research on "social loafing" (the phenomenon of some group members exerting less effort) points to three influencing factors: project size, group size, and the use of peer evaluations (Aggarwal & O'Brien, 2008). This research indicates that projects too large in scope open up more opportunities for social loafing. Students may be inclined to "disconnect" from projects so large that their individual contributions may not be recognized. Additional study on group size points to three to five individuals as optimal in promoting student involvement and accountability (Margolis, 2011), a group size that also resonates as ideal with faculty experienced in teaching with team-based strategies. The use of multiple peer evaluations during the course of the project has also been shown to reduce incidence of social loafing. Evaluation processes as a whole will be more directly addressed later in this chapter.

There are several strategies faculty can employ to bring groups of students together, all with potentially different impacts on student project team development. One option is to allow students to find their own project partners. This strategy, while possibly the easiest, has many pitfalls. Students are likely to choose their friends or those they perceive as similarly high achieving, resulting in groups that are more homogeneous. Some students will struggle to find others to work with and possibly face rejection in their efforts. Self-selected teams do not expose students to the real-world experience of being placed on projects teams based on factors related to business interests. Faculty can randomize the formation of student project teams simply by counting off within the classroom, but this may result in the formation of teams that will experience significant problems due to personality clashes or awkward groupings of gender, race, or culture that may form randomly.

Most faculty attempt to "craft" groups partly based on factors such as project interest, student demographics, apparent personality factors, and student preference for teammates. Typically faculty will provide students with questionnaires (see Appendix 12.1) that allow them to rate preferences for particular projects, suggest classmates they would prefer *not* to work with, and generally share time availability. Faculty can then attempt to select students for teams based on these stated preferences while weighing apparent demographic and personality factors. Generally, faculty seek to fashion diverse teams in terms of demographics and academic abilities while avoiding isolating single underrepresented individuals (race, culture, gender). This method is far more time intensive than those described in the previous paragraph, but most faculty say that the time spent is worthwhile in improving overall student experience and potential for success. Online tools, such as the CATME (Ohland, Pomeranz, & Feinstein, 2006), can greatly aid faculty in the complicated process of student selection, as well as in other aspects of project team support.

Once teams are formed, faculty must choose how much structure and support they will provide the students as they begin their work. They may provide group assignments oriented to helping students share information about themselves to foster connections within the group. Team building exercises can be assigned within and outside the classroom to promote group cohesion (see Appendix 12.2).

In their uncertainty, students often look to faculty for concrete instruction and answers in terms of project definition and approach. Faculty are encouraged to keep these responsibilities on the project teams but may provide support, encouragement, and time for teams to find more security in project definition and team development. Assigning a "team contract" exercise as the group is forming is helpful in clarifying team expectations of one another and in outlining consequences associated with team members not meeting these expectations (see Appendices 10.1, 11.3, and 12.3). These contracts can prove invaluable as a resource later on if project teams encounter group dynamic challenges.

Storming Project Teams

In the next class you notice apparent tension within the group. Priya and Vanessa are sitting together and appear to be getting along quite well; Javier is sitting with friends across the classroom; and Laurie is sitting separately, looking angry, with her arms folded. During group work time you notice a similar dynamic playing out, where Priya and Vanessa appear to be carrying the conversation, Javier appears disengaged and distracted on his cell phone, and Laurie continues to sit quietly with her arms folded. After class you approach the group and ask how things are going with their work together. Vanessa says the research section has been difficult for them, but they're working through it just fine. Others in the group nod in agreement. You remain unconvinced.

The next day Priya and Vanessa ask to meet with you during your office hours. They are visibly upset as they share with you that Laurie and Javier are not pulling their weight within the group. They describe that it was, in fact, Laurie's and Javier's fault that their research section was incomplete, as they were responsible for researching resources and cultural elements. Priya shares that neither of them submitted material until just before the research write-up was due, and what they submitted was of such poor quality it could not be incorporated into the paper.

Vanessa shares that Laurie has been late for or absent from several recent team meetings, and even when she's there, she's disengaged and angry. In addition, Vanessa shares that Javier just doesn't seem invested in working hard, constantly making jokes and distracting the group from the task at hand. They're both fed up and not sure they can continue working with Laurie and Javier. You ask Priya and Vanessa if they've talked to their project partners about these concerns, and they provide a vague response about it being too late to fix the problem.

Student Experience

Tension and potential conflict will predictably emerge as student teams begin the serious work of digging into the project and producing early deliverables. Just as predictable is the fact that most teams will ignore and avoid dealing with these tensions and in all likelihood will not share their struggles with faculty or project sponsors. These predictable sources of tension may include the following: personality differences, assigning roles within the project, leadership and power struggles, differing work ethic and styles, control of the project, and expectations in terms of outcomes (grades). More deeply rooted tensions may emerge centered on conscious or unconscious biases associated with race, gender, and differing cultural backgrounds.

Most of these tensions can and will be worked out without directly addressing them; healthier teams will demonstrate flexibility in adjusting to these differences in constructive ways. Quite often, though, avoiding discussion and problem-solving around persisting sources of tension leads to the buildup of resentment and anger within the team. A most important telltale sign of this is a breakdown in team communication. These factors can then lead to group members' physical and emotional withdrawal from project work (under functioning) and, conversely, other group members attempting to take control and save the project (over functioning). This dynamic generates further resentment among all members of the team, bringing them closer to total team breakdown. Unfortunately, this may be the first evidence, to the project team and the faculty, that the team has major problems.

Faculty Roles and Strategies

Faculty should consider how their assessment strategies for student project teams will affect the teams' ability and motivation to manage tension and conflict and their willingness to seek outside support when significant conflict is encountered. Applying a single grade to the entire team, regardless of individual efforts and contributions, may contribute to a sense of unfairness within the group and allow "social loafing," as described earlier in this chapter, to occur. At the other extreme, attempting to apply individual grades to each group member, based on time spent, contribution to outcomes, and quality of work, may discourage the dynamic interactions within the group that will propel the group toward its best work. Assessment approaches that balance team outcomes and individual efforts, such as those described in chapter 6, are ideal in reinforcing equity within the group while recognizing the importance of outcomes generated by synergistic collaboration.

In addition, faculty should build opportunities into the course of the project for periodic peer and team assessment. Peer assessment provides a structured opportunity for students to reflect and report on their teammates' contributions to the project, in terms of both content and process. Students should be supported in openly discussing these assessments with one another as an opportunity to grow in their ability to provide reinforcing and constructive criticism. Team assessment assignments can provide additional opportunities for students to reflect on and share their perspectives on how the team as a whole is functioning. Structured assignments that guide students to reflect on peer and team performance can be critical in breaking through teams' tendency to avoid tension and conflict and help student teams recognize and address areas of tension before they escalate to destructive levels. Examples of peer and team evaluation tools can be found in Appendix 12.4. Chapter 11 has additional tools that incorporate issues of identity and equity.

Also relevant is the manner in which faculty frame their expectations of student teams as it relates to team dynamics and tension. Faculty can share the Tuckman paradigm outlined in this chapter within the classroom as a way of introducing a model that helps students understand the various stages of team development and normalizes the emergence (and importance) of tension as the project progresses. Faculty should affirm the importance of students actively managing team dynamics and that student teams will not be penalized if they encounter tension and conflict. Messaging in class discussion and the course syllabus that the team will be judged on many different factors, including their recognition and management of tension and conflict, can help project teams feel safe and supported in the difficult task of approaching interpersonal conflict.

Faculty can also present to the class a model to help students learn and remain cognizant of important conflict management strategies. A quick overview of conflict management strategies can help students become more flexible and thoughtful in their approach to managing team tension and conflict. One way of helping students understand their "conflict styles" is by administering and discussing the Thomas–Kilmann Instrument (TKI) (Kilmann & Thomas, 1977). This tool points to five different conflict management styles that can be used depending on the level of cooperativeness and assertiveness individuals may want to employ in a given situation. The chart shown in Figure 12.1 depicts these five styles of conflict management. This model helps students recognize that a particular style of conflict management,

Figure 12.1 Conflict management styles.

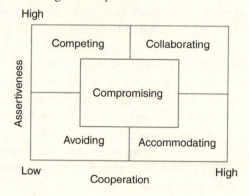

which may be relatively more comfortable to employ, is not always the most effective approach in a given situation.

Even after providing all the structure and resources previously outlined, faculty will find themselves attempting to support project teams whose functionality has been significantly impaired by tension and conflict. Assigning group work during class time and casually observing project team dynamics may help faculty get a read on the group's functionality. Providing behavioral observations to groups (e.g., "I've noticed that Daniel does much of the talking within the group while Alex says very little.") may help teams work on fine-tuning their dynamics. Inevitably, there will be teams wherein tension is so high and dysfunction so severe that students will seek out faculty intervention, often hoping that faculty will "fire" an underperforming team member. Here, faculty may be pulled into a mediator role, attempting to help the group address sources of conflict and supporting more effective communication. In some instances it may be helpful to bring in an outside consultant to help restore group functionality. This role may be filled by a faculty colleague or by seeking resources within student life (counseling, residential services, dean's office, trained student peers) who may have the skills and willingness to provide project group interventions. A sample format for such consultations can be found in Appendix 12.5.

Norming Project Teams

During a regularly scheduled faculty–team meeting with the Namibia Rainwater group, tension within the group is very apparent. Laurie continues to appear angry and disengaged, and upon your making this observation to her in the group, she breaks down in tears. Priya and Vanessa both seem angry and contemptuous of Laurie at this point. Javier, shifting uncomfortably in his seat, dismisses himself to go to the bathroom. You decide the whole group could use a break and ask Laurie to remain so you can talk to her individually.

Laurie shares that from the start of the project, Priya and Vanessa, who are close friends, have taken control and have been dismissive of any input and ideas she has put forward. She describes them both as perfectionists who become bossy and controlling whenever the group meets. They routinely criticize and reject her input, making her feel unwelcome. She feels they don't like her, and group meetings have become very uncomfortable for her. Laurie states that the stress associated with being part of this group has made a chronic medical condition flare up and prevented her from attending several recent meetings.

Having spoken with Priya, Vanessa, and Laurie, at this point you're curious about Javier's perspectives on the team's functioning. After having scheduled a follow-up meeting with the team as a whole, you ask Javier to remain behind. He shares that project group meetings have been more and more tense as the weeks have gone on and that he's tried to help out the group by injecting humor into the meetings. Javier also states that Vanessa or Priya have completely rewritten everything he's submitted to the group thus far, without providing him any feedback as to why they're doing so. At this point Javier believes that Priya and Vanessa would prefer to finish the project on their own, doing all the work themselves. He admits that he's given up trying to fix the situation and is just riding things out.

Student Experience

The project team at the norming phase has "worked out the bugs" in terms of their functioning together. Ground rules have been established around logistics: how often and how long the group will meet, the balance of group and individual work, the roles and responsibilities team members will take on, and how work will be assigned. The project team has a shared vision of what is to be accomplished and an agreed-on plan of how the team might get there. Leadership is typically shared at this point, depending on variables, including expertise and the task at hand. Leadership may also be delegated to or assumed by a team member; on healthy teams there is an awareness and agreement about this model. Teams at this phase begin to be highly productive, and a sense of cohesion, pride, and camaraderie emerges within the group.

Knowledge, respect, and support of team members' strengths and weaknesses also develop during the norming phase of team development. Within their strength sets, group members are contributing equitably to the progress of the project, which is to say at various times in the project one or more team members may be working "harder" than others on the team, but there remains a sense of balance of overall effort and commitment to agreed-on outcomes. Norming project teams generally enjoy working together and are able to produce results and meet deadlines.

Nonetheless, there remain some challenges and potential pitfalls at the norming stage. To preserve their comfort and cohesion, project teams in the norming phase may be reticent to "rock the boat." Disagreements about approach and priorities may be swept under the rug in an attempt to preserve harmony within the group. Groups at the norming stage are susceptible to "groupthink," a psychological phenomenon wherein groups of individuals can be found to prioritize group harmony and cohesion to the degree that critical evaluation is minimized, potentially resulting in irrational and dysfunctional conclusions and behaviors (Janis, 1972). An antidote to groupthink is found in the dynamics of the fourth stage of Tuckman and Jensen's (1977) model, *performing*, to be discussed later.

Faculty Roles and Strategies

Norming project teams require far less faculty involvement, support, and intervention than teams at the forming and storming phases. In fact, it can be very enjoyable to witness teams engaging meaningfully in project team conversations, meeting deadlines, and producing quality outcomes. Yet, as reported earlier, there are two great dangers to effective team dynamics within this phase: First, project teams may be avoiding and covering up significant conflict within the team, with mounting frustration and resentment; second, teams that may have been swept up by the earlier described groupthink phenomenon are bypassing critical information and perspectives that may negatively affect outcomes of the project.

As mentioned earlier, periodically building in peer and team assessment assignments may help teams identify and address dysfunctional behaviors and patterns. These assignments may seem superfluous to teams who perceive themselves as highly functional but, nonetheless, may have value in identifying problems and in helping functional teams move to their highest level of performing. Periodic assessments help project teams appreciate the importance of taking time to step away from the enmeshed work of the project to make critical adjustments to their approach and work together, while recognizing and celebrating their strength and accomplishments as the project proceeds.

Faculty can help students understand and avoid the pitfalls of groupthink by explaining the concept and making constructive recommendations as to how groups might avoid its dangers. A basic step toward this end involves building in opportunities for teams to engage in critical analysis of their approach and strategies. Project teams can rotate assigning someone the role of "devil's advocate" in each team meeting. In addition, teams can be assigned the task of bringing in an "expert" to consult on their current work together. This could be done in the context of a classroom assignment where other students within the class are assigned the role of team consultant, which would offer a learning opportunity for these students as well.

Faculty may also consider adding in project team presentations during the norming phase, essentially assigning teams the task of making a brief presentation to the professor and the class on how they've conceptualized their project, strategies they've developed, and expected outcomes. In doing this, faculty may get a read on team dynamics and functionality in the students' ability to articulate in a clear fashion a well-thought-out description and plan of their work together. Project teams who are under functioning— perhaps still storming—will have a difficult time articulating a cohesive view of their work together. Encouraging constructive critical feedback from others in the classroom may provide yet another opportunity to identify and break through groupthink.

Performing Project Teams

As part of the next group meeting, you're determined to attempt to help the Namibia Rainwater group talk about their differences and how to work together more effectively. After consulting with a colleague about the situation, you decide to ask each group member to directly address his or her concerns with each other. You're also quite concerned that the team could blow up, and you are feeling a bit out of your element in promoting such a conversation, but you forge ahead.

Vanessa takes the lead and says that the biggest problem within the group is that Laurie and Javier are not carrying their fair share of the work. Laurie immediately responds defensively, saying that Vanessa and Priya have taken full control of the project and there's no room for her to contribute. The tension immediately escalates. You intervene to establish a ground rule for this conversation: Each group member must first acknowledge what has just been shared before moving ahead with comments (a deescalating strategy taught in marriage counseling).

With some ongoing prompting from you, the conversation becomes more constructive—team members begin to listen more to each other's perspectives, and the tension within the group remains relatively low. Each of the team members begins to share more personally how difficult the project has been and how it has adversely affected his or her well-being. Vanessa and Priya eventually acknowledge that their close friendship may have negatively affected the team's dynamic, and the two of them joke that perhaps they need to let go of some of their perfectionism and control. Javier chimes in with a well-timed quip about their "letting go," and the group as a whole has a good laugh. Eventually Laurie discloses to the group that she's been struggling with a medical condition exacerbated by the stress of this team. Her heartfelt disclosure clearly generates compassion from all.

You share your appreciation for the group members' willingness to address their difficulties honestly and ask them to develop an agreement outlining expectations of each other moving ahead. You also suggest that they discuss how they're doing as a team in each of their upcoming meetings and try to constructively address concerns as they emerge.

Student Experience

When, and if, a project team reaches the performing stage, its confidence and energy are high. Deadlines and final deliverables loom, but the group pulls together in a highly functional manner to produce an outcome that is synergistic and that challenges the group members in a manner that propels results and outcomes that are far better than any of the group members could have achieved on their own. At the performing stage, team members are "in the zone"—their work together is highly energized, and the resulting quality of the work is recognized as a product of their synergistic functioning. Team dynamics in this stage, though, can still be quite challenging and sometimes exhausting. Group members can see the project approaching completion, and they're beginning to experience the rewards of all the work that has led up to this point.

The team remains cohesive and is relatively freed of interpersonal issues and conflicts. It's not that tensions have disappeared; team members channel all their energy toward project completion and understand that interpersonal tension is an artifact of their mutual passion for excellence. Tension within the group is appreciated as dynamic inasmuch as it propels and sustains their elevated level of performance. Group members instinctively challenge one another to think out of the box and take risks, fully realizing that mistakes might be made and appreciating each mistake as an opportunity for growth. Project team members appreciate that something special is happening within the group during these often short-lived bursts of synergistic energy.

Faculty Roles and Strategies

The faculty's main role with teams in the performing stage is to provide positive feedback about outcomes and recognition of synergistic dynamics while reflecting the toll this level of achievement can take on the team and providing ongoing encouragement and support. It's not uncommon that highly performing teams will briefly slip back into norming or storming phases, and faculty can expect that teams will readily return to performing relatively quickly and without the need for faculty intervention. It is essential that faculty recognize the importance that risk-taking and tension play in this highly functional phase of group work and to reward this dynamic as opportunities arise.

One excellent indicator of highly performing teams is reflected in their written outcomes, which tend to read with continuity and singularity of voice but not the voice of one team member. Faculty should encourage members of teams that submit more disjointed work, indicative of norming, to work together and provide each other with more constructive feedback about each other's sections and the work as a whole. Faculty may want to spend some time with members of groups that appear to be functional but are stuck in a norming phase to witness team dynamics and help them move toward challenging each other a bit more.

Adjourning Project Teams

This particular project team scenario demonstrates just how complicated and layered student team dynamic issues can be. It provides a fair depiction of student avoidance of conflict with mounting tension and dysfunction within a team.

All four students were considered "very high performing" but ran into difficulties together as Priya and Vanessa took control of the project. We see the dynamic of Laurie gradually disengaging (under functioning), which prompted more control from Priya and Vanessa (over functioning) as the project progressed. Javier was instinctively trying to alleviate this tension with his humor, which was not well received, and eventually he moved toward disengaging from the group.

Faculty intervention eventually went well, effectively addressing and deescalating the tension and allowing for honest communication and ownership about core issues within the group. The group's sudden shift into more effective communication may appear overly dramatized, but this type of shift is typical when we can effectively "blow up" team tension and promote direct conversations about team issues. Not all team issues will be resolved with this type of approach, especially when there is one team member under functioning for reasons not associated with team dynamics. But the greater majority of under functioning teams can and will improve when they are able to break through tension and have honest discussions about their differences.

Student Experience and Faculty Strategies

All student project teams, no matter how far along Tuckman and Jensen's stages they've progressed, will experience the adjourning phase. For many project teams, whose experience has involved significant storming, adjourning can provide much needed relief. Most project teams, though, having functioned within the norming and performing stages, will have a sense of pride in their accomplishments and may experience a sense of loss as the class ends and the group dissolves. This can be expected, especially in groups that managed to establish high cohesion and the exhilaration of being part of a highly functional team.

An opportunity to create and make a final presentation or poster presentations in front of the class can help adjourning groups begin to reflect on their experience together as a team. Teams may wish to gather and celebrate their accomplishments as a group. Opportunities for such gatherings may be interrupted by the end of the class and semester and leave teams with a sense of incompleteness and disappointment. This is especially true of teams who may have completed their projects in the context of a study abroad experience and may be understood in the context of reverse culture shock. Providing encouragement for teams to reengage and celebrate upon their return to campus can help address this sense of incompleteness.

One highly recommended faculty assignment for adjourning project teams is a final group evaluation of project team dynamics. A sample format of such an assignment can be found in Appendix 12.6. This exercise, by encouraging students' reflection on the process of working together, will help promote closure for the team and provide an invaluable opportunity for students to learn more about team dynamics in general and their own tendencies as it relates to project team functioning. Faculty may even underscore the importance of such an exercise by offering additional grading credit to teams who complete this assignment in an invested and thoughtful manner.

Conclusion

The concept of synergy, cited frequently throughout this chapter in describing highly functional teams, provides an important manner of understanding the essential value of differences. Student project teams, in the context of students' work together, learn important lessons about the value of embracing differences as a dynamic means of achieving outcomes that surpass the work of an individual. But embracing differences requires significant effort. Students must take the time to recognize and acknowledge differences and be able to bear the tension that differences generate. Perhaps the most straightforward example of differences within project teams has to do with personality preferences that can be described in the MBTI (Myers, 1995).

I often make use of the MBTI in classroom discussions with student project teams to demonstrate the inherent tension and the value of personality differences within the teams. For instance, a quick test to provide individuals a measure of themselves on the introversion–extroversion scale (comfort with internal versus external locus of attention) of the MBTI (see Appendix 11.2) is followed by a discussion of how these differences can be a source of tension. Extroverts will be quick to share how uncomfortable they feel when introverts are not sharing their thoughts and ideas. Extroverts may perceive introverts as withholding and uncaring. At the same time, introverts will share that they are often taken aback by some of the outrageous ideas and opinions of extroverts and that they get frustrated when they feel that extroverts are controlling the conversation. The tension becomes apparent in this discussion.

Yet, students are also quick to recognize the potential synergy inherent in these personality differences in a discussion of how these differences play into each other in a constructive manner. When prompted, students recognize how extroverts provide much needed energy for group discussions and the generation of ideas and possibilities (brainstorming), while introverts naturally synthesize these ideas into meaningful new concepts and possibilities. Students are quick to recognize the value of the dynamic interplay of these personality differences but that this may come to fruition only when there is an appreciation for these differences and an ability to make room for, even welcome, dynamic tension.

This appreciation for differences can also be applied to forming a better understanding of the importance of diversity within our campus communities, which are often a mix of differing ages, races, cultures, genders, sexual orientations, and socioeconomic backgrounds. We do well to promote the value and richness of our campus communities by welcoming students, faculty, and staff from diverse backgrounds not because it makes us "look better" but, most important, because it is these differences that put us in position to "be better" and synergistically achieve greater outcomes than we could without these differences. But this doesn't happen without a commitment to truly engaging differences within our communities, approaching different others with curiosity and compassion and with the courage to approach the tension inherent in difficult conversations that help us embrace the value of diversity. These issues are more explicitly addressed in the preceding chapter.

EXAMPLE PROJECT SELECTION SHEET

The following information will be used in the formation of teams for your project. Place an X along the scale to indicate your level of interest in each project. A rating of 0 means "I would rather stay home than do this project"; a rating of 100 indicates that "I would choose to work on this project rather than go to the beach or watch my favorite movie." All projects must be ranked; ties are allowed. We will make every effort to assign you to one of your first three choices, but there are many constraints, and some flexibility is required. Please e-mail this form to Prof. A (prof-email@wpi.edu) by 5:00 p.m. on Wednesday, September 9. You will be notified of your project team assignment and partners on Friday, September 11.

Name   Class Year and Major

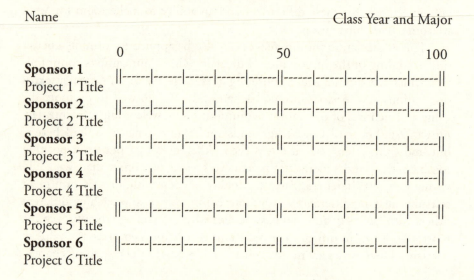

Write: For *each* project, please write a *paragraph* or two describing the reasons why you are or are not interested in the project and identify the skills that make you uniquely qualified for each project.

Personal Data

1. Complete the following schedule. This information will be used to set up weekly team meetings with the project advisers.
2. List any specialized *skills* such as website design, database programming, or statistical analysis.
3. List any people with whom you would like to work.
4. Identify *one* person (if any) with whom you would prefer *not* to work.
5. List any person with whom you have a personal relationship (romantic, business, etc.).
6. Greek affiliation, if any.
7. Provide other comments that you think the advisers may find useful in forming teams.

Instructions

Enter the *activity name* (course number, work study, etc.) in the cells for all times that you are *not* available for team meetings. Please include *only* those commitments that *absolutely cannot be changed*. Normally these are limited to academic commitments. Note any athletics, cocurricular, or other personal commitments in the comments section.

	Monday	Tuesday	Wednesday	Thursday	Friday
8:00–9:00					
9:00–10:00					
10:00–11:00					
11:00–12:00					
12:00–1:00					
1:00–2:00					
2:00–3:00					
3:00–4:00					
4:00–5:00					
5:00–6:00					

TEAM BUILDING EXERCISES

The Mine Field (15–30 minutes). The idea behind this exercise is to improve team members' trust, to improve their relationship, and to communicate in a more effective way. You will need an open space such as an empty room or hallway in which you will distribute "mines," placing them haphazardly around the area. The mines can be cones, balls, bottles, and so on. Participants are paired into teams: A is blindfolded, B can see and talk but is not allowed to enter the field or touch A. The challenge is for A to walk from one side of the field to the other, avoiding the mines by listening to the verbal instructions of B. (*Optional:* Have more than one pair walking through the mine simultaneously, so the difficulty of focusing and listening to the right instructions increases.)

Two Truths and a Lie (15–30 minutes). Start by having team members secretly write down 2 truths and a lie about themselves on a small piece of paper. Then allow 10 to 15 minutes for open conversation—much like a cocktail party, where everyone quizzes each other on their three questions. The idea is to convince others that each lie is actually a truth. After the conversational period, participants gather in a circle and one by one repeat each one of their three statements and ask the group members to vote on which one they think is the lie. You can play this game competitively and award points for each lie you guess or for stumping other players on your own lie.

Classification Game (10–15 minutes). This activity is a quick icebreaker. Before splitting the group into teams of four, explain the concept of pigeonholing or stereotyping someone. (It should be made clear that this type of classification is subjective and unhelpfully judgmental.) Instruct the participants to introduce themselves to teammates and quickly discuss some of their likes, dislikes, and so on. After the introductions, reveal to the teams that it will be their job to discover how they should classify themselves *as a team* into two or three subgroups by using criteria that contain no negative, prejudicial, or discriminatory judgments. Examples of these subgroups might include night owls and morning people, pineapple pizza lovers and sushi lovers, and so forth. This activity encourages members to get to know each other better and enables them to collectively consider the nature of all individuals within the team.

SAMPLE TEAM CONTRACT

Team Contract

Class: _____

Team Name: _____ Date: _____

Goals: What are the team goals for this project? What are the team member skill development goals for this project? Write team and individual goals with specific and measurable language. What would be an ideal teamwork experience?

Expectations: What do we expect of one another in regard to attendance at meetings, participation, frequency of communication, the quality of work, and so on? How much effort are we willing to expend? How important is the final grade?

Structure and approach: What rules can we agree on to help us meet our goals and expectations? How will we decide to fairly distribute the workload? How will team leadership and management be handled? How will agendas and record keeping be managed?

Consequences: How will the team resolve disagreements? How will the team manage missed deadlines? How will the team address concerns about distribution, amount, and quality of work?

We have all discussed and agree to these goals, expectations, structure and approach, and consequences.

Team member name:

Team member name:

Team member name:

Team member name:

TWO EVALUATIONS OF TEAM DEVELOPMENT

Evaluate Your Team Development

How do you feel about your team's progress? (Circle rating.)

1. Team's purpose
   I'm uncertain   1   2   3   4   5   I'm clear
2. Team membership
   I'm out   1   2   3   4   5   I'm in
3. Communications
   Very guarded   1   2   3   4   5   Very open
4. Team goals
   Set from above   1   2   3   4   5   Emerged through team interaction
5. Use of team member's skills
   Poor use   1   2   3   4   5   Good use
6. Support
   Little help for individuals   1   2   3   4   5   High level of support for individuals
7. Conflict
   Difficult issues are avoided   1   2   3   4   5   Problems are discussed openly and directly
8. Influence on decisions
   By few members   1   2   3   4   5   By all members
9. Risk-taking
   Not encouraged   1   2   3   4   5   Encouraged and supported
10. Working on relationships with others
    Little effort   1   2   3   4   5   High level of effort
11. Distribution of leadership
    Limited   1   2   3   4   5   Shared
12. Useful feedback
    Very little   1   2   3   4   5   Considerable

Teamwork and Teamwork Assessment

Your career success will largely depend on your ability to work effectively with people who have different perspectives, attitudes, and backgrounds from yours. One of the most challenging and important skills you will be asked to develop during this project is that of effective teamwork. The basis of good teamwork is a shared desire for the team, and not just individuals, to excel. *Although you will receive individual grades for this project, you will be evaluated on how well you have worked within the context of the team, not as an individual achiever.*

Effective teamwork does not mean avoiding conflict; it means drawing out all viewpoints and ideas, having commitment to informed debate and analysis, actively listening, having the ability to give constructive feedback, being open to changing your mind, and managing conflict. In fact, if your team is getting along quite peacefully, it may actually mean that you are not thinking critically as a team.

It is important to have lots of team discussion time prior to meetings with advisers and liaisons and as major decisions about the report need to be made. Your partners should always know what you are going to say during a meeting—*never "spring surprises" on each other*. Do not pass in material that you have worked on alone and not shown to your partners. Put everyone's name on everything, in alphabetical order. Do not denigrate the performance of your partners in front of your advisers or liaisons. Do not spend your part of the meeting trying to make yourself look good; spend it trying to make the whole team look good. In this context you should find yourself using "we" more than "I"—just make sure that you have discussed and agree on statements where you use "we."

A major challenge that advisers face is evaluating the teamwork component of projects. Although we will see you in action during formal and informal meetings and will see the outcomes of your work, we rarely see the "daily grind" and process of teamwork behind the scenes. Some teams try to hide concerns about individuals' efforts or their team processes, thinking that bringing it out in the open will reflect poorly on their group dynamics. Judgments that advisers make in such situations can be inaccurate and unintentionally unfair. Of even more concern in these situations is the fact that teams do not learn much about effective teamwork. Even teams that work effectively together may not, in fact, learn much about teamwork if they do not reflect on the processes they used. Imagine yourself in an interview with a potential employer: "I was lucky. My team got along really well!" does not convey that you learned anything whatsoever about teamwork development.

To address these limitations of advisers' evaluation of teamwork, to promote deeper learning about teamwork, and to prepare you for professional work environments, *each team will be responsible for developing and proposing its own teamwork assessment process.*

The assessment process must have the following components and characteristics:

- It must include a formative (i.e., for purposes of improvement) component at least once during the term, as well as a summative component at the end of the project.
- Individual contributions to the team must be assessed, as well as the team as a whole. Your assessments of each other and of the team must be shared and discussed with team members before being given to advisers.
- The assessment reports must be persuasive to advisers. There should be tangible evidence of learning about teamwork. *Actions* planned or taken as a result of the assessment process should be stated clearly.
- The assessment reports should be sincere and self-critical, showing introspection about multiple aspects of teamwork.

MODEL FOR OUTSIDE CONSULTATION FOR UNDERFUNCTIONING PROJECT TEAMS

This two-part model for team consultation was developed by staff at WPI's Student Development and Counseling Center (SDCC) as a resource for faculty who are concerned about underfunctioning project teams. Faculty refer (often mandate) students to arrange these consultations with SDCC staff when they observe significant tension and/or persistent problems within the group dynamic that are negatively affecting outcomes.

Part One: Individual Meetings (One Hour)

Faculty contact the SDCC to share concerns about a particular project team, then inform the team of their expectation that they seek consultation from the SDCC. The team schedules an initial assessment meeting at the SDCC, where all group members attend an initial, one-hour consultation together. The consultant meets initially with the whole team to explain the process, assuring the team that he or she is working for the team and not conducting an investigation on behalf of the professor. They are told a single report reflecting the two-part consultation (see following example) will be provided to all group members and the faculty.

The consultant then meets individually with each group member for 10 to 15 minutes. The students are told this is their time to succinctly "air out" their perceptions of the group's functioning as a whole and the individual's contributions within. Individual group members are assured that what they say in this session will remain between each individual and the consultant, so "name names" and "try to be as open and honest about thoughts, feelings, and perceptions as you can."

The following are facilitating questions that may be included:

- How has the group been functioning together since your work began?
- What different roles have individual members of the group assumed?
- Does everyone appear to be contributing equally to the effort?
- Have you noticed any tension between group members?
- What would you like to see done differently within the group?
- Is this concern something you think you could share with the group as a whole?

The consultant's role at this point is to be an active listener and gather information. All group members remain together in the waiting room while each individual meets with the consultant. After individual meetings are concluded, a follow-up meeting is scheduled for the group to meet as a whole with the consultant within the next week.

Part Two: Group Meeting (30 Minutes to 60 Minutes)

The group meets as a whole to talk with the consultant about observations and concerns about the group's functioning. The group is also asked to develop an agreed-on plan to address concerns and therefore improve overall group functioning.

The consultant's role is to keep the group on task and to skillfully mediate escalating tensions that may emerge within the conversation. This can be accomplished by ensuring that each group member is able to demonstrate understanding of others' observations and concerns before expressing his or her own opinions. In addition, the consultant ensures each group member has ample time and opportunity to contribute to the group discussion. The consultant holds faithfully to the promise to each individual to not share information gained from the initial meeting but does attempt to direct the conversation toward critical issues if the group is not doing so on its own.

Finally, the consultant writes a report that goes to all group members and the faculty that summarizes the consultation (see the following example; all names were changed).

IQP Group Consultation

Group members: Mariano Olivier, Patrick Jones, Serena Davis, Emily Roberson

Faculty advisers: Sam Vatrano, Jennifer Carter

Date: 4/23/2014

Individual Meeting Summary

All group members completed individual interviews on 4/18 to share their perceptions of group dynamics. Their comments converged on the following themes:

- The group had started strong with high expectations but experienced external stress associated with shifting project expectations during the term.
- Personality differences appear to contribute to some degree to the tension within the group; both men are somewhat more laid back and flexible in their work styles, while the women are more structured, timely, and organized.
- There was some tension within the group associated with perceptions of differences between how much each group member was prioritizing the project.

Group Meeting Summary

Group members met with me as a whole on 4/22. The group as a whole appeared to be experiencing a good deal of pressure as the term approaches completion and there is much left to do. The group had worked for about an hour before the SDCC meeting, and some members were concerned about lack of progress. Emily expressed her frustration with Patrick that he had made plans to be away from campus Friday through Sunday of this coming weekend. Serena and Mariano agreed that this would place unfair strain on the rest of the group, as they expected they would need to work closely together to complete project expectations. Patrick explained that he had planned this trip and told group members long ago he would be away, though other group members expressed they had only recently learned of just how long he would be off campus. Patrick agreed to reassess his plans to travel based on progress made in the upcoming week.

Group/Consultant Observations and Recommendations

There appears to be ongoing tension within the group resulting from personality and work style differences, as well as external project pressures. This tension may contribute to group members moving more to their differing "comfort zones" of structure, organization, and control versus flexibility, creativity, and comfort. The group will need to work very hard to reach the potential for excellence in the project that they all aspire to.

Group members should maintain open communication about expectations and deadlines in finishing up the work.

Moving ahead, group members should balance differing work styles, recognizing and respecting the importance of both structure and deadlines *and* flexibility and managing stress levels within the group to sustain open communication.

Completed by Charles Morse, Director, WPI SDCC

TEAM DYNAMICS
REFLECTION ASSIGNMENT

Team Dynamics Reflection

To be completed as a team:

1. Describe team strengths and how they supported successful completion of the project.
2. Describe team weaknesses and challenges and how they were recognized and addressed.
3. Identify differences within your group (gender, culture, race, personality, etc.) and provide analysis of how these differences may have contributed to both tension and success within the group.
4. Describe what you learned from your group experience on this project that you will carry into your next group experience.

REFERENCES

ABET. (2017). *Criteria for accrediting engineering programs, 2016–2017.* Retrieved from http://www.abet.org/accreditation/accreditation-criteria/criteria-for-accrediting-engineering-programs-2016-2017/#students

Adams, N. E. (2014). A comparison of evidence-based practice and the ACRL information literacy standards: Implications for information literacy practice. *College and Research Libraries, 75*(2), 232–248.

Adams, S. (2014, November 12). The 10 skills employers most want in 2015 graduates. *Forbes Magazine.* Retrieved from https://www.forbes.com/sites/susanadams/2014/11/12/the-10-skills-employers-most-want-in-2015-graduates/#3e2acd262511

Aggarwal, P., & O'Brien, C. L. (2008). Social loafing on group projects: Structural antecedents and effects on student satisfaction. *Journal of Marketing Education, 30*(3), 255–264.

Al-Atabi, M., Shamel, M. M., Younis, O., & Chung, E. (2010). Corporate style team-building activities for undergraduate engineering programmes. In *Proceedings of the 21st Annual Conference for the Australasian Association for Engineering Education* (p. 391). Barton, Australia: Engineers Australia.

Alexander, M. (2011). *The new Jim Crow: Mass incarceration in the age of colorblindness.* New York: NY: New Press.

Ambrose, S. A., Bridges, M. W., DiPietro, M., Lovett, M. C., & Norman, M. K. (2010). *How learning works: Seven research-based principles for smart teaching.* San Francisco, CA: Jossey-Bass.

American Library Association. (1989). *Presidential committee on information literacy: Final report.* Retrieved from http://www.ala.org/acrl/publications/whitepapers/presidential

American Library Association. (2000). *Information literacy standards for higher education.* Retrieved from http://www.ala.org/acrl/sites/ala.org.acrl/files/content/standards/standards.pdf

Anaya, G., & Cole, D. G. (2001). Latina/o student achievement: Exploring the influence on student–faculty interactions on college grades. *Journal of College Student Development, 42*(1), 3–14.

Anderson, K., & May, F. A. (2010). Does the method of instruction matter? An experimental examination of information literacy instruction in the online, blended, and face-to-face classrooms. *Journal of Academic Librarianship, 36*(6), 495–500.

Arreola, R., Theall, M., & Aleamoni, L. M. (2003, April). *Beyond scholarship: Recognizing the multiple roles of the professoriate.* Paper presented at the annual meeting of the American Educational Research Association, Chicago, IL.

Ash, S. L., & Clayton, P. H. (2009). Generating, deepening, and documenting learning: The power of critical reflection in applied learning. *Journal of Applied Learning in Higher Education, 1*(1), 25–48.

Association of American Colleges & Universities. (n.d.-a). VALUE rubrics. Retrieved March 2017 from https://www.aacu.org/value-rubrics

Association of American Colleges & Universities. (n.d.-b). What is a liberal education? Retrieved from https://www.aacu.org/leap/what-is-a-liberal-education

Association of American Colleges & Universities. (2002). *Greater expectations: A new vision for learning as a nation goes to college.* Washington DC: Author.

Association of Colleges and Research Libraries. (2015). *Framework for information literacy in higher education.* Retrieved from http://www.ala.org/acrl/standards/ilframework

Bain, K. (2004). *What the best college teachers do.* Cambridge, MA: Harvard University Press.

Bain, K. (2012). *What the best college students do.* Boston, MA: Belknap Press.

Bakermans, M. H., & Ziino Plotke, R. (2018). Assessing information literacy instruction in interdisciplinary first year project-based courses with STEM students. *Library and Information Science Research, 40*(2), 98–105.

Bakhtin, M. M., Holquist, M., & Emerson, C. (2014). *The dialogic imagination: Four essays.* Austin, TX: University of Texas Press.

Barrows, H. S. (1992). *The tutorial process.* Springfield, IL: Southern Illinois University School of Medicine.

Bass, R., & Elmendorf, H. (n.d.). *Designing for difficulties: Social pedagogy as a framework for course design.* Retrieved May 26, 2018, from https://blogs.commons.georgetown.edu/bassr/social-pedagogies/

Benkler, Y., & Nissenbaum, H. (2006). Commons-based peer production and virtue. *Journal of Political Philosophy, 14*(4), 394–419.

Birmingham, C., & McCord, M. (2002). Group process research: Implications for using learning groups. In L. K. Michaelsen, A. B. Knight, & L. D. Fink (Eds.), *Team-based learning: A transformative use of small groups.* Westport, CT: Greenwood Publishing Group.

Blum, S. D. (2016). *"I love learning, I hate school": An anthropology of college.* Ithaca, NY: Cornell University Press.

Bok, D. (2003). *Universities in the marketplace: The commercialization of higher education.* Princeton, NJ: Princeton University Press.

Boruff, J. T., & Thomas, A. (2011). Integrating evidence-based practice and information literacy skills in teaching physical and occupational therapy students. *Health Information and Libraries Journal, 28*, 264–272. Retrieved from http://dx.dio.org/10.1111/j.1471-1842.2011.00953.x

Bourne, P. E. (2007). Ten simple rules for making good oral presentations. *PLoS Computational Biology, 3*(4), e77.

Bowles-Terry, M. (2012). Library instruction and academic success: A mixed-methods assessment of a library instruction program. *Evidence Based Library and Information Practice, 7*(1), 82–95. Retrieved from http://dx.doi.org/10.18438/B8PS4D

Brookfield, S. D. (2012). *Teaching for critical thinking*. San Francisco, CA: Jossey-Bass.

Bruce, C., Hughes, H., & Somerville, M. M. (2012). Supporting informed learners in the twenty-first century. *Library Trends, 60*(3), 522–545. doi:10.1353/lib.2012.0009

Bruff, D. (2011). *Social pedagogies: Authentic audiences and student motivation*. Retrieved from https://derekbruff.org/?p=808

Brundiers, K., Wiek, A., & Redman, C. L. (2010). Real-world learning opportunities in sustainability: From classroom into the real world. *International Journal of Sustainability in Higher Education, 11*(4), 308–324.

Buck Institute. (n.d.). What is PBL? Retrieved from http://bie.org/about/what_pbl

Burkhardt, J. M. (2007). Assessing library skills: A first step to information literacy. *portal: Libraries and the Academy, 7*(1), 25–49. Retrieved from http://dx.dio.org/10.1353/pla.2007.0002

Callison, R., Budny, D., & Thomes, K. (2005). Library research project for first-year engineering students: Results from collaboration by teaching and library faculty. *The Reference Librarian, 43*, 93–106. Retrieved from http://dx.doi.org/10.1300/J120v43n89_07

Cannon, A. (1994). Faculty survey on library research instruction. *RQ, 33*(3), 524–541.

Carlson, C. R., & Wilmot, W. W. (2006). *Innovation: The five disciplines for creating what customers want*. New York, NY: Crown Business.

Cho, K., & Schunn, C. D. (2007). Scaffolded writing and rewriting in the discipline: A web-based reciprocal peer review system. *Computers and Education, 48*(3), 409–426.

Colvin, J. W., & Ashman, M. (2010). Roles, risks, and benefits of peer mentoring relationships in higher education. *Mentoring and Tutoring: Partnership in Learning, 18*(2), 121–134.

Cook, J. M. (2014). A library credit course and student success rates: A longitudinal study. *College and Research Libraries, 75*(3), 272–283.

Cooper, K., & McNab, S. L. (2009). Questioning as a pedagogical tool. In S. G. Kouritzin, N. A. C. Piquemal, & R. Norman (Eds.), *Qualitative research: Challenging the orthodoxies in standard academic discourse(s)* (pp. 199–216). New York, NY: Routledge.

DaCosta, J. W. (2010). Is there an information literacy skills gap to be bridged? An examination of faculty perceptions and activities relating to information literacy in the United States and England. *College and Research Libraries, 71*(3), 203–222.

Dasgupta, N., Scircle, M. M., & Hunsinger, M. (2015). Female peers in small work groups enhance women's motivation, verbal participation, and career aspirations in engineering. *Proceedings of the National Academy of Sciences, 112*(16), 4988–4993.

Daugherty, A. L., & Russo, M. F. (2011). An assessment of the lasting effects of a stand-alone information literacy course: The students' perspective. *Journal of Academic Librarianship, 37*(4), 319–326. doi:10.1016/j.acalib.2011.04.006

Davidson, N., Major, C. H., & Michaelsen, L. K. (2014). Small-group learning in higher education—Cooperative, collaborative, problem-based, and team-based learning: An introduction by the guest editors. *Journal on Excellence in College Teaching, 25*(3–4), 1–6.

Deci, E. L., & Flaste, R. (1995). *Why we do what we do: The dynamics of personal autonomy.* New York, NY: Putnam's Sons.

Dehler, G. E. (2006). Using action research to connect practice to learning: A course project for working management students. *Journal of Management Education, 30*(5), 636–669.

Dent, S. M. (2002). What is your Conflict Resolution Style?. The CEO Refresher . . . brain food for business! Retrieved from http:// www.refresher.com/asdconflict .html

Dewey, J. (1997). *How we think.* Mineola, NY: Dover Publications.

Douglas, K. A., Rohan, C., Fosmire, M., Smith, C., Van Epps, A., & Purzer, S. (2014). "I just Google it": A qualitative study of information strategies in problem solving used by upper and lower level engineering students. In *Proceedings of the Frontiers in Education Conference.* Madrid, Spain: IEEE. Retrieved from http://dx.doi.org/10.1109/FIE.2014.7044298

Drew, C. (2011, November 6). Why science majors change their minds (it's just so darn hard) [Education Life]. *New York Times,* p. ED16.

Duckworth, A. (2016). *Grit: The power of passion and perseverance.* New York, NY: Scribner.

Durkin, K., & Main, A. (2002). Discipline-based study skills support for first-year undergraduate students. *Active Learning in Higher Education, 3*(1), 24–39.

Eddy, E. R., & D'Abate, C. (2016, November 16). Stop assigning team projects . . . unless . . . [Blog post]. The Scholarly Teacher: Applying Evidence-Based Strategies to Enrich Student Learning. Retrieved from http://scholarlyteacher .com/2016/11/10/stop-assigning-team-projects-unless/

EL Education. (2012, March 9). *Austin's butterfly: Building excellence in student work* [Video file]. Retrieved from https://vimeo.com/38247060

Ellis, J., & Salisbury, F. (2004). Information literacy milestones: Building upon the prior knowledge of first-year students. *The Australian Library Journal, 53*(4), 383–396. doi:10.1080/00049670.2004.10721685

Erren, T. C., & Bourne, P. E. (2007). Ten simple rules for a good poster presentation. *PLoS Computational Biology, 3*(5), e102.

Fain, M. (2011). Assessing information literacy skills development in first year students: A multi-year study. *Journal of Academic Librarianship, 37*(2), 109–119. Retrieved from http://dx.doi.org/10.1016/j.acalib.2011.02.002

Fallows, S. J., & Steven, C. (2000). The skills agenda. In S. J. Fallows & C. Steven (Eds.), *Integrating key skills in higher education: Employability, transferable skills, and learning for life* (pp. 3–12). New York, NY: Psychology Press.

Farrington, C., Roderick, M., Allensworth, E., Nagaoka, J., Keyes, T. S., Johnson, D. W., & Beechum, N. O. (2012). *Teaching adolescents to become learners: The role of noncognitive factors in shaping school performance: A critical literature review.* Chicago, IL: University of Chicago Consortium on School Research. Retrieved from https://consortium.uchicago.edu/sites/default/files/publications/Noncognitive %20Report.pdf

Felix, E. R., Bensimon, E. M., Hanson, D., Gray, J., & Klingsmith, L. (2015). Developing agency for equity-minded change. *New Directions for Community Colleges, 2015*(172), 25–42.

Finnegan, M. (2017, August 1). It's good till it's not: Does group work really help all students? *Inside Higher Ed.* Retrieved from https://www.insidehighered.com /advice/2017/08/01/helping-diverse-learners-navigate-group-work-essay?utm _source=Inside+Higher+Ed&utm_campaign=1b0d729230-DNU20170801 &utm_medium=email&utm_term=0_1fcbc04421-1b0d729230-198477221& mc_cid=1b0d729230&mc_eid=47613e59d6

Fleischmann, K. (2015). Developing on-campus work-integrated learning activities: The value of integrating community and industry partners into the creative arts curriculum. *Asia-Pacific Journal of Cooperative Education, 16*(1), 25–38.

Freeman, S., Eddy, S. L., McDonough, M., Smith, M. K., Okoroafor, N., Jordt, H., & Wenderoth, M. P. (2014). Active learning increases student performance in science, engineering and mathematics. *Proceedings of the National Academy of Sciences of the United States of America, 111*(23), 8410–8415.

Gallup–Purdue. (2014). *Great job, great lives: The 2014 Gallup–Purdue index report.* Retrieved from http://www.gallup.com/services/176768/2014-gallup-purdue-index-report.aspx

Gaytan, J. (2010). Instructional strategies to accommodate a team-teaching approach. *Business Communication Quarterly, 73*(1), 82–87.

Georgas, H. (2014). Google vs. the library (Part II): Student search patterns and behaviors when using Google and a federated search tool. *portal: Libraries and the Academy, 14*(4), 503–532. Retrieved May 18, 2017, from Project MUSE database.

Goddard, R. H. (1904, June). *On taking things for granted.* Graduation oration, South High Community School, Worcester, MA.

Greer, K., Hess, A. N., & Kraemer, E. W. (2016). The librarian leading the machine: A reassessment of library instruction methods. *College and Research Libraries, 77*(3), 286–301. Retrieved from http://dx.doi.org/10.5860/crl.77.3.286

Guerin, C., Xafis, V., Doda, D. V., Gillam, M. H., Larg, A. J., Luckner, H., . . . & Xu, C. (2013). Diversity in collaborative research communities: A multicultural, multidisciplinary thesis writing group in public health. *Studies in Continuing Education, 35*(1), 65–81.

Hanlan, L. R., & Boudreau, K. (2014). *A game-based approach to information literacy and engineering in context.* Paper presented at the Frontiers in Education Conference, IEEE. Retrieved from http://digitalcommons.wpi.edu/gordonlibrary-pubs/4

Hanrahan, S. J., & Isaacs, G. (2001). Assessing self-and peer-assessment: The students' views. *Higher Education Research and Development, 20*(1), 53–70.

Hanusch, F., Obijiofor, L., & Volcic, Z. (2009). Theoretical and practical issues in team teaching a large undergraduate class. *International Journal of Teaching and Learning in Higher Education, 21*(1), 66–74.

Hardesty, L. (1995). Faculty culture and bibliographic instruction: An exploratory analysis. *Library Trends, 44*(2), 339–367.

Hart Research Associates. (2015). *Falling short? College learning and career success.* Washington DC: Association of American Colleges & Universities.

Hays, P. A. (2004). Case study research. In K. deMarrais & S. D. Lapan (Eds.), *Foundations for research: Methods of inquiry in education and the social sciences* (pp. 217–234). Mahwah, NJ: Lawrence Erlbaum.

Heifetz, R., Grashow, A., & Linsky, M. (2009). *The practice of adaptive leadership: Tools and tactics for changing your organization and the world.* Boston, MA: Harvard Business School.

Hemlin, S., Allwood, C. M., & Martin, B. R. (2008). Creative knowledge environments. *Creativity Research Journal, 20*(2), 196–210.

Hennink, M., Hutter, I., & Bailey, A. (2010). *Qualitative research methods.* Thousand Oaks, CA: Sage.

Hesse, D. (n.d.). Response to student writing: 13 Ways of looking at it. Retrieved from https://www.niagara.edu/wc-response-to-student-writing/

Higgins, R., Hartley, P., & Skelton, A. (2001). Getting the message across: The problem of communicating assessment feedback. *Teaching in Higher Education, 6*(2), 269–274.

Hrycaj, P. L., & Russo, J. F. (2007). A survey of LSU faculty attitudes toward library research instruction. *Louisiana Libraries, 69*(4), 15–25.

Hugo, V. (1862). *Les misérables.* Paris, France: A. Lacroix, Verboeckhoven & Cie.

Hurtado, S., Cabrera, N. L., Lin, M. H., Arellano, L., & Espinosa, L. L. (2009). Diversifying science: Underrepresented student experiences in structured research programs. *Research in Higher Education, 50*(2), 189–214.

Hyun, E. (2011). Transdisciplinary higher education curriculum: A complicated cultural artifact. *Research in Higher Education Journal, 11.* Retrieved from http://works.bepress.com/eunsook_hyun/1/

Jacobson, T. E., & Mark, B. L. (2000). Separating wheat from chaff: Helping first-year students become information savvy. *Journal of General Education, 49*(4), 256–278.

James, W. (1981). *Pragmatism.* B. Kuklick (Ed.). Indianapolis, IN: Hackett. (Original work published 1907.)

Janis, I. L. (1972). *Victims of groupthink: A psychological study of foreign-policy decisions and fiascoes.* Boston, MA: Houghton Mifflin.

Jonassen, D. H., & Hung, W. (2008). All problems are not equal: Implications for problem-based learning. *Interdisciplinary Journal of Problem-Based Learning, 2*(2).

Junisbai, B., Lowe, M. S., & Tagge, N. (2016). A pragmatic and flexible approach to information literacy: Findings from a three-year study of faculty-librarian collaboration. *Journal of Academic Librarianship, 42*(5), 604–611. doi:10.1016/j.acalib.2016.07.001

Katehi, L. (2015, May 26). Liberal arts and our future. *Huffington Post.* Retrieved from http://www.huffingtonpost.com/linda-katehi/liberal-arts-and-our-futu_b_7444758.html

Kilmann, R., & Thomas, K. W. (1977). Developing a forced-choice measure of conflict-handling behavior: The "MODE" instrument. *Educational and Psychological Measurement, 37,* 309.

Kingsley, K., Galbraith, G. M., Herring, M., Stowers, E., Stewart, T., & Kingsley, K. V. (2011). Why not just Google it? An assessment of information literacy skills in a biomedical science curriculum. *BMC Medical Education, 11*(1), 17. doi:10.1186/1472-6920-11-17

Knight, L. A. (2002). The role of assessment in library user education. *Reference Services Review, 30*(1), 15–24.

Koufogiannakis, D., & Wiebe, N. (2006). Effective methods for teaching information literacy skills to undergraduate students: A systematic review and meta-analysis. *Evidence Based Library and Information Practice, 1*(3), 3–34.

Krimsky, S. (2003). *Science in the private interest: Has the lure of profits corrupted biomedical research?* Lanham, MD: Rowman & Littlefield.

Kuh, G. D. (2008). *High-impact educational practices: What they are, who has access to them and why they matter.* Washington, DC: Association of American Colleges & Universities.

Lang, J. (2013). *Cheating lessons.* Cambridge, MA: Harvard University Press.

Larkin, J. E., & Pines, H. A. (2005). Developing information literacy and research skills in introductory psychology: A case study. *Journal of Academic Librarianship, 31*(1), 40–45. Retrieved from http://dx.doi.org/10.1016/j.acalib.2004.09.008

Larmer, J., Mergendoller, J. R., & Boss, S. (2015). *Setting the standard for project based learning: A proven approach to rigorous classroom instruction.* Alexandria, VA: ASCD.

Laursen, S., Hunter, A. B., Seymour, E., Thiry, H., & Melton, G. (2010). *Undergraduate research in the sciences: Engaging students in real science.* San Francisco, CA: Jossey-Bass.

Leckie, G. J., & Fullerton, A. (1999). Information literacy in science and engineering undergraduate education: Faculty attitudes and pedagogical practices. *College and Research Libraries, 60*(1), 9–29.

Lester, J. N., & Evans, K. R. (2009). Instructors' experiences of collaboratively teaching: Building something bigger. *International Journal of Teaching and Learning in Higher Education, 20*(3), 373–382.

Lightfoot, E., McCleary, J. S., & Lum, T. (2014). Asset mapping as a research tool for community-based participatory research in social work. *Social Work Research, 38*(1), 59–64.

Logo Company, The. (2017). *Color emotion guide.* Retrieved from https://thelogocompany.net/blog/infographics/psychology-color-logo-design/

Lundstrom, K., & Baker, W. (2009). To give is better than to receive: The benefits of peer review to the reviewer's own writing. *Journal of Second Language Writing, 18*(1), 30–43.

Manuel, K., Beck, S. E., & Molloy, M. (2005). An ethnographic study of attitudes influencing faculty collaboration in library instruction. *The Reference Librarian, 43*(89–90), 139–161.

Margolis, S. (2011, January 24). What is the optimal group size for decision-making? Retrieved May 18, 2017, from https://sheilamargolis.com/2011/01/24/what-is-the-optimal-group-size-for-decision-making/

Markham, T., Larmer, J., & Ravitz, J. (2003). *Project based learning handbook: A guide to standards-focused project based learning for middle and high school teachers.* Novato, CA: Buck Institute for Education.

Mateos, M., & Solé, I. (2009). Synthesising information from various texts: A study of procedures and products at different educational levels. *European Journal of Psychology of Education, 24*(4), 435–451. doi:10.1007/BF03178760

Mathews, B. (2015, June 10). Practicing critical information literacy: An interview with Troy Swanson [from "The Ubiquitous Librarian," a blog of the *Chronicle of Higher Education*]. Retrieved from http://chronicle.com/blognetwork/the ubiquitouslibrarian/2015/06/10/practicing-critical-information-literacy-interview-with-troy-swanson/

Maton, K. I., & Hrabowski, F. A., III. (2004). Increasing the number of African American PhDs in the sciences and engineering: A strengths-based approach. *American Psychologist, 59*(6), 547.

Maybee, C., Bruce, C., Lupton, M., & Renmann, K. (2013). Learning to use information: Informed learning in the undergraduate classroom. *Library and Information Science Research, 35*(3), 200–206. Retrieved from http://dx.doi.org/10.1016/j.lisr.2013.04.002

McDonough, W., & Braungart, M. (2009). *Cradle to cradle: Remaking the way we make things.* London, UK: Vintage.

McGuinness, C. (2006). What faculty think: Exploring the barriers to information literacy development in undergraduate education. *Journal of Academic Librarianship, 32*(6), 573–582.

McNair, T. (2017). *Examining equity gaps in high-impact practices: Access, design, and student success.* Workshop PowerPoint, 2017 American Association of College and Universities (AAC&U) High Impact Practices (HIPs) and Student Success Institute. Retrieved from http://www.aacu.org/sites/default/files/files/hips/HIPs%20 2017%20Session%202.pdf

Meadows, L. A., Sekaquaptewa, D., & Paretti, M. C. (2015). *Interactive panel: Improving the experiences of marginalized students on engineering design teams* (Paper ID # 11803). Paper presented at the American Society for Engineering Education Annual Conference and Exhibition, Seattle, WA.

Megwalu, A. (2013). Undergraduate research, Part II: A technique for synthesizing information. *The Reference Librarian, 54*(4), 349–352. doi:10.1080/02763877. 2013.809291

Moore, D., Brewster, S., Dorroh, C., & Moreau, M. (2002). Information competency instruction in a two-year college: One size does not fit all. *Reference Services Review, 30*(4), 300–306.

Myers, I. B. (with Myers, P. B.). (1995). *Gifts differing: Understanding personality type*. Mountain View, CA: Davies-Black Publishing.

National Association of Colleges and Employers. (2016). Job outlook 2016: The attributes employers want to see on new college graduates' resumes. Retrieved from http://www.naceweb.org/career-development/trends-and-predictions/job-outlook-2016-attributes-employers-want-to-see-on-new-college-graduates-resumes/

National Humanities Alliance and the Federation of State Humanities Councils. (2017, November). National Humanities Conference, Boston, MA. Retrieved from http://www.statehumanities.org/news/nhc-2017-call-for-proposals/

Nicol, D., Thomson, A., & Breslin, C. (2014). Rethinking feedback practices in higher education: A peer review perspective. *Assessment and Evaluation in Higher Education, 39*(1), 102–122.

Oakleaf, M. (2009). The information literacy instruction assessment cycle: A guide for increasing student learning and improving librarian instructional skills. *Journal of Documentation, 66*(4), 539–560. doi:10.1008/00220410910970249

Oakleaf, M., & Kaske, N. (2009). Guiding questions for assessing information literacy in higher education. *portal: Libraries and the Academy, 9*(2), 273–286. Retrieved from http://dx.doi.org/10.1353/pla.0.0046

Ohland, M. W., Pomeranz, H. R., & Feinstein, H. W. (2006, June). The Comprehensive Assessment of Team Member Effectiveness: A new peer evaluation instrument. In *Proceedings of the American Society of Engineering Education Annual Conference*, Chicago, IL.

Palmer, P. J. (2007). *The courage to teach: Exploring the inner landscape of a teacher's life*. San Francisco, CA: Jossey-Bass.

Patton, L. D., Harper, S. R., & Harris, J. Using critical race theory to (re)interpret widely-studied topics related to students in U.S. higher education. In A. M. Martínez Alemán, E. M. Bensimon, & B. Pusser (Eds.), *Critical approaches to the study of higher education* (pp. 193–219). Baltimore: Johns Hopkins University Press.

Paul, A. M. (2015, September 12). Are college lectures unfair? *New York Times*, p. SR12.

Perry, B., & Stewart, T. (2005). Insights into effective partnership in interdisciplinary team teaching. *System, 33*(4), 563–573.

Petersen, J., & London, N. (2003). *First in flight, last in wetlands preservation?* Buffalo, NY: National Center for Case Study Teaching in Science, University at Buffalo, State University of New York.

Pfeifer, G., & Rosbach, D. (2016). The Great Problems Seminars: Connecting students with external stakeholders in project-based approaches to sustainable development education in the first year. In W. L. Filho & L. Brandli (Eds.), *Engaging stakeholders in education for sustainable development at university level* (pp. 233–242). New York, NY: Springer.

Phillips, K. W., Liljenquist, K. A., & Neale, M. (2010, October 1). *Better decisions through diversity*. Kellogg School of Management at Northwestern University, Kellogg Insight. Retrieved from https://insight.kellogg.northwestern.edu/article/better_decisions_through_diversity

Plank, K. M. (Ed.). (2012). *Team teaching: Across the disciplines, across the academy*. Sterling, VA: Stylus.

Plank, K. M. (2013). Team teaching [Idea Paper #55]. Retrieved from www.ideaedu.org/Portals/0/Uploads/Documents/IDEA%20Papers/IDEA%20Papers/PaperIDEA_55.pdf

Predmore, S. R. (2005). Putting it into context. *Techniques: Connecting Education and Careers, 80*(1), 22–25.

Ramaley, J. A. (2016). Navigating the rapids: On the frontiers of the knowledge revolution. *Liberal Education, 101–102*(4–1). Retrieved from https://www.aacu.org/liberaleducation/2015-2016/fall-winter/ramaley

Rhodes, T. (Ed.). (2010). *Assessing outcomes and improving achievement: Tips and tools for using rubrics*. Washington DC: Association of American Colleges & Universities.

Riegle-Crumb, C., & Morton, K. (2017). Gendered expectations: Examining how peers shape female students' intent to pursue STEM fields. *Frontiers in Psychology, 8*, Article 329.

Rittel, H., & Webber, M. (1973). Dilemmas in a general theory of planning. *Policy Sciences, 4*, 155–169.

Rock, D., & Grant, H. (2016, November 4). Why diverse teams are smarter. *Harvard Business Review, 4.*

Rossing, J. P., & Lavitt, M. R. (2016). The neglected learner: A call to support integrative learning for faculty. *Liberal Education, 102*(2). Retrieved from https://www.aacu.org/liberaleducation/2016/spring/rossing

Rowley, J. (2002). Using case studies in research. *Management Research News, 25*(1), 16–27.

Ryan, R. M., & Deci, E. L. (2000). Self-determination theory and the facilitation of intrinsic motivation, social development, and well-being. *American Psychologist, 55*(1), 68–78.

Salisbury, F., & Karasmanis, S. (2011). Are they ready? Exploring student information literacy skills in the transition from secondary to tertiary education. *Australian Academic and Research Libraries, 42*(1), 43. Retrieved from http://dx.doi.org/10.1080/00048623.2011.10722203

Sandholtz, J. H. (2000). Interdisciplinary team teaching as a form of professional development. *Teacher Education Quarterly, 27*(3), 39–54.

Schoenfeld, A. H. (1985). *Mathematical problem solving*. Cambridge, MA: Academic Press.

Schoenfeld, A. H. (1992). Learning to think mathematically: Problem solving, metacognition, and sense making in mathematics. In D. Grouws (Ed.), *Handbook for research on mathematics teaching and learning* (pp. 334–369). Reston, VA: National Council of Teachers of Mathematics.

Segev-Miller, R. (2004). Writing from sources: The effect of explicit instruction on college students' processes and products. *L1: Educational Studies in Language and Literature, 4,* 5–33.

Selingo, J. J. (2013). *College (un)bound: The future of higher education and what it means for students.* Las Vegas, NV: Amazon Publishing.

Shibley, I. A. (2006). Interdisciplinary team teaching: Negotiating pedagogical differences. *College Teaching, 54*(3), 271–274.

Siegel, D. J. (2007). Constructive engagement with the corporation. *Academe, 93*(6), 52–55.

Siegel, D. J. (2012). Beyond the academic–corporate divide. *Academe, 98*(1), 29–31.

Simmons, C. S. (2015). *Using CATME Team-Maker to form student groups in a large introductory course.* Conference Paper, ASEE Southeast Section Conference, Tuscaloosa, AL.

Singh, A. B. (2005). A report on faculty perceptions of students' information literacy competencies in journalism and mass communications programs: The ACEJMC survey. *College and Research Libraries, 66*(4), 294–311.

Skorton, D., & Bear, A. (Eds.). (2018). *The integration of the humanities and arts with sciences, engineering, and medicine in higher education: Branches from the same tree.* Washington, DC: National Academies of Science, Engineering, and Medicine.

Snow, C. (1998). *Two cultures: With introduction by Stefan Collini.* Cambridge, UK: Cambridge University Press. (Original work published 1959.)

Soria, K. M., Fransen, J., & Nackerud, S. (2013). Library use and undergraduate student outcomes: New evidence for students' retention and academic success. *portal: Libraries and the Academy, 13*(2), 147–164. Retrieved from http://dx.doi.org/10.1353/pla.2013.0010

Spivey, N. N. (1997). *The constructivist metaphor: Reading, writing and the making of meaning.* San Diego, CA: Academic.

Steinemann, A. (2003). Implementing sustainable development through problem-based learning: Pedagogy and practice. *Journal of Professional Issues in Engineering Education and Practice, 129,* 216–224.

Stoddard, E. A., & Pfeifer, G. (2018, April). *Working towards more equitable team dynamics: Mapping student assets to minimize stereotyping and task assignment bias.* Paper presented at the meeting of CoNECD-The Collaborative Network for Engineering and Computing Diversity Conference, Arlington, VA.

Stolk, J. D., & Martello, R. T. (2015). Can disciplinary integration promote students' lifelong learning attitudes and skills in project-based engineering courses? *International Journal of Engineering Education, 31*(1), 434–449.

Thomas, J. (1994). Faculty attitudes and habits concerning library instruction: How much has changed since 1982? *Research Strategies, 12*(4), 209–223.

Thomas, J. W. (2000). *A review of research on project-based learning.* Retrieved from the Buck Institute for Education, http://www.bie.org/object/document/a_review_of_research_on_project_based_learning

Thoms, F. (2010). *Teaching from the middle of the room: Inviting students to learn.* Lowell, MA: Stetson Press.

Tinto, V. (1993). Principles of effective retention. *Journal of the Freshman Experience, 2*(1), 35–48.

Tinto, V. (2010). From theory to action: Exploring the institutional conditions for student retention. In J. C. Smart (Ed.), *Higher education: Handbook of theory and research* (Vol. 25, pp. 51–89). New York, NY: Springer.

Tomlinson, C. A. (2011). One to grow on: Every teacher a coach. *Educational Leadership, 69*(2), 92–93.

Tough, P. (2012). *How children succeed: Grit, curiosity, and the hidden power of character.* New York, NY: Houghton Mifflin.

Tough, P. (2016). *Helping children succeed: What works and why.* Boston, MA: Houghton Mifflin Harcourt.

Traver, R. (2016). Power of peers. *Educational Leadership, 73*(7), 68–72.

Tuckman, B. W., & Jensen, M. A. C. (1977). Stages of small group development revisited. *Group and Organizational Studies, 2*, 419–427.

Tufte, E. (2006). *Beautiful evidence.* Cheshire, CT: Graphics Press.

UCLA. (n.d.). Urban Humanities Initiative. Retrieved from http://www.urban humanities.ucla.edu/?/urban-humanities/

Van den Berg, I., Admiraal, W., & Pilot, A. (2006). Design principles and outcomes of peer assessment in higher education. *Studies in Higher Education, 31*(3), 341–356.

Vance, J. M., Kirk, R., & Gardner, J. G. (2012). Measuring the impact of library instruction on freshman success and persistence: A quantitative analysis. *Communications in Information Literacy, 6*(1), 49–58. Retrieved from http://dx.doi .org/10.7548/cil.v6i1.189

Vander Meer, P. F., Perez-Stable, M. A., & Sachs, D. E. (2012). Framing a strategy: Exploring faculty attitudes toward library instruction and technology preferences to enhance information literacy. *Reference and User Services Quarterly, 52*(2), 109–122.

Veldof, J. (2005). *Creating the one-shot library workshop: A step-by-step guide.* Chicago, IL: ALA Editions. Retrieved from http://site.ebrary.com/lib/wpi/doc Detail.action?docID=10194720&ppg=1

Wakefield, C. R. (2016). *Agentic engagement, teacher support, and classmate relatedness: A reciprocal path to student achievement* (Doctoral dissertation). Retrieved from UNLV Theses, Dissertations, Professional Papers, and Capstones, http:// digitalscholarship.unlv.edu/thesesdissertations/2757

Wang, L. (2006). Sociocultural theories and information literacy teaching activities in higher education. *Reference and User Services Quarterly, 47*(2), 149–158.

Washburn, J. (2006). *University, Inc: The corporate corruption of higher education.* New York, NY: Basic Books.

Wazwaz, N. (2015, July 6). It's official: The U.S. is becoming a minority–majority nation. *U.S. News and World Report.* Retrieved from http://www.usnews.com/news/ articles/2015/07/06/its-official-the-us-is-becoming-a-minority-majority-nation

Wellmon, C. (2016). *Organizing enlightenment.* Baltimore, MD: Johns Hopkins University Press.

Wenger-Trayner, E., & Wenger-Trayner, B. (2015). *Introduction to communities of practice*. Retrieved from http://wenger-trayner.com/introduction-to-communities-of-practice/

Wentworth, J., & Davis, J. R. (2002). Enhancing interdisciplinarity through team teaching. In C. Hayes (Ed.), *Innovations in interdisciplinary teaching* (pp. 16–37). Westport, CT: Oryx Press.

Westra, L., & Lawson, B. (Eds.). (2001). *Faces of environmental racism: Confronting issues of global justice*. New York, NY: Rowman & Littlefield.

Wiggins, G. P. (1998). *Educative assessment: Designing assessments to inform and improve student performance*. San Francisco, CA: Jossey-Bass.

Williams, J. C. (2015, March 24). The five biases pushing women out of STEM. *Harvard Business Review*. Retrieved from https://hbr.org/2015/03/the-5-biases-pushing-women-out-of-stem

Williams, J. C., Philips, K., & Hall, E. (2014). *Double jeopardy? Gender bias against women of color in science*. Tools for Change: Boosting the Retention of Women in the STEM Pipeline. Retrieved from http://worklifelaw.org/publications/Double-Jeopardy-Report_v6_full_web-sm.pdf

Wilson, E. O. (1999). *Consilience: The unity of knowledge*. New York, NY: Vintage Books.

Wingate, U. (2006). Doing away with "study skills." *Teaching in Higher Education, 11*(4), 457–469.

Wingate, U., Andon, N., & Cogo, A. (2011). Embedding academic writing instruction into subject teaching: A case study. *Active Learning in Higher Education, 12*(1), 69–81.

Withgott, J. H., & Laposta, M. (2015). *Essential environment: The science behind the stories*. Hoboken, NJ: Pearson Education.

Wolfe, J. (2010). *Team writing: A guide to working in groups*. Boston, MA: Bedford/St. Martin's.

Wolfe, J., Powell, B., Schlisserman, S., & Kirshon, A. (2016, June). *Teamwork in engineering undergraduate classes: What problems do students experience?* Paper presented at the American Society for Engineering Education 123rd Annual Conference and Exposition, New Orleans, LA. Retrieved from https://www.asee.org/public/conferences/64/papers/16447/view

Wolniak, G., Flores, S., & Kemple, J. (2016, September). How can we improve college success for underserved students? *Education Solutions Initiative*, 1–8.

Wong, S. H. R., & Cmor, D. (2011). Measuring association between library instruction and graduation GPA. *College and Research Libraries, 5*, 464–473.

Zainal, Z. (2007). Case study as a research method. *Jurnal Kemanusiaan, 9*, 1–6.

CONTRIBUTORS

Diran Apelian is the Alcoa-Howmet professor of engineering and founding director of the Metal Processing Institute (MPI) at WPI. He has been in leadership positions at both Drexel University and WPI: department head, associate dean, provost at WPI (1989–1997). MPI is an industry–university alliance dedicated to materials processing with over 90 corporate partners. He is credited with pioneering work in various areas of materials and metals processing. During the past decade, he has worked on sustainable development issues and, particularly, resource recovery and recycling. Apelian is the recipient of many distinguished honors and awards; he has over 700 publications to his credit, 18 patents, and 16 books. He serves on several technical and corporate boards. With his colleagues and students, he has founded 5 companies: Materials Strategies LLC, Battery Resourcers Corp, Melt Cognition LLC, Solvus Global LLC, and Kinetic Batteries. During 2008–2009 he served as president of The Minerals, Metals, and Materials Society (TMS). Apelian is a fellow of TMS, ASM, and APMI, and he is a member of the National Academy of Engineering (NAE), European Academy of Sciences, and Armenian Academy of Sciences.

Marja Bakermans is an associate teaching professor at WPI, where she is an instructor in both the GPS program and the biology and biotechnology department. Bakermans possesses a strong commitment to student education and research, and a goal of hers is to stimulate students' critical thinking and problem-solving abilities while addressing ecological problems. She has presented work related to her teaching at multiple conferences and workshops, including AAC&U, Science Education for New Civic Engagements and Responsibilities (SENCER), Ecological Society of America (ESA), and WPI's Institute on Project-Based Learning. In addition, she is a member of WPI's Faculty Learning Community, where she is developing online modules to improve student comprehension of primary research literature and is an ESA education scholar working on integrating research data into undergraduate classrooms.

Randall Bass is vice provost for education and professor of English at Georgetown University, where he leads the Designing the Future(s) initiative and the Red House incubator for curricular transformation. For 13 years he was the founding executive director of Georgetown's Center for New Designs in Learning and Scholarship (CNDLS). He has been working at the intersections of new media technologies and the scholarship of teaching and learning for nearly 30 years, including serving as director and principal investigator of the Visible Knowledge Project, a 5-year scholarship of teaching and learning project involving 70 faculty on 21 university and college campuses. In January 2009, he published a collection of essays and synthesis of findings from the Visible Knowledge Project under the title, "The Difference that Inquiry Makes," (coedited with Bret Eynon) in the digital journal Academic Commons. Bass is the author and editor of numerous books, articles, and electronic projects, including recently, "Disrupting Ourselves: the Problem of Learning in Higher Education" (*Educause Review*, March/April 2012). He is currently a senior scholar with AAC&U.

Kristin Boudreau is the Paris Fletcher Distinguished Professor of Humanities and head of the Department of Humanities and Arts at WPI. A teacher and scholar of nineteenth-century American literature, she is also involved in transdisciplinary and integrative teaching and scholarship. Her most recent work concerns pedagogy that integrates STEM and the humanities. Her recent publications in this field include "To See the World Anew: Learning Engineering Through a Humanistic Lens" in *Engineering Studies* (2015); "A Game-Based Approach to Information Literacy and Engineering in Context" (with Laura Hanlan) in *Proceedings of the Frontiers in Education Conference* (2015); and "The Theatre of Humanitarian Engineering" (written with a transdisciplinary team), which was named best paper in the Division of Liberal Education/Engineering and Society and in the PIC 3 Division at the 2017 American Society for Engineering Education conference. A classroom game she developed with WPI students and colleagues, "Humanitarian Engineering Past and Present: Worcester's Sewage Problem at the Turn of the Twentieth Century," was chosen by the National Academy of Engineering as an Exemplary Engineering Ethics Activity that prepares students for ethical practice, research, or leadership in engineering.

Arthur Heinricher joined the mathematical sciences faculty at WPI in 1992 and has served as dean of undergraduate studies since 2008. He earned a BS in applied mathematics from the University of Missouri–St. Louis and a PhD in mathematics from Carnegie Mellon University. He was a founding member and served as director of the Center for Industrial Mathematics and Statistics at WPI. He has advised more than 100 students on more than 30 different mathematics projects sponsored by business and industry. Those projects provide the raw material for many outreach programs, including Mathematics in Industry Institutes for High School Teachers and the Mathematics Research Expos developed in partnership with Boston University and five Boston-area school districts. He is a member of the steering committee for WPI's Institute on Project-Based Learning and was a corecipient of the 2016 Bernard M. Gordon Prize for Innovation in Engineering and Technology Education awarded by the National Academy of Engineering.

Charlie Morse has been with WPI's Student Development and Counseling Center since 1993 and assumed the role of director of counseling in 2005. He is a licensed mental health counselor (LMHC), with an MA in counseling psychology from Assumption College. Morse works directly with students and also oversees WPI's innovative training and consultation programs on recognizing and responding to student distress. He has an expertise in acceptance and commitment therapy (ACT), which helps students move toward their values with openness and acceptance. In addition, his focus includes leadership development and performance enhancement for students.

Svetlana Nikitina is an associate teaching professor of English and of international and global studies at WPI. She joined WPI after serving as a senior researcher on the national study of interdisciplinary programs and initiatives at the Harvard Graduate School of Education. Nikitina's professional interests lie in three main areas: new forms of narrative emerging in our multimedia age, comparative and environmental literature, and interdisciplinary pedagogy. She teaches a variety of writing and literature courses in the humanities and arts department and coteaches Recycle the World: Recovering Earth's Resources for All Species and for All Time in the GPS with Diran Apelian. Apelian and Nikitina have been involved with the First-Year Experience and GPS program at WPI from inception. Nikitina has previously coauthored a chapter on the contribution of the humanities and arts to WPI's unique pedagogy and PBL in *Shaping Our World*, with David Spanagel (John Wiley and Sons, 2012). She also serves on the board of the Museum of Russian Icons and directs the Moscow Project Center for WPI.

Geoff Pfeifer is an associate teaching professor of philosophy at WPI, where he holds a joint appointment between the undergraduate studies department and the humanities and arts department. He teaches philosophy courses and also for the GPS program. He has been the recipient of two teaching-related grants at WPI and is constantly looking for ways to improve his courses and teaching methods. He also has been involved in curriculum development for the GPS program and is a faculty member for the WPI/AAC&U

Summer Institute on Project-Based Learning. Pfeifer has also given a number of teaching-related presentations at various conferences. In addition to this, he has published a number of book chapters, and his work can also be found in the *Journal of Global Ethics, Human Studies, Crisis and Critique*, and *The European Legacy*. He is also the author of *The New Materialism: Althusser, Badiou, and Žižek* (Routledge, 2015) and coeditor of *Phenomenology and the Political* (Rowman and Littlefield International, 2016).

Derren Rosbach earned a PhD in planning governance and globalization from Virginia Tech, an MS in biology from Western Carolina University, and an undergraduate degree in human ecology from College of the Atlantic. He is currently an associate teaching professor at WPI in the departments of civil and environmental engineering, social sciences and policy studies, and undergraduate studies. His main teaching and research is focused on collaborative environmental governance, sustainability, water resources, environmental policy, and transdisciplinary research approaches.

Jill Rulfs has been a professor of biology and biotechnology at WPI for 25 years. She was the principle investigator on an NSF-funded initiative to introduce graduate students as mentors in grades K through 6 and to design an engineering and technology curriculum for the Worcester Public Schools. She has incorporated the use of active learning and educational technology into her classroom and was a coprinciple investigator on a foundation-funded effort to incorporate teaching technology in the undergraduate laboratory. In her current role as associate department head, her focus is on undergraduate teaching and learning, including curriculum development and delivery. She helped establish the Teaching and Learning Journal Club at WPI and has been engaged in teaching in the GPS at WPI since its inception. She has been a frequent presenter at the Lilly Conferences on College and University Teaching and was a charter member of the Society for the Advancement of Biology Education Research.

David Spanagel is an associate professor of history in the Department of Humanities and Arts at WPI. He has been active as an innovator in curriculum and instructional approaches. He codeveloped the Power the World course (one of the first GPS themes offered as part of WPI's First-Year Experience) back in 2007. He has pioneered collaborative learning approaches in the history capstone projects that he advises for students completing the humanities and arts requirement. He worked with colleagues to overhaul and update WPI's history of science and technology course offerings in 2009 and is currently engaged in a new round of discussions about revising those courses and their structure yet again (in 2017). Prior to acquiring a PhD in the history of science at Harvard (1996), Spanagel's first graduate degree (an MS Ed) involved academic research in mathematical problem-solving techniques and pedagogy. Thus, his very first publication was the article "Solving Extreme Value Problems Without Calculus," published in *The Mathematics Teacher* (1988).

Elisabeth (Lisa) A. Stoddard is a geographer and an assistant teaching professor at WPI, where she holds a joint appointment between undergraduate studies and the environmental and sustainability studies program. She has been the recipient of multiple grants to examine issues of bias and stereotyping on student project teams and the impact this has on student learning and has developed tools and strategies to empower students and faculty to create more equitable team dynamics. Stoddard has also worked with faculty to develop active and project-based learning techniques through conferences, workshops, and WPI's Institute for Project-Based Learning. She has published a number of book chapters and articles that focus on food, environmental, and social justice, particularly in the area of livestock production in the rural southern United States. Her work can be found in *The Annals of the Association of American Geographers*, *Political Ecologies of Meat*, and *Critical Animal Geographies*.

Rob Traver is a teaching professor within the Office of Undergraduate Studies and the project center director for Asunción, Paraguay, WPI. Formerly he was principal of the Massachusetts Academy of Mathematics and Science at WPI, a statewide public magnet high school for high-ability math and science students. Before that he held positions at the Harvard Graduate School of Education as lecturer on education and program administrator of the Harvard College Undergraduate Teacher Education Program. He served two years on the board of editors of the *Harvard Educational Review*. His academic education publications appear in *Educational Theory*, *Teachers College Record*, and the *Handbook of Research on Teacher Education* (2nd ed., Macmillan Library Reference, 1996). Practitioner-oriented papers appear in *The Science Teacher* and *Educational Leadership*. He is a consultant with Teachers, where he has offered professional development workshops in curriculum, instruction, assessment, mentoring, and data-informed schools in 7 states and more than 40 school districts in Massachusetts.

Kristin Wobbe is associate dean for undergraduate studies and the director of the GPS program. She has been involved in the program since its inception but has a much longer history with project-based learning, having introduced projects into her biochemistry classes early in her career as a professor almost two decades ago. She has given workshops and seminars on using projects in the first year at conferences and several colleges and universities. She is a member of the WPI Institute on Project-Based Learning and a member of the Center for Project-Based Learning advisory committee. Her teaching awards include the Moruzzi Prize for Innovation in Undergraduate Education, and she a corecipient of the 2016 Bernard M. Gordon Prize for Innovation in Engineering and Technology Education awarded by the National Academy of Engineering. She received her BA in chemistry from St. Olaf College and her PhD in biochemistry and molecular biology from Harvard University. Recent publications appear in *Change: The Magazine of Higher Learning* and *Diversity and Democracy*.

Rebecca Ziino Plotke is a research and instruction librarian at WPI with an MS in library science. She primarily works with first-year students in an interdisciplinary project-based first-year seminar, teaching students about the depth and intricacies of the research process. She focuses on the development of information literacy curriculum and coordinates, designs, implements, and assesses the information literacy learning outcomes against the wider WPI learning outcomes. She continues to support student success by working collaboratively with faculty to facilitate the effective use of curriculum-specific information resources and to embed information literacy practices within instruction. In addition, as a science librarian she, works with the Biology and Biotechnology Department in introductory and upper-level courses, helping to teach science literacy research skills.

Project Kaleidoscope (PKAL), 51
projects. *See also* sponsored projects;
    student project teams; students,
    with success in projects
  advising for equity faculty, 237–38
  blog post on team, 208–9
  Dengue Project, 38
  "Energy Source Types Project,"
    80–81
  eWaste, 158, 166–67
  food bank, 155–58, 168–69
  IQP, 3–4, 11, 27, 288–90
  MQP, 3, 27
  selection sheet example, 280–81
  sponsor and project roster, 164–65
  student guide for mid-project group
    discussion, 217
  support with student needs and
    success in, 174–75
  team teaching and sponsorship of,
    69–70
  transdisciplinary approach for first-
    year project-based courses, 40–43
  worth of, 117
  WPI, 2–3
promotion, materials for institutional,
  49–50
proof by intimidation, 7
PubMed, 200
Purdue OWL, 118
purpose
  ethnic food market assignment and,
    23
  as motivator, 14, 15
  PBL, 22–24, 25

question reformulation, for open-ended
    problems, 175–77
quizzes, tests and, 111

race. *See also* students of color
  bias based on, 241
  faculty and, 239
  population, multi-ethnic groups, 222
racism, environmental, 207

rainwater collection systems, 266
Ramalay, J. A., 44, 46–47
rapport, PBL assessment and, 107
recognition, lack of work, 223–24
Redman, C. L., 40
reflections
  research notebook and, 180–81
  self-, 161–62
  team dynamics and students, 230–31
  team management and dynamics,
    291
relatedness
  as motivator, 14, 15
  PBL, 22
research
  ACRL, 125
  case studies to guide undergraduate,
    177–78
  course content and, 200–202
  identifying gap in, 178–79
  labs and sponsorship, 145
  student engagement with, 179–82
  student guide for allocating group
    tasks, 216
  student guide for mid-project group
    discussion on, 217
  water pollution, 201–2
  Zika virus and credible sources for,
    200–201
Research Experience for
    Undergraduates (REU) programs,
    26–27
research notebooks
  assignment, 218–19
  concept map and, 183
  reflections and, 180–81
  transdisciplinary approach and, 42
resources
  CR3, 145, 150–51
  institutional support and, 49–50
  student teams, 256–58
REU programs. *See* Research
    Experience for Undergraduates
Reuse, Recover, Recycle (GPS course),
    33

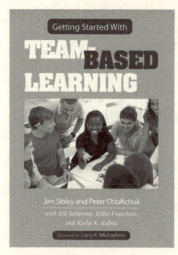

Getting Started with Team-Based Learning

Jim Sibley, Pete Ostafichuk

With Bill Roberson, Billie Franchini, Karla Kubitz

Foreword by Larry K. Michaelsen

"The book is full of practical advice, however, which is well-grounded in literature about teaching and learning so that faculty members who are hesitant to transform a course to TBL can still benefit from reading (advice such as how to write effective multiple choice questions and how to facilitate discussions). ...after reviewing the book, I am motivated to try this model in my teaching." —*David B. Howell*, *Ferrum College, Wabash Center for Teaching & Learning in Theology and Religion*

Team-based learning (TBL) is a uniquely powerful form of small group learning. It harnesses the power of teams and social learning with accountability structures and instructional sequences. This book provides the guidance, from first principles to examples of practice, together with concrete advice, suggestions, and tips to help you succeed in the TBL classroom. This book will help you understand what TBL is and why it is so powerful. You will find what you need to plan, build, implement, and use TBL effectively. This book will appeal to both the novice and the expert TBL teacher.

Sty/us

22883 Quicksilver Drive
Sterling, VA 20166-2019

Subscribe to our e-mail alerts: www.Styluspub.com

Creating Wicked Students

Designing Courses for a Complex World

Paul Hanstedt

In this work, Paul Hanstedt argues that courses can and should be designed to present students with what are known as "wicked problems" because the skills of dealing with such knotty problems are what will best prepare them for life after college. As the author puts it, "this book begins with the assumption that what we all want for our students is that they be capable of changing the world. . . . When a student leaves college, we want them to enter the world not as drones participating mindlessly in activities to which they've been appointed, but as thinking, deliberative beings who add something to society."

This is a course design book centered on the idea that the goal in the college classroom—in all classrooms, all the time—is to develop students who are not only loaded with content but also capable of using that content in thoughtful, deliberate ways to make the world a better place. Achieving this goal requires a top-to-bottom reconsideration of courses, including student learning goals, text selection and course structure, day-to-day pedagogies, and assignment and project design. *Creating Wicked Students* takes readers through each step of the process, providing multiple examples at each stage, while always encouraging instructors to consider concepts and exercises in light of their own courses and students.

(Continues on preceding page)

Also available from Stylus

COURSE-BASED
UNDERGRADUATE
RESEARCH
*Educational Equity and
High-Impact Practice*

Edited by NANCY H. HENSEL
Foreword by CATHY N. DAVIDSON

**Course-Based Undergraduate
Research**

*Educational Equity and High-Impact
Practice*

Edited by Nancy H. Hensel

Foreword by Cathy N. Davidson

Undergraduate research has long been recognized as a high-impact practice (HIP),
but has unfortunately been offered only to
juniors and seniors, and very few of them.
This book shows how to engage students
in authentic research experiences, built into
the design of courses in the first two years, thus making the experience available to a much greater number of students.

The book addresses all aspects of the topic, including the following:
- The appropriate expectations for research in the first two years
- How to design appropriate course-based research for first- and second-year
  students
- How to mentor a class rather than individual students
- How students can disseminate the results of their research
- Possible citizen-science projects appropriate for the first and second years
- Providing additional resources available to support course-based research
  in the first two years

(Continues on preceding page)